Tay Bridge
DISASTER

Tay Bridge
DISASTER

The People's Story

Robin Lumley

The History Press

*For Debra, Johanna, Charlie and
Daniel and Robert Allanson (1929–2013)*

*And in memory of Bill Dow, 'the Grand Old Man of the Tay Bridge',
who sadly passed away on 21 June 2013*

Cover illustrations. Front: The River Tay surging between the new and old bridge piers. (Alistair Nisbet) Back: The gap at the southern end of the high girders illustrating the search for bodies. (Alistair Nisbet)

First published 2013

The History Press
The Mill, Brimscombe Port
Stroud, Gloucestershire, GL5 2QG
www.thehistorypress.co.uk

© Robin Lumley, 2013

The right of Robin Lumley to be identified as the Author of this work has been asserted in accordance with the Copyright, Designs and Patents Act 1988.

All rights reserved. No part of this book may be reprinted or reproduced or utilised in any form or by any electronic, mechanical or other means, now known or hereafter invented, including photocopying and recording, or in any information storage or retrieval system, without the permission in writing from the Publishers.

British Library Cataloguing in Publication Data.
A catalogue record for this book is available from the British Library.

ISBN 978 0 7524 9946 8

Typesetting and origination by The History Press
Printed in Great Britain

Contents

	Foreword by Terry Jones	6
	Acknowledgements	8
	Preface	13
	Introduction	16
1	Working on the Railway	19
2	Tay to Forth: Across Fiobha, the Kingdom of Fife	34
3	Crossing the Forth	46
4	Duress Non Frango	56
5	Strangers on a Train	69
6	The Tay and Two Cities	81
7	The Rainbow Bridge	92
8	Heavy Weather	105
9	Iron and Cupar	114
10	The Last One Across	124
11	Train of Tumbrils	134
12	The Long Drop	145
13	Who Saw What?	154
14	Inquiry	167
15	The Rebuild	183
16	Coda	190
	Appendix	201
	Chapter Notes	204
	Bibliography	220
	Index	222

Foreword
by Terry Jones

This is a stopping train, calling at all stations from Edinburgh (in the late nineteenth century) to Perth (in which town King James IV lifted the ban on playing golf in 1502) and Dundee (Perth's great rival). On the way, the reader is taken on many detours down fascinating branch lines, as we follow the story of the ill-fated 5.27 Burntisland to Dundee train on that stormy night of Sunday 28 December 1879.

We get to know many of the passengers on that doomed train: giving us a peep-show of the lives of ordinary Victorian folk in stereoscopic detail, including Lady Baxter's maid, Ann Cruikshanks, who, on that very day, may (or may not) have stolen her mistress's entire collection of jewellery.

We discover the problems of early train travel – especially the perils of first-class passengers who were wearing rubber soles, and, when they reached their station, would find their feet stuck to their foot-warmers.

At the centre is the story of a reckless and arrogant designer, Thomas Bouch, and the catalogue of mistakes, errors of judgement and corner-cutting that led to the Tay Bridge Disaster.

After reading Robin Lumley's detailed account of the correct method of iron casting, I feel like I've gone through quite an apprenticeship. I certainly now know that, when buying iron for bolts from the Cleveland Iron Works, 'Best Iron' is a euphemism for 'Worst Iron', since they grade their iron 'Best', 'Best Best' and 'Best Best Best'.

Useful to know.

There is the dramatic story of the last train across, with the force of the wind ramming the carriages to the rails and producing showers of sparks, and the fact that the passengers and train crew wouldn't know what a narrow escape they'd had when they reached the other side. And in the middle of the drama there is a wonderfully ludicrous moment, when the Rev. George Grubb, in the only first-class carriage, is subjected to a demonstration by a fellow passenger of the effect of opening a window facing the storm! If only they'd known how close they were to death.

FOREWORD

And finally the fatal train itself makes its way across the already destabilised bridge, and meets its end plunging 88ft into the freezing black waters of the River Tay.

The final irony is that two of the members of the inquiry, sitting in judgement on what had happened, were hardly able to criticise the construction of the bridge, since they had approved Thomas Bouch's designs, and indeed supplied information on which he had based those designs.

This is a slow train and not a 125mph express, with the result that you see more of the countryside, have more time to enjoy the details and ultimately have a more interesting journey for the same ticket.

Terry Jones

Terry Jones is a writer, broadcaster, historian, film maker and a founder member of the Monty Python team.

Acknowledgements

Serious and heartfelt thanks to everyone listed here, without whom the book would never have happened. For omissions I do apologise to anyone left out. But I must at the outset apportion some blame for the inspiration of this book. It's all Kevin Ormsby and Julie Carter's fault. Some years ago they ran a second-hand bookshop in Melbourne where I would occasionally browse and one day I bought a copy of *The High Girders* by John Prebble from them which jogged my memory about my great-grandfather Jamie Lee and his chance escape from death on the doomed train 133 years ago. Re-reading that book inspired me to write this one. Throughout the research and writing Kevin and Julie provided non-stop enthusiastic support.

So, big thanks to (and in no particular order):

David Kett, formerly Head of Reference Services at Dundee Central Library, who over the several years this book has taken to write, has been the prime mover par excellence in 'on the spot' research in Dundee. Ably assisted by Eileen Moran and the staff of the Dundee Local History Library, David has constantly come up with priceless information, gems of history and an ongoing e-mail dialogue about the whole subject of the Tay Bridge event, probably wearing out the library's photocopy machine on my behalf. As time has passed, David and I have discovered much in common, not least a pleasantly warped and irreverent sense of humour. It is amusing to re-read the formality of our earlier correspondence and compare it to the lunacy of our current missives! Truly he is now a real pal and an utterly invaluable one for this book. I've constantly pestered him and probably been responsible for his early retirement and the shortening of his life.

Dr Peter Lewis, whose own book *The Beautiful Railway Bridge over the Silvery Tay* was published a few years ago: this is a paragon of meticulous forensic analysis about the Tay Bridge collapse, and Dr Lewis has been another long-term correspondent, providing a sounding board for some of my more madcap theories and allowing a healthy repartee with some sparky moments on the whole subject. He was kind enough to acknowledge this by including me in his own book's 'Thank You' list, a fact of which I am most proud.

ACKNOWLEDGEMENTS

Ted Thoday is a magazine editor in his own right as well as being a walking encyclopaedia of all things railway, both model and 12in to the foot scale. He's also a long-time friend and a great proof reader. Not only that, his constant faith in the project kept me going when I lapsed into despair. He was always there to supply the occasional gems of information. What a pal! Ta lots Teditor!

Alan Porter is a railway modeller with an encyclopaedic knowledge of the prototype. My thanks to him for always answering my questions.

Kylie Robertson rendered the map of the 5.27 train's route on the fateful night. Using her formidable computing skills she transformed my biro scrawl into the cartographic perfection which now graces these pages. Many many thanks, Kylie!

Dr Mal Clark is another of those well-lettered chaps who didn't mind demeaning themselves and having the patience to have long dialogues with a non-academic like me. Years of happy e-mail exchanges with Mal taught me lots, including how to remain wide-minded when perusing evidence. He must think I'm OK because we're both busy working on the early stages of his own book about scapegoats in the world of engineering. If I can be of use to him, that will be small thanks for all the help he's been to me.

Bill Dow, now a retired physicist, is the doyen of all Tay Bridge Disaster investigators. A local to the Dundee area, he's been fascinated for ever by the night of 28 December 1879. His article in *The Scotsman* magazine in 1989 certainly inspired me to research further and although I haven't always agreed with his conclusions, he remains the 'Grand Old Man of Tay Bridge' (that's a compliment, Bill!) and he is someone for whom I have the deepest and greatest respect. I do so hope he enjoys this book, although he may fume a bit that an upstart should muscle in like this! In cahoots with Professor Rob Duck, Bill wrote the scientific paper on side-scan sonar analysis featured in the appendices. Rob is the only Dundee mentor I've actually met to date and is a geologist at St Andrews University. He helped me on the subject of river borings and is a splendid fellow. In fact absolutely everyone I've had dealings with deserves that epithet.

It's said that one cannot choose one's in-laws. Well that may be true but I couldn't have been luckier with mine. My wife Debra's parents, Bob and Beryl Allanson, have both been oracles for me. Bob is a retired steam locomotive driver and carefully checked all my footplate data while Beryl's knowledge of historical clothing and footwear helped me immensely. Thanks to you both.

I'm very grateful to some folks who've been of significant help on specific subjects. Like husband-and-wife medical professors John Mills and Suzanne Crowe, who advised me on the physiology of drowning and burn damage to human flesh. And Professor Jeff Cooke from the Metallurgy Department of the University of Western Australia, who filled me in about casting iron and all the snags therein. Dr Dennis Wheeler from Sunderland University is a climatologist with a special interest in the impact of weather on historical events and through his correspondence I learned about the gusts inside a main storm that can wreak unexpected havoc. Thank you Dennis.

The help I've had from other meteorologists has been a tremendous boon. Like Sara-Jane Harris at the UK Met Office, who helped me decipher the language of synoptic charts, and the guidance from Bruce Underwood at the Australian Bureau of Meteorology.

You couldn't write a book which involves the North British Railway without consulting the NBR Society, a historical club dedicated to that company. My contact there was Arch Noble, who was utterly marvellous in supplying information and a happy interchange of ideas. To him and the NBR Society as a whole, thank you all.

Ewan Crawford is a man who is passionate about the history of Scotland's railways. His website RAILSCOT (http://railbrit.co.uk/) is a must destination for anyone researching that subject. But Ewan's input went beyond allowing me to trawl his site; he's been so very willing to help me personally. Ewan, you're a star!

Thanks to Terry Jones for agreeing to write the Foreword after a bit of blackmail on my part. I reminded him that I'd sat through six episodes of his television series *Ripping Yarns* in one go (hardly a difficult task!) in order to help record a laughter track and he caved in, because he thought he owed me something. However, it's nice to get an academic stamp of approval from such a well-accredited historian. Ta, TJ!

Audrey Brown at Kirkcaldy Central Library kindly provided loads of background information on Mr Linskill and his lucky escape from the train at Leuchars Junction, while the staff at Cheltenham Library sent contemporary newspaper clippings all about William Henry Beynon. All other books have him as 'Benyon', so I'm glad that his name has finally been spelt correctly in print.

Ian Nimmo White and Stuart Morris, Laird of Balgonie, have both been involved with the setting up of permanent memorials to the Tay Bridge victims and were most helpful to me.

Earlier in my research, Angus Kidd and I had a lively e-mail correspondence in which his local knowledge proved to be a boon. Ta, Angus!

Dundonian Cliff Blackburn, now a resident of Western Australia, gave me a large-scale streetmap of Dundee, which enabled me to work out the routes the people in the book used to get to work or to their homes. He also sent me a little book of historical Dundee photographs which helped to flavour my descriptive prose.

Janette Fly discovered the details of John Gosnell's toothpaste containers while wandering through a *Titanic* artefacts exhibition.

Felicity Allen, an author in her own right, was kind enough to peruse some of my early drafts and helped my learning curve as a first-time writer in no small way.

Robert Styles has been a lifelong friend and eagerly followed the progress of my book, supplying constant encouragement and impetus. I hadn't heard of the Ashtabula Bridge Disaster in the USA but Robert turned me on to it and I was able to incorporate the event into my story. Full marks, brave Sir Robert!

ACKNOWLEDGEMENTS

Andrew Holmes is a London-based film producer and supplied agent contacts for various 'star names' while I was searching for someone to write the Foreword.

Professor Charles McKean was a source of advice and vignettes concerning Tay Bridge, while Professor G. Sewell has written several books on NBR rolling stock. I happily used the information they supplied.

Historian David Swinfen has written his own book, *The Fall of the Tay Bridge*, which I gleefully raided with his permission.

Friend and neighbour Mick Bolto, himself a consummate man of letters, read a late draft and gave me some excellent advice on pacing and content.

Ian Biner, another old friend and author, was always there at the end of a phone to urge me forward on those occasions when I was flagging somewhat.

Jan van Schaik lent me a plethora of coloured diagrams on the workings of the Westinghouse Brake System, which cleared up a lot of mysteries for me.

Pillaging access to Alistair Nisbet's photographic archives was most kindly permitted by the man himself and I have availed myself freely! Many of his pictures have never been published. Finding such items is always a problem with illustrating a book about the Tay Bridge. Alistair's private archive solved everything. He is also the author of magazine articles and papers on the Tay Bridge subject and is a fellow aficionado of the event. Small wonder he's turned out to be an e-mail friend at the very least and I'm very much looking forward to meeting him in person. So many thanks to Alistair Nisbet for all his photos and his efforts in sending them to me: my book is very much the richer for their inclusion.

Anna Carmichael and Chloe Day are my UK agents at Abner Stein who have been indefatigable in their help at the latter stages of the book. The History Press has an editor in Chrissy McMorris who is second to none and who imaginatively thought up the book's title when I floundered and couldn't think of anything new.

Finally the two most important girls involved: without my wife Debra Allanson and her long-term help with my analogue and non-computer mind I'd have tried to write this in longhand, I'm sure! Sorting out my pagination problems, proof-reading and general morale boosting were fundamental assistances which ensured an arguably sentient manuscript. She also endured seven years of rooms cluttered with research notes, piles of reference books and sheaves of NBR timetable photocopies from the National Archive of Scotland amongst other mess-making impedimenta. Debra put up with all this in a highly patient manner although, as a neat and tidy worker herself, her temper was probably bordering on homicidal.

Finally Lyn Tranter, my indefatigable agent who runs Australian Literary Management in Sydney and with only a ten-page resumé of the projected book, took me on as a client. Somewhat reckless of her I thought at the time, me being an unpublished first-time author. Even when I defaulted many times on deadlines, she always patiently kept the faith with the project and has endlessly supplied morale boosts when my enthusiasm flagged, as well as constantly providing valuable editorial advice. Always available on the end of a phone when I ran into problems, she was ever a mentor and ideas person and has now become a friend. Lyn made this book happen and for that I am deeply in her debt.

Preface

In 1879 a man called Jamie Lee lived at number 83 Peddie Street, Dundee, Scotland, only three doors away from a man called David Mitchell who was an engine driver for the North British Railway (NBR) Company. These men's fates are bound together in this tale. Mr Lee was a butcher by trade and owned a number of shops in Dundee and across the county of Fife. Apart from a wife, he had a cat, a ferret, two white mice and a canary. His children had not at that time been conceived.

Early on the morning of Saturday 27 December 1879, he paid 12s 9d for a first-class return railway ticket from Dundee to Burntisland. He was on his way to a meeting with some business associates which was scheduled to be completed by the following day, when he planned to return home to Dundee. But the agenda took longer than anticipated, the meeting continued throughout Sunday 28 December and Mr Lee decided to postpone his trip home to Dundee until Monday morning, 29 December.

So it was that he didn't catch the Sunday 5.27 p.m. Burntisland–Dundee train. As it was this locomotive and carriages which fell with the great Tay Bridge that night, killing everyone aboard, Jamie Lee believed he could discern the 'Arm of Providence' at work, preserving his life when so many had perished. So he kept the unused return half of the ticket in his wallet for the rest of his days as a reminder of God's hand, his own mortality and proof that miracles can happen.

When I was a very small child growing up in Rosyth, Fife, in the early 1950s, Jamie Lee's son, by then an old man, showed me the ticket that had been passed to him by his father. The son in this anecdote was my grandfather and Jamie Lee my great-grandfather. By not catching the 5.27 p.m. train that Sunday night, Jamie enabled my birth sixty-nine years later.

Ever since then, I have been entranced by my grandfather's story of the primitive little steam engine pulling its train of tiny fragile wooden carriages which were only a small step up from stage coaches. Lit by guttering paraffin lamps, they lurched bumpily along on their four and six wheels, a world away from the monocoque, all-metal, air-conditioned, neon-lit bogie coaching stock of the twenty-first century.

Out they went across the longest bridge in the world on a black fierce night, only to be dashed to pieces into the River Tay during one of the worst storms in Scottish history. The Tay Bridge Disaster remains to this day the most catastrophic failure of a civil engineering structure in Britain – the land equivalent of the sinking of the *Titanic*, given its repercussions not only in Britain but around the world in the sphere of engineering. Indeed, there are many parallels between the *Titanic* and the Tay Bridge Disaster: hubris, arrogance, incompetence and the ignoring of warning signs to name but a few.

Previous and subsequent accidents have taken a far heavier toll of human life and have caused a stir for a time, only to be forgotten. A good example is the SS *Princess Alice* disaster of September 1878.[1] This accident occurred just fifteen months prior to the Tay Bridge collapse. Over 600 people (more than seven times the death roll in the River Tay) were drowned in broad daylight on a sunny summer Sunday evening in the River Thames near Woolwich. Yet this terrible catastrophe is now largely forgotten, while Tay Bridge has entered the world of legend.

This book's narrative takes the form of a journey on the out-and-back 'Edinburgh' train from Dundee to Burntisland and return – well almost. This format enables us to meet many of the passengers and crew who would lose their lives in the disaster to come, as well as railway employees like signalmen, wheel tappers, stationmasters, ticket collectors and engine shed staff. As the trip progresses, we sidetrack to learn about the factors involved in the demise of the Tay Bridge. For example, how the great storm that blasted Scotland that night developed and why, the current state of weather forecasting, the character of bridge designer Thomas Bouch, the story of how the bridge was built and the intense rivalry between the two cities of Perth and Dundee, and how that affected the way the Tay Bridge was constructed. At the heart of the whole story is the River Tay itself and so we'll learn of its influence on the whole matter. I've been able to weave into the narrative many pieces of Scottish history and observations on Scottish life at the time, including some fascinating anecdotal material concerning the city life of Edinburgh, Perth and Dundee, all of which, while being background, serve to enrich the whole story and add to the tapestry of the minutiae of a Victorian age now long gone.

This book is designed as a kind of living history to give readers an experience of the Tay Bridge event that is subjective and to make them feel part of it. Back then people were doing things that folk today will understand because in similar circumstances they may have reacted in the same way.

Period books tend to focus on the differences between 'then' and 'now'. But folk were the same. Human nature was the same. People's loves, hates and fears were the same.

Connecting to a momentous event in this way gives so much more resonance if the reader is there and aboard the train, as it were.

C.P. Scott, the editor of the *Manchester Guardian* in 1916, advised his journalists: 'comment is free but facts are sacred.'

In writing *Tay Bridge Disaster: The People's Story*, I have tried to adhere to that precept.

An old proverb used by Josephine Tey (pronounced 'tay') as a book title in 1955 says it all, since I'm writing this from a distance of over 130 years from the event: 'Truth is the daughter of time.'

Introduction

AD 1879: THE YEAR IN PERSPECTIVE

To put 1879, the year of the Tay Bridge Disaster and the forty-second year of Queen Victoria's reign, into a historical perspective, here's a list of some of the events, anniversaries and trivia that occurred during that year, so one can see just what was going on in the world at the time.

In Britain, people were having a rough time in socio-economic terms compared to the present day with much of the population in bad health. Many suffered from tuberculosis, cholera, whooping cough, scarlet fever, measles, syphilis and a host of other infectious diseases. A man in the industrial working classes might only expect to live on average to thirty-eight years. Agriculture, once the main source of work, had been in decline for many years and by the 1870s less than 15 per cent of the population was still so employed. Many in these social strati decided upon emigration to pastures new, such as Canada and Australia. Disgruntled young men joined the army where, although discipline was severe and flogging still extant, they did have at least regular if paltry pay plus food and quarters. At the time of our story, the Prime Minister of Britain was the Conservative Benjamin Disraeli, whose government had held power since 1874.

The year 1879 saw the birthdays of some significant people, several of whom would have a great influence in the new century to come. Amongst these was writer Edward Morgan Forster – E.M. Forster, later to struggle with his homosexuality of which we only recently have cognisance – who shared a birthday on 1 January with William Fox, the founder of the Twentieth Century Fox Film Corporation. Two giants of Communism breathed their first in that year: Josef Vissarionovich Dzhugashivi – later known to the world as Stalin – in Gori, Georgia on 21 December, and Lev Davidovitch Bronstein in Ianovka, Ukraine on 7 November; subsequently he would call himself Leon Trotsky.

Albert Einstein was born in Ulm, Germany on March 14, Paul Klee, the influential expressionist and surrealist painter, in Munchenbuchsee bei Bern, Switzerland, on 18 December and Frank Bridge, the British composer, arrived into the world in Brighton on 26 February.

Canadian Max Aitken, later in life Lord Beaverbrook, the newspaper magnate and Minister for Aircraft Production during the crucial months of the Battle of Britain (1940), was born on 26 March.

In the world of politics and warfare, after the catastrophic defeat of a British army at Isandlwana, South Africa by Zulu forces under King Cetewayo on 22 January, the following day saw the now legendary successful defence of the mission station at Rorke's Drift by a handful of the South Wales Borderers under Lieutenant John Chard. This became the subject of Stanley Baker's classic 1964 film, *Zulu*. The Zulu Wars ended on 4 July when Lord Chelmsford's army defeated King Cetewayo at Ulundi. A peace treaty was signed on 1 September. Two days later and in another part of the world, Afghani forces massacred the British Legation in Kabul and the British invaded Afghanistan in October in an attempt to restore order, an activity which is still ongoing and an example of the lessons of history not being learned which, as we'll see, was a factor in the fall of the Tay Bridge.

Meanwhile, Chile invaded Peru and Bolivia on 1 November. Between 24 November and 9 December in Scotland during the Midlothian constituency campaign, opposition leader and Scot William Ewart Gladstone denounced Disraeli's government for imperialism and the mishandling of domestic affairs. The fall of the Conservatives came very soon after in 1880, helped to some degree by the stigma of the Tay Bridge Disaster.

An alliance between Germany and Austria was signed in Vienna on 7 October.

Science and inventions had a bumper 1879. German physician Albert Neisser discovered the bacteria responsible for gonorrhoea, US chemist Ira Remson discovered saccharin (which is 500 times sweeter than sugar), Henry Fleuss developed the first self-contained oxygen re-breather for divers – the forerunner of SCUBA, the acronym for Self-Contained Underwater Breathing Apparatus – and Scotsman Dugald Clark invented the two-stroke petrol engine. Mitosis cell division was observed by Walter Flemming. On 4 November American bar owner James Jacob Ritty of Dayton, Ohio, patented the cash register, known as 'Ritty's Incorruptible Cashier', while French engineer François Hennebique was the first to use reinforced concrete for floor slabs. Chemist Robert Chesebrough produced a petroleum jelly he called Vaseline. Werner Von Siemens demonstrated the electric street car in Berlin and Thomas Edison turned on the first electric light bulb in the USA, as did Joseph Swan in England – both illuminations in October. And the first telephone exchange for general use, as opposed to business use only, opened in London during August.

Amongst important personages' death dates in 1879 were Rowland Hill (of Penny Black postage stamp fame) on 27 August, Saint Bernadette of Lourdes on 16 April and William Lloyd Garrison, anti-slavery campaigner, on 24 May.

When Scottish physicist James Maxwell Clerk, who was the pioneer of electromagnetic theory and who ushered in the age of modern physics, died on 5 November, it was a significant loss to the field of science.

Finally, here are a number of interesting things happened in the year that fall into the 'miscellaneous' category:

The Bishop of Durham proudly announced that the world was created at 9 a.m. on 23 October, 4004 BC.

The use of the 'cat o' nine tails' lash as a Royal Navy punishment was abolished.

The British Goat Society was formed.

In Britain, Henry John Lawson marketed the 'safety bicycle', recognisably the forerunner of the modern bicycle, with pedals and a chain-drive. It cost around £12, about five weeks' wages for an ordinary British working man in 1879.

The first Bulgarian postcard was printed on 1 May.

An eccentric jeweller in Iowa, USA, invented the airbrush.

Gilbert and Sullivan's comic operettas *HMS Pinafore* and *The Pirates of Penzance* were both premiered.

The science of psychology was founded by Wilhelm Wundt of Leipzig while, again in Germany, Wilhelm Marr coined the term 'anti-Semitism'.

The first funicular railway was opened on the slopes of Mount Vesuvius, Italy.

On 19 July, 'Doc' Holliday (made famous by the film based on true events *Gunfight at the O.K. Corral*) killed his first man in a shoot-out, and 30 May saw the renaming in New York of Gilmore's Garden to Madison Square Garden. Still in the USA, a businessman called Frank Woolworth opened his first 'Five and Dime' store in Utica, New York State. His businesses were to proliferate worldwide as Woolworths and eventually Safeways supermarkets to this day (although in the UK Woolworths is not now trading, and Safeways has been taken over by Morrisons supermarkets).

On Monday 29 December, an 18-year-old badly deformed youth named Joseph Carey Merrick, later to be known as the 'Elephant Man', was admitted in a state of destitution to the Leicester Union Workhouse on a day when the whole of Britain was in shock, reeling from the 'morning after' news of the Tay Bridge collapse. That event provided the sorry climax to 1879.

Working on the Railway

Unlike the motor car, which can be adequately controlled by a backward child, the steam locomotive needs intelligence and man-handling if it is to run at all.

Dr W.A. Tuplin

Dundee, Scotland, 5 a.m. Sunday 28 December, 1879. A cold, pitch-black winter's morning and the upstairs bedroom windows at 89 Peddie Street were steamy with condensation. Mr and Mrs David Mitchell were fast asleep, but a continuous thudding noise against the glass panes woke David and made him scrabble in the dark for his matches.

Outside on the front wall below, a 14-year-old boy was wielding a long broomstick handle with a wad of cotton waste bound to the top end. He gently bumped this against the window glass, hoping that Mr Mitchell would wake up quickly so that he wouldn't have to stand for too long in the chilly morning air. The sheets of old newspaper that were swathed around his legs and body beneath his clothing were marvellous for keeping out the wind but he was still very cold.

With the bedside candle now glowing through the window, the lad knew at once that Mitchell was up and about. Off he went to bang at another man's window, for he was a 'knocker up' or callboy from Dundee North British Railway engine shed and every night he scuttled around the streets in the wee small hours to wake up engine crews rostered for early duties.

David Mitchell and his family had been living in Peddie Street since moving across the river from Tayport (formerly called Ferryport On Craig) nineteen months earlier. This was just as the 'Stupendous New Tay Railway Bridge' had opened as 'The Wonder of The Age' as the North British Railway described the structure in its advertising material. Indeed, the bridge had been the very reason for their moving home, for Mitchell was an engine driver for the North British Railway Company.

The son of a miller at Balbirnie Flour Mill in Leslie, Fife, 37-year-old Mitchell was a senior member of the locomotive department and, as such, earned about 7s a day. He drove the prestigious express trains between Burntisland and Dundee, nicknamed 'The Edinburghs', as they connected with the Edinburgh ferries crossing the Firth of Forth. He'd done the same sort of trips before the bridge opened and when Tayport had been the northern terminus but now, with the railway link extended across the Tay, he was based at the newly built Dundee (Tay Bridge) Engine Shed, just under a mile's walk from his front door.

The duty Mitchell had pulled today was irksome. He was to take the out-and-back run of the Sunday 'Edinburgh', a turn of duty which he often performed. Ironically, this particular Sunday he wasn't actually rostered for the job but had swapped shifts with Driver William Walker as a return favour for a previous exchange of duties. How such little moments decide life for one man and death for another ... and this was indeed going to happen again on this raw morning as we'll see.

On a weekday, his usual 'Edinburgh' train was scheduled to leave Dundee Tay Bridge station for Burntisland at 1.30 p.m. There was only a two-hour layover there until the train returned to Dundee at 5.02 p.m., having met the Edinburgh passengers off the ferry across the Firth of Forth from Granton.

But on Sundays the timetable was very sparse, with only two Edinburgh services each way as compared with eight on a weekday. Scottish railway companies, under pressure from the Sabbatarians, found it convenient to discourage Sunday travel. It seems that tardiness and discomfort were deliberately contrived. Branch line connections were few and infrequent – in fact most branch or feeder lines didn't run on Sundays at all. Mitchell's outward trip began at 7.30 a.m. and involved an eight-hour wait at Burntisland until the homeward leg at 5.27 p.m. With the need to book on ninety minutes before departure for engine preparation, this meant a total duty time of over fourteen hours, much of it mooching around at Burntisland, where there was really nothing to do. A gloomy ferry port in the middle of a winter Sunday was no place to be stuck all day but at least the enginemen could have an afternoon nap in the shed crew room.

Having lit his bedside candle David rolled out of bed, trying not to disturb his sleeping wife Janet. Mitchell, along with the rest of the working classes, couldn't afford the new-fangled gas lighting which illuminated the streets and the houses of the wealthy.

Dressing quickly, he took a perfunctory wash, using the china water bowl. Then, thanks to a Christmas present just three days ago from Janet, he cleaned his teeth with John Gosnells's Cherry Toothpaste, which came in a pale grey ceramic bowl with a lid. The wording on the top of the container proclaimed that the contents were 'For beautifying and preserving the teeth and gums as well as being extra moist' and that the 'Cherry Toothpaste is patronized [sic] by The Queen'. In 1879 this was an expensive gift.[2]

Mitchell savoured the cherry taste as he brushed his teeth with a bone-handled toothbrush with horsehair bristles. Then he tiptoed towards the stairs.

On the way, he couldn't resist taking a quick peek into the other bedroom where his children, boys David, Thomas and Andrew, aged 8, 7 and 5 years respectively, and wee 2-year-old lassie Isabella were all sleeping soundly. The youngest, Margaret, was still a babe-in-arms and slept in a cradle in her parents' bedroom.

David Mitchell Junior had kicked out his blankets during the night so Mitchell Senior gently tucked his lad in once more. Smiling softly to himself, he went downstairs to make some breakfast and find his food for the rest of the long day ahead.

After lighting the kitchen oil-lamp, he raked through the glowing embers of the cooking-range fire and, with a couple of lumps of coal, soon coaxed it back into life. Mitchell put a kettle of water on to boil and opened a drawer in the kitchen dresser. The drawer was lined with thick brown paper and contained several soft grey lumps of cold porridge and buttermilk, each about the size of a cricket ball.

Janet had made these the night before, along with some 'potted hough' which was a stew of meat off-cuts and pig's trotters that had now set solid in its own gelatine. Mitchell cut off a sizeable wedge, selected a couple of porridge lumps and wrapped the lot in more brown paper. He placed the little parcels in his food (or 'tummy') bag, sometimes called a 'piece box'. For pudding, he made up some 'jeely pieces' – basically jam or marmalade sandwiches. These were a popular working-class dessert ever since the firm of James Keiller and Sons had begun producing marmalade and jam in Dundee at the dawn of the nineteenth century. Now the company's factory in Chapel Street exported the preserves all over the world.

While waiting for the kettle to boil, Mitchell took a cardboard packet of Epp's Cocoa Powder from the larder and tipped two liberal spoonfuls of it into a mug. He idly scanned the wording on the packet which extolled the virtues of Epp's Cocoa as an excellent breakfast: 'a delicately-flavoured beverage which may save us heavy doctor's bills.'

With the boiling water, he made both his breakfast cocoa and a pot of tea, which, after cooling sufficiently, he decanted into two empty whisky bottles to be enjoyed as his drink while on the footplate of the engine. The tea would be drunk cold and without milk or sugar, for the era of the tea-can for footplate brew-ups was many years in the future – during the Second World War, in fact.

Warmed against the raw morning by his cocoa, Mitchell set off into the darkness and down the hill towards Perth Road and Nethergate, thinking that Sunday duties were a bit of a nuisance for a family man such as he. No matter, he'd be back home just after eight that night and would at least be able to tuck in his brood with a quick bedtime story: with his children all being under 10 years old they still believed in magic and fairytales. Then he would have a bite of supper with Janet, and some peace and quiet. For Mitchell was a sober and careful man with a gentle face and he had a great love for his family.

But now, the crisp December air was in his lungs as he walked purposefully to work to earn his 7s a day, dressed in clean white moleskin trousers, tweed peaked cap, blue pilot jacket, strong boots and a dark tweed waistcoat with albert watch-chain clinking. What with his jaw-line beard in the fashion of the day, he looked every inch the professional railwayman he most certainly was. A little earlier, his workmate for the day had left his own home at 18 Hunter Street, just over half a mile from the engine sheds. Bachelor John Marshall was 24 years old and had eight years' service with the North British Railway, first as an engine-cleaner and now as a fireman.[3]

Mitchell and Marshall worked easily together on the footplate, as teamwork was essential in every way to the successful operation of a steam locomotive. Indeed that bonding continued in off-duty hours as the tall young fireman with dark hair was a frequent and welcome visitor to the Mitchell fireside. There, the talk was inevitably about engines, engines and more engines: the types and classes on the North British compared with those on the rival Caledonian Railway, their features and foibles and every aspect of driving and firing them.

Janet Mitchell often remarked that she might as well be living in the engine shed itself and if railwaymen lavished half the care on their womenfolk as they did on their engines, then there wouldn't be a happier set of wives in the world! But at least husband David's earnings from driving engines had enabled her to buy a new mangle from G.H. Nicholl's Ironmongery Store in Bank Street. The Monday washing day chores were thus made a little easier and the big iron machine with its winding handle now dominated the kitchen.

Mid-Victorian enginemen were the elite amongst the ranks of the working class. Recently enfranchised in 1867, they were on a par with the policeman or schoolteacher: respectable, sober and God-fearing. The craftsmen of the steam age, they didn't just go to work as other men did – they 'proceeded to go on duty'.

It was the high noon era of engine smartness, with the gleaming brass and paintwork only seen nowadays on preserved railways. Engine cleaning, using 'sockers' of cotton waste and tallow, was a ritual strictly supervised and scrutinised. Dirty and unkempt engines were almost unheard of on goods trains, let alone on passenger services.[4]

Not only were the driving wheels and spokes cleaned but also the areas behind the spokes received attention. The inside-cylinder covers were scoured with brick dust until they shone like chrome.

Smoke box rings, brackets, dart handles, handrails and buffers all received the same treatment. The engine-cleaners would climb onto the smoke box footstep and pull themselves up by the grab rail until they could stand precariously on the boiler barrel itself, clasping the chimney to polish it, and the brass whistles at the front of the cab roof were burnished until they gleamed.

Unlike today, fourteen-hour shifts for enginemen were not uncommon. One driver spoke of being on pilot-engine duty for forty hours and complained, not surprisingly, that his faculties were impaired. When he reported his condition to his Superintendent, he was asked to retract his words or face dismissal. He refused and was fired!

Fatigue was found to be the cause of a nasty accident in 1873, in which the guard of the train had been on duty for nineteen hours and the driver and fireman had clocked up thirty-two hours. Some drivers had only six hours of sleep in a week.

In 1877, a Royal Commission was set up to investigate railway accidents and staff fatigue was found to be a frequent cause. The Commission displayed a peculiar reluctance for 'any legislative interference prescribing particular hours for railway working'. Instead, the Commission thought: 'It must be left to the companies to work the men as they feel best and most convenient.'

Often there was no proper uniform issue and a driver could be fined if his train arrived late or if he let an axle box run hot.[5] However, pride in their craft and job security motivated the men over and above any of these hardships. One railwayman reputedly went to church on Sundays proudly carrying his shunter's pole as his badge of office, so that all should know what he did.

So it was that, having enjoyed a pleasant if dark walk along Nethergate, passing the Morgan Tower and the new Gothic slab of St Andrew's Roman Catholic Cathedral, David Mitchell turned down the lane leading to the Caledonian Railway's engine shed at Dundee West station (the terminal of that line coming from Perth), passing in front of it and across its tracks to reach the NBR Tay Bridge engine shed which, named like the railway station lying adjacent to it, was a brand-new structure built for, and at the same time as, the bridge was constructed.

Greeting James Robertson, the Locomotive Shed Foreman, with a cheery, 'Here for the Seven-Thirty', Mitchell booked on duty at around 6 a.m., ready to drive the 7.30 a.m. departure for Burntisland. The round trip, which carried Her Majesty's Royal Mail in both directions, was over by 7.20 p.m. on arrival at Dundee and was the last main-line train due to cross the Tay Bridge on a Sunday night. The last scheduled movements across the bridge were the branch-line trains to Tayport, the 'church trains' as they were nicknamed, leaving Dundee at 8 p.m. and returning by 8.50.

All very normal indeed – a rather ordinary train stopping at all intermediate stations, not really running to express schedules as if the North British Railway was loath to disturb the lethargy of a Scottish Sunday. So Mitchell concluded that he should be back home in the bosom of his family by mid-evening, as usual. What wasn't usual was the choice of engine for the train.

Mitchell was informed that the previous night Locomotive Inspector James Moyes had failed engine No 89 Ladybank (or perhaps it was No 314 Lochee – accounts vary on this point) because of a minor mechanical fault. The small 0-4-2 tank-engine had been diagrammed[6] for the job as was normal for the lightly laden Sunday 'Edinburghs'.

David Mitchell carefully read the 'Special Notices to Enginemen' board, which listed any temporary speed restrictions, permanent way work, changes in signalling or alterations to timings. He then called in at the stores to draw oil bottles (actually made of tin) plus cotton waste in quarter-pound balls for cleaning hands and wiping down control levers. He found his mate John Marshall already busy preparing the replacement engine which Moyes had earmarked the night before and pronounced to be in first-class condition.

It was No 224, a 4-4-0 tender engine designed by Thomas Wheatley and one of a pair on the North British with that type of wheel arrangement. Built in 1871 at Cowlairs Works in Glasgow, Nos 224 and 264[7] were now specifically diagrammed to work the weekday 'Edinburghs' and usually had Sundays off for minor maintenance and tube cleaning.

She was not a particularly big steam railway engine by twentieth-century standards, but for her day, No 224 was quite a monster. Sitting on the rails, she stretched along 27ft 6in of track, with another 17ft 10in of tender. She was powered by two inside cylinders, each measuring 17in bore by 24in long each in large iron castings. Considered in comparison to your car, it would be like having two dustbin-sized cylinders under your bonnet instead of an engine block.

The engine, including the boiler, which had 208 heating tubes running its length, and the firebox with a grate area of 15.75sq. ft, was carried on four 6ft 6in diameter driving wheels suspended on laminated springs under each axle box. Via connecting rods, the two inside cylinders drove the front crank axle.

Power was transmitted to the rear axle by a pair of coupling rods on the wheels themselves. A bogie of four 2ft 9in solid cast-iron wheels held up the front end. This front bogie helped to ease the engine through the sharp curves that abounded on the North British main line across Fife.

No 224 weighed 37 tons 1cwt in full working order – that is, with her boiler filled with water and her firebox stuffed with half a ton of incandescent coal. Of this weight, some 22 tons 8cwt was available for adhesion through the four-coupled driving wheels centred 7ft 7in apart. She towed a six-wheeled tender weighing in at 24 tons 17cwt, which was the supply cart for both firebox and boiler, carrying 3 tons of coal and 1,650 gallons of water.

She looked very handsome in her coat of pea-green paint, lined out in black and white. Her tender sides sported the gold letters 'N B R' and her combined number and works plates in cast brass were bolted to her cab side-sheets. The big dome on top of the boiler barrel was to collect the steam generated by the boiler itself and inside the dome was the regulator valve, which apportioned the amount of steam to reach the cylinders. The safety valves, which 'blew off' excess steam when full boiler pressure had been reached, were also fitted inside the top of the dome.

Imagine you are aboard No 224's footplate and watching how the enginemen worked. The driver would be standing on the left side of the footplate with the fireman on his right in keeping with standard British railway practice. An exception was the Great Western Railway, whose footplate men stood the other way around.[8]

You'll notice that the controls for a nineteenth-century steam engine were very few and basic. You'll also notice that they all seem too robust and heavy for their purposes. This is because they have to withstand being belted with a coal pick, which is the most grab-able footplate tool to deal with a sticking control in an emergency. In the middle of the boiler back plate above the fire hole, the regulator handle controlled how much steam reached the cylinders, in effect the direct equivalent of your car's accelerator. To the left by the cab side stood the 4ft-long steel reversing lever, which could be pushed forwards and backwards through several set positions of cut-off,[9] these being marked on a brass quadrant. A 'car' comparison here would be the gearbox. In the middle of the boiler back plate, centrally positioned so that both driver and fireman could see it easily, was the boiler water gauge glass. This instrument was a thick glass tube standing vertically in a small metal frame. The water level in the tube corresponded exactly with the level of water in the boiler and was perhaps the most vital instrument on the footplate, considering the dire and literally explosive results should the water level be allowed to fall too low. In an emergency, if the gauge glass should shatter and no convenient moment was found to replace it, three test-cocks, mounted vertically above each other about 6in apart, could give a rough idea of the boiler water level.

Then there were two more levers on the driver's side: the steam brake – which allowed steam-driven pistons to push cast-iron brake blocks against the driving wheels – and the other lever, that operated the Westinghouse continuous brake system.[10]

This 'continuous brake system' lever not only worked the engine brakes (through a device called a 'triple valve') but also all the brakes on the carriages of the train. The equipment was powered by compressed air from a pump fitted on the right-hand running-plate just in front of the cab, and this air was piped down the train by a series of flexible hoses. It formed a marvellous safety device because, should the couplings part and the train become divided, all the brakes would automatically go on and stop the train. The North British Railway was one of the earliest British companies to adopt this new American-designed system but by 1879 not all rolling stock had yet been fitted with it.

On the right side of the footplate was the live-steam injector handle. When the fireman turned on the water from the tender and then activated the steam jet to urge water via the injector into the boiler, there was initially a gurgling and then a sweet whistle. Footplate men have described this sound as 'whistling like a linnet'.

Next to the injector[11] was the blower control. Opening this tap allowed live steam to blow into the smoke box through a small-diameter copper pipe, pulling more air through the boiler tubes and thus the fire, acting like a set of bellows. Nicknamed 'the fireman's friend', it was very useful if you needed to brighten up the fire and create more steam pressure in a hurry. Down near the floor on the right were the damper handles, which allowed the fireman to regulate the amount of cold air entering the fire grate from below, while down on the left were the cylinder draincock handles. As water cannot be compressed, any condensed steam in the cylinders could literally blow off the cylinder covers when the engine next moved, so on starting away, the draincocks were opened to allow any water to escape safely. Two small levers allowed dry sand to run down through pipes onto the rail under the driving wheels to prevent them slipping on wet days. The sand was stored in sandboxes, just under the running plate and in front of the leading driving wheel splashes on both sides of the engine. Finally, a pair of chains up in the roof sounded the whistles when pulled, one for goods, braking and shunting codes, the other for general warning use.[12]

There were but three instruments to watch. The steam pressure gauge was known as 'the clock' because it looked like one with its circular face graduated with increments of boiler pressure in lb/sq. in and indicated by a sweeping needle like the second hand on a watch. A red line against the poundage showed full boiler pressure and was the point when the safety valves, set at this maximum pressure, started to 'blow off' to vent excess steam. In No 224's case this was at 150lb/sq. in.

The Westinghouse air gauge looked similar but its twin needles gave readings on the air pressure in the train pipe and the compressed air reservoir. The last instrument was the boiler water-level gauge or gauge glass, which we've just looked at above. There were no speedometers in use generally on British locomotives until the 1920s. Drivers were expected to 'know' how fast they were going.

Now Mitchell and Marshall didn't have a little 0-4-2 tank engine as their mount, the two friends had to work a mite faster to prepare No 224, as she was a much bigger engine altogether. Booking on with the 'wee tankie' in mind, they'd allowed about an hour for the job, whereas the big Wheatley bogie would take longer to be ready for the road.

Unlike a diesel locomotive or a motorcar, both of which can be started with a key, a steam engine required a lot of skill and effort before it could move at all.

The cavernous engine shed had the stillness of a cathedral, with flickering weak gaslight cutting through the gloom to sparkle back from engines adorned with polished brass and copper. The peace was broken as Marshall's shovel rasped through coal and the firebox doors were clanked open.

The fire had been lit a few hours previously by the night-turn shed crew. When he wasn't 'knocking up' engine crews, the callboy would help with such duties. The firebox was lined with small lumps of coal, leaving a space in the middle. Firelighters, made from small strips of old timber nailed together and stuffed with paraffin-soaked cotton waste, were lit, placed on a shovel and lowered into that space in the firebox. Choice lumps of coal were then placed on top, the dampers opened and the firebox doors closed to within an inch. The gap increased the draught and brought the fire up more quickly. Four hours after lighting up, No 224 was on the simmer with about 40lb of steam showing on the pressure gauge, all ready for the fireman to build up his fire for the journey.

So now Marshall got out the pricker – which was like an overgrown domestic poker that was 8ft long – to reach right down the firebox and spread the fire more thinly over the grate. Thick 'haycock' fires are fine once on the road but don't provide as much heat as a thin fire bed. With a half-turn on the blower, steam pressure soon started to rise more rapidly and No 224 was gurgling to herself and beginning to come alive. Meanwhile, Mitchell had disappeared into the access pit under the engine with his oil-feeder and a flare lamp to see his way. He filled up lubrication pots, checked the worsted trimmings[13] and bearings and made sure that the ash pan wasn't clogged. He called up to the footplate to get Marshall to move her forwards an inch as the spokes of the driving wheels were fouling his reach to the axle-box oilways. With Mitchell's arm stretched through those spokes, there could be no risk of the engine moving even a quarter-inch, so his mate checked that the big reversing lever was in mid-gear, the hand-brake screwed hard on and the cylinder draincocks wide open.

After about forty-five minutes, the engine had been oiled all round, injector tested, sand-boxes topped up, smoke box door tightened, ashes swept off the front framing, footsteps and footplate cleaned and the tender coal 'trimmed': this term means that the coal is broken up with the coal pick into fist-sized pieces, the ideal dimension for effective combustion in the firebox.

The two men stowed their food bags and drinks before checking all their equipment – spare gauge glass, red flags, detonators,[14] bucket, coal pick, pricker and firing shovels. Two shovels were always carried in case of accidental loss, either into the firebox or overboard, by slipping from the fireman's hands; this could easily happen on a rough piece of road. An engine could get along without a lot of things but certainly wouldn't go far without a shovel to stoke the fire. The second shovel had an unofficial use, for when nature called, enginemen would disappear into the dubious privacy of the tender with it!

With No 224 nicely on the boil, Mitchell, pleased as usual with Marshall's careful preparation of the fire, took the locomotive off-shed to join the train of carriages waiting at Dundee Tay Bridge station.

Backing down gently onto the six carriages, the engine's wheels squealed in protest against the sharp curves of the points as the flanges bit into the bullhead rail. Mitchell opened and shut the regulator in a series of short 'blips', keeping the engine just moving at about 3mph. He eased up No 224's tender buffers to those of the leading carriage, so that they kissed gently with a solid double clunk. At the instant of contact, the regulator was opened and the steam brake applied at the same moment. This had the effect of compressing the buffers and catching the engine hard up against the train, making it easier to 'hook on'.

Marshall hopped off the footplate and got down onto the track to hoist the heavy grease-laden screw coupling on No 224's tender buffer-beam over the front carriage hook and then to wrestle together the fat black Westinghouse brake hoses.

Even at this hour of the morning, there were at least twenty passengers waiting to board the train. Most of them were making day trips to Fife or Edinburgh to visit kith and kin. The paucity of the Sunday service had enforced this early start but at least it gave them more time to spend with their friends and relatives on their only day off.

Some, like Robert Syme and William Threlfell, were travelling right through to Edinburgh. Twenty-two-year-old Robert, a clerk at The Royal Hotel, Nethergate, was visiting his father Adam. Robert was wearing a dark grey suit and a felt hat and carried a travelling bag initialled 'RS'. William was 18 years old. He was a thin young man with fair hair and wore a black corded shooting coat, black doeskin trousers and a white shirt. Employed as a confectioner's apprentice, he lived in Union Street with his mother and was making the trip to see his brother Andrew, a trooper in the Inniskillen Dragoons, whose barracks were at Edinburgh Castle.

Travelling together, David Cunningham and John Fowlis weren't going far at all, only to St Fort, the first station after crossing the Tay Bridge. The name St Fort was actually a corruption of the old words 'sann forde', meaning sandy ford and indeed the area abounded in sand pits and shallow crossings of Motray Water.

David and John had been firm friends since childhood. They were now both 21 years old, both stonemasons and shared the same lodgings at 23 Pitalpin Street, Lochee. They did most things in life together and indeed they were both due to start work building the new asylum at Lochee. They'd decided to spend the day visiting their parents who both lived near Newport on the south bank of the Tay and so bought their nine-penny green third-class return tickets for the 7.30. Robert wore a felt hat, a muffler and a pair of gloves against the sharp December air and, apart from 19s 1d in cash, had his pipe, two books and a number of letters from his sweetheart. He was 5ft 10in tall and inclined to stoutness. David, at 5ft 9in, was also on the plump side and wore a silver watch with a leather 'albert' strap, scarf pins and had 11s and a ha'penny in money. Their close association ironically continued after death when they were buried together at Kilmany, Fife.

Also going to St Fort was 25-year-old mechanic George Johnston, 5ft 6in tall with fair hair and wearing light tweed trousers and a blue topcoat. He was paying a visit to his father, a keeper on the St Fort estate at Sandford. However, he was also looking forward to the return journey that coming night because he'd arranged to meet his sweetheart, Eliza Smart, on the evening 'Edinburgh' when it arrived there at 7.08 p.m. She was going to be travelling from Cupar, where she worked nearby at Kilmaron Castle as Lady Baxter's housemaid.

A lot of folks were off to visit their parents. These people had left the small town or village of their birth to seek better work and career prospects in the big city of Dundee. Nevertheless the imbued Victorian sense of 'family' ensured that they went home as often as possible, even if only for the day. People like James Crichton (one of two men of that name to be aboard the doomed train later that night), off to see his dad in Leven; grocer William H. Jack going to visit his Mum in Dairsie;

brothers William and Alexander Robertson to see their father William in Abernethy; and Annie Spence going to visit her parents in Newburgh. Plasterer John Lawson, who was 25 years old, was also off to Newburgh to see his parents. Mr Lawson lived with wife Mary and their two children at 39 Lilybank Road, Dundee, and he had reddish curly hair and wore a tweed coat. Timber-merchant clerk James Smith was going to Springfield to visit his grandfather.

Some were simply making social calls to friends. John Sharp, a 35-year-old joiner who lived at 76 Commercial Street, Dundee, with his ageing parents, worked for the jam-makers James Keiller in Castle Street. He was off to see his pal Robert Brown who shared the same trade and lived in Abbey Close, St Andrews. Because the branch line there was closed on Sundays, John would have to walk the 5 miles from Leuchars Junction.

William MacDonald was taking his 11-year-old son David to see their friend Peter McLaren, a hotelier in Newburgh. Foreman Saddler Walter Ness from Bain Square had friends in Auchtermuchty which was on another branch line that was shut on a Sunday, so he'd have to walk the 5 miles from Ladybank Junction.

Two men called Watson though unrelated, Robert and David, were Fife-bound for the day. Robert, a 34-year-old iron moulder, was taking his two sons, David aged 9 and 6-year-old Robert, to Cupar. Back home at 12 Lawrence Street, Mrs Watson had opposed the idea of the trip but Robert had promised his boys they were going and he would not break his word. The two lads were very excited at the thought of crossing the great Tay Bridge twice in one day!

The other Watson was David, an 18-year-old commission agent from Newport who doesn't enter the story until the train's return trip in the evening.

David Neish, 37 years old, from 51 Coupar Street, Dundee, was a schoolteacher and registrar. He was taking his 5-year-old daughter Isabella (whom everyone called Bella) to visit a relative, Mrs Robert Baxter in Maryhall Street, Kirkcaldy. He had the usual array of pocket contents for a Victorian gentleman – watch, pocketknife, tobacco pouch, pipe and a bunch of keys, plus just over a pound in cash. Fair-haired little Bella was wearing boots, a pillbox hat decorated with crêpe feathers, a black satin dress, white shawl and black stockings.

The net result of all these different arrivals was a flurry of carriage-door slamming as everyone found seats and settled down for the trip.

On the footplate, Marshall could see the fruits of his labours – a lovely fire about a foot thick all over the flat grate and burning through nicely, three-quarters of a gauge glass of water and boiler pressure close to maximum. Perfect. He started the injector, which picked up with that sweet singing sound beloved of footplate men, feeding cold water into the boiler to keep her from blowing off steam. Dundee Stationmaster James Smith had hard words for crews who allowed their engines to roar off steam from the safety valves. It frightened lady passengers and turned tearful goodbyes into shouting matches.

The Westinghouse brake pump was gently panting with a slow asthmatic rhythm. You'd recognise the sound straight away from Western cowboy movies when engines stand at frontier-town stations.

Marshall placed two white paraffin headlamps on their brackets, one on each side of the front buffer beam, and gave the red lenses a quick buff with a piece of cotton waste. This head code, as it was known, meant the train was officially an express passenger service although on a Sunday, the 'Edinburghs' were stopping trains calling at all stations.

The guard for today's 7.30 a.m. train to Burntisland and the return service to Dundee at 5.27 p.m. was 44-year-old bachelor David McBeath. He'd only had a very short walk from his home in 46 Castle Street – a mere 350yd to his booking-on point at the Traffic Department Office at Dundee Tay Bridge station.

Keiller's Jam and Marmalade shop was also in Castle Street, very convenient for him as he liked 'jeely pieces' and had stocked his food bag with them for today's lunch. A thickset man, 5ft 11in tall with a bushy full beard, he was dressed in his North British Railway passenger guard's uniform of navy blue coat with red piping with the legends 'NORTH BRITISH' on one collar and 'GUARD' on the other, the words stitched over a quatrefoil of gold thread. His navy blue trousers were made from 'Oxford Mixture' doeskin. To top it off, he wore a Zouave-style cap. Goods guards wore pilot jackets with cord waistcoats and trousers.

Macbeath's watch and chain were NBR brass issues and the watch itself was made by the John Walker Company in Princes Street, Soho. It was marked 'E&GR', the initials of the Edinburgh and Glasgow Railway. This company had amalgamated with the NBR back in 1865 so McBeath had probably originally worked as a guard on the E&GR, thus having at least fourteen years' service to his credit.

A guard's wages might be anywhere between 18s to 30s (depending on longevity of service) for a seventy-two-hour week. With his seniority, McBeath would have been on the top scale.

Up he came to the engine with the train details and weight and to take the driver's name for his guard's journal.

'Six on, 55 tons'[15] he tersely reported to Mitchell and walked back down the platform to his van. A little taciturn by nature, he eschewed the banter usual between train crews at the start of a trip.

Back again by his guard's van, he checked the three red tail-lamps were lit and burning brightly and then helped himself to a liberal pinch from his silver snuffbox.

His official companion for today's round trip was Donald Murray, who was a mail guard and supervised the carriage and security of Her Majesty's Royal Mail. Murray was 49 years old and lived with his wife and three children in South Ellen Street, Dundee. Ironically and, just like Driver Mitchell, he wasn't actually listed for duty that morning and came to work at the last moment. Murray had been on his way to an early church service when a railway messenger intercepted him and told him that the rostered mail guard for the 7.30 to Burntisland was ill and could he take over? So, still carrying his prayer book, which was all that was ever found of him after the disaster, he joined the train for the last day of his life.

Stern Sabbatarians in Scotland were critical of the railways running on a Sunday but did admit: 'Carrying the mail helps them out. But is it necessary to keep up the Sabbath violation in order to forward the mail?' The passengers, whose only day off work was the Sabbath, were only too pleased that there were any Sunday trains at all. Otherwise, working six-day weeks, they wouldn't be able to see their friends and relatives from one year's end to another.

David Johnston, aged 24, was yet another NBR guard but was today travelling off-duty to Edinburgh to spend the day with his wife, 5-year-old son and 9-week-old babe-in-arms. His posting to Dundee had split up his family life, but soon Mrs Johnston and the children would be moving up to join him. Meanwhile, he was only able to visit them once a week on his Sunday off. He climbed aboard the guard's van to keep McBeath and Murray company for the trip, as he would again on the return journey later that afternoon.

The station clock came round to 7.30 and the signal arms ahead tumbled off into their 'clear' positions, their lamps pricking the early morning darkness. They showed a white light in those days. Although red has always meant 'danger', green for 'go' didn't come into use until 1892 but was used on distant signals to indicate 'caution'. A little memory-jog phrase used by railway staff at the time explained the colour code perfectly:

> White is Right and Red is Wrong,
> Green means gently go along.

With the starting signal in the down or 'off' position, McBeath blew a warning blast on his pea-whistle[16] and waved the train away with a flourish of his flag. Both men on the footplate were looking back down the train, double-checking that all doors were shut and no one on the platform was too near the edge. Marshall, seeing and hearing McBeath's permission to start, shouted 'Right Behind, Right Away!!' So Mitchell pushed the long reversing lever into full forward gear, opened the regulator and yanked the whistle chain, the hoot sending a thin column of steam straight up into the still air. The North British Railway whistles provided for engines were of a very mellow tone, a deep rich baritone in contrast to the bass of the rival Caledonian locomotives.

For the first few beats of the engine, Mitchell left the cylinder drain cocks open and the reversing lever fully forward. Barking happily out of her tall stovepipe chimney, No 224 stamped out of the station until Driver Mitchell shut the drain cocks and moved the reversing lever back a little from full gear. Called 'notching up', a car driver would refer to this practice in his vehicle as 'changing gear'.

Fireman John Marshall then continued his firebox preparations for the journey ahead. Everything about driving and especially firing a steam locomotive is anticipation. A thorough knowledge of the route, gradients and speed restrictions is essential so that steam in plenty is available for the driver's use when needed and not blown off wastefully through the safety valves when not required.

Firstly, he gave a quick stir-up to the fire with the pricker and then worked on the back corners of the firebox, sticking several shovelfuls of coal to build up a 'tump' or thickening of the fire just inside the firebox doors. He then put four good shovelfuls down to each front corner of the firebox, six down the front end and six more straight down the middle. The 'hump' of the haycock fire began to take shape. He carried on in this fashion with shovel-shots to the front, middle and back until he was satisfied that he had a good fire bed to work on further. The journey could now begin in earnest.

Notes

1. Refer to Preface (i) the *Princess Alice* disaster in the chapter note section.
2. The working classes normally used charcoal or a recipe from *The Farmer's Almanac* of 1855, which recommended one ounce of myrrh powder, two spoonsful of honey and a pinch of sage.
3. All footplate crew started off their service as engine cleaners/call boys. They had to be able to read and write and earned about 16*s* to 20*s* per week depending on seniority. They couldn't become a fireman until aged 19 years, when they could earn 3*s* 4*d* a day. After many more years they may get promotion to driver, starting at 4*s* 6*d* per day, rising to 7*s* like Mitchell.
4. The North British Railway claimed it had no locomotives, no coaches and never ran freight trains. How did they do anything? Well, they called the items engines, carriages and goods trains.
5. Railway employees' rights were badly protected in 1879. The unions were in their infancy and the railway companies wouldn't tolerate or recognise them. The Engine Drivers & Firemen's United Society was formed in 1865 but only lasted two years. The Amalgamated Society of Railway Servants followed in 1871 and managed to survive. In Edwardian times it renamed itself The National Union of Railwaymen and exists today as the biggest British railway union. Its brother organisation ASLEF (Associated Society of Locomotive Engineers and Firemen) would be formed in 1880. As there was no State machinery in place, the new unions would soon set up accident, orphan and sick funds to support their members at times of distress. But back in 1879 there was nothing. If a railway worker was injured, sick or even died, the whole family was thrown on the mercy of the community and alms from the churches.
6. An engine's 'diagram' referred to its list of duties over a twenty-four-hour period.
7. The pair were *not* the first 4-4-0 engines built in Britain as asserted by many historians. 4-4-0 locomotives were built for the Great Western in the 1840s and for the Stockton & Darlington Railway in 1860. Coincidentally, these latter were designed by Sir Thomas Bouch's elder brother William. However, Wheatley's engines *were* the first 4-4-0s with inside frames and inside cylinders. The type proliferated on railways worldwide for many years to come.
8. The GWR was always individualistic, with its 7ft and a ¼in broad gauge track until 1892. Even Thomas Bouch had shares in the company.
9. 'Cut-off' was the point in the piston's stroke when the valve gear cut off the steam supply to the cylinders. 'Full gear', when steam was admitted for 75 per cent of the stroke, was only used for starting away. When a train was on the move the reversing lever was moved back through its quadrant so that the steam admission to the cylinders was 'cut off' earlier in the stroke. An analogy here is a heavy door which you must imagine two people are trying to swing backwards

and forwards. To get it moving they need to push for nearly the whole swing but once it is going it's better for each pusher to give a shorter shove in the early part of the swing.

10   Refer to 1(i) 'Westinghouse Brakes' in the chapter note section.
11   Refer to 1(ii) 'Injectors' in the chapter note section.
12   Whistles were first used on the Leicester & Swannington Railway in the English Midlands after a train hauled by the engine *Samson* was in collision at a level crossing on Saturday 4 May 1833. It hit a cart laden with 50lb of butter and 80 dozen eggs en route to Leicester Market – all the makings of a gigantic omelette. The accident happened primarily because the engine had no audible warning of approach and the cart driver didn't hear the train coming before setting out across the line of rails. To avoid a repetition of such an event, Ashlin Bagster, the railway manager, suggested to George Stephenson (the line's engineer and major shareholder), that it might be possible to fit a steam whistle to engines. He visited a musical instrument maker in King Street, Leicester who devised a 'steam trumpet', 18in long by 6in across the top. When this was fitted to *Samson* it proved so successful that all railway companies soon adopted the idea. Credit for the invention is due not to Stephenson, who never laid claim to it anyway, but to Bagster.
13   Trimmings were the driver's responsibility. He both made them and used them. Basically they allowed a flow of oil down a pipe to where it was needed, such as an axle box or the horn cheek bearings. They were made from worsted yarn wrapped around copper wire. Their sizes determined the rate of oil-flow and were set to be an easy fit inside the oil pipe.
14   Detonators cost a penny each and were flat hollow metal discs about 2in across containing three fulminate of mercury caps. In an emergency they were fixed to the running rail by means of lead tags. When crunched by an engine's wheels they would go off with a loud bang, giving a positive warning of danger ahead. Invented by E.A. Cowper in 1841.
15   'Six on' meant six vehicles and 55 tons meant the total weight of the train, not including the engine.
16   *Not* the world-famous 'Acme Thunderer' whistle used the world over and still in production today. They weren't available until 1883.

2

Tay to Forth:
Across Fiobha, the Kingdom of Fife

A fringe of gold on a beggar's mantle.

(King James VI (1542–1625) writing of Scotland but referring to the Kingdom of Fife as the fringe of gold)

For the first quarter-mile or so, after a brief stiff climb at 1 in 68 out of Dundee Tay Bridge station, the train headed west on the flat, running parallel with the River Tay and the Esplanade, with extensive goods yard sidings on one side and the engine shed on the other.

The double-track main line branched into two at Buckingham Junction, the pair of lines to the right joining the Caledonian Railway main line coming from its own Dundee West station and heading off to Perth.

The left lines were for Fife and climbed steeply on 1 in 66 and 1 in 74 gradients to the start of the Tay Bridge. Mitchell opened the engine out until she rasped up the grade to reach Tay Bridge North Signal Box.

The train slowed down to the regulation 3mph to allow Marshall to lean from the cab to collect the 'Train Staff' (see below) from Signalman Henry Somerville, for here the double line of rails ended and merged into one for the crossing of the bridge. Somerville had been stationed at the North Box for a year, having previously been the signalman at Leuchars Junction. He'd come on duty on the Saturday night and then only came to the box when required to pass trains which were very few on Sundays. In between times, he went home.

Single lines of railway like the Tay Bridge have the inherent danger of two trains speeding in opposite directions and colliding. The worst-case scenario would be two trains meeting head-on in the middle of this 88ft-high bridge across an arm of the North Sea. To obviate such horrors, British railway signalling practice had evolved a system where two signal boxes, one at each end of the single track, passed a 'Train Staff' to the driver entering the section between them as physical authority to be on that single track. As there was only one 'Staff', theoretically there could only ever be one train at a time on the stretch of line.[1]

So the Staff shuttled backwards and forwards with each service. In the case of two trains timetabled to head in the same direction one after the other, the Staff was shown to the driver of Train 1, who was then given a written ticket to prove he'd seen the staff, and the driver of Train 2 carried the Staff in the usual way.

The Tay Bridge Train Staff collected by John Marshall was an 18in-long hollow brass tube with a 4in T-bar at one end and a hexagonal swelling in the middle bearing, separately on each of the six flat surfaces, the engraved inscriptions: 'TAY BRIDGE', 'TRAIN STAFF' and 'No 4'. A wooden rod ran inside the length of the brass piece and protruded from either end. One wooden end was slotted to receive the single-line ticket when necessary. The staff weighed about 4½lb and was later recovered from the Tay. It can be seen to this day at Glasgow Transport Museum.

Rumbling across two separated bow-string girder spans onto the beginning of the bridge proper, the train continued to steam against a gradient of 1 in 73 as it turned through 90 degrees on a very tight twenty-chain radius curve, finally to head south out across the river.

Mitchell kept No 224 chugging away at a steady 25mph, which was the speed limit for trains crossing the bridge. Many other drivers were liberal in their interpretation of this regulation, often getting up to 40mph, especially with the weekday morning northbound commuter trains on the downgrade during and after the high girder section. But Driver Mitchell was a diligent man when it came to the rules of the road and anyway the schedule for the Sunday mail trains was easy, with no need to paste along.

An example of Mitchell's qualities as a driver was his foresight. He always carried six little India-rubber rings and a piece of stiff brass wire in his waistcoat pocket, against the possibility of the boiler water gauge glass breaking. The rubber rings were required as seals for re-seating the replacement glass, and the wire was for digging out the old perished rings. Not every driver was so conscientiously well prepared.

Although sunrise wasn't due for another hour, the oyster light of pre-dawn caused the dark-maroon red-lead paint of the bridge girder work to glisten. Below, the river waters were calm. Their colour was dilute saffron as they slopped gently against the brick pier bases.

Squadrons of seagulls wheeled and cawed around the bridge with air-show precision, prompting Marshall to remark about the possibility of a coming storm. He was thinking of the old sailors' tale about seabirds coming inland if a 'blow' was imminent. But that morning there were also several large black cormorants lurking on the pier bases and lazily orbiting in and out of the girders. The cormorant or sea raven has always been regarded as a bird of sinister reputation and a harbinger of death.

In *Paradise Lost* John Milton compared Satan to a cormorant and Charlotte Brontë's Jane Eyre pictured a cormorant perched above a drowned body. Staunch Scottish Presbyterians would have approved these ironies as omens to those people who broke the Sabbath by daring to travel.

You'd think that an engine's footplate would be a warm haven on a cold day with its roaring fire. Not so, especially on a nineteenth-century engine like a Wheatley bogie. For a start, the cab was a very rudimentary structure indeed, not much more than a weatherboard with the top bent over into a tiny roof. These early locomotives look very archaic to us now, given the scanty footplate protection provided. The engine designers of the day agreed with Isambard Kingdom Brunel, he of Great Western Railway fame, who'd said that to pamper engine crews by giving them a cab would invite accidents as their attention would wander! There was nothing like a cold wind, with the liberal addition of smoke, smuts and steam, for keeping men alert.[2]

So No 224's footplate was a very cold and draughty place to work, even on a fine day. The only parts of your body likely to be at all warm were your legs and this would be the case only when the firebox doors were open for firing. But even so, you'd be alternately scorched or frozen. In such an open cab the crosswind was vicious – the skin on the hands could split with the contrasting temperatures of cold wind and the heat from the fire. Both men would be pretty miserable by the time they reached the Tay Bridge that night on the northward journey – but it was all part of their job – 3s 6d a day for Marshall, and 7s a day for Mitchell.

Mitchell, on the left side of the footplate, maintained his gaze ahead through the spectacle glass in the cab front, watching for signals, with one hand on the regulator and the other resting lightly but ready to respond on the Westinghouse brake handle. Marshall, to his right, plied the shovel, carefully placing 'shots' of coal where the fire needed them. He glanced regularly at the steam pressure needle and the water gauge glass.

The train continued to climb the gradient on the bridge away out across the river, with prosaic-sounding sandbanks to the left and right – The Binns of Blackness, Dog Bank, Naughton Bank, Middlebank and My Lord's Bank, a favourite spot for basking seals at low tide. By contemporary accounts, crossing Thomas Bouch's Tay Bridge could be quite an alarming experience for a first-time passenger.

The bridge deck was very narrow, 'not much wider than a respectable dining-room table', said a columnist in the *Dundee Advertiser*.[3]

Which meant that the view from a carriage window resembled flying across the river with no visible means of support as all the girder and pier work was below the passengers' line of sight. But after about half a mile and still climbing, the train reached the 'high girders', thirteen long spans which enclosed the track like a latticework tunnel, which was more reassuring to a nervous traveller. The first five of these spans were still on a 1 in 73 rising gradient which levelled off at the start of span six. After clearing these spans, the gradient started to fall at 1 in 365 towards the north shore. To the left, a passenger could see a permanent resident of the river. This was the training ship *Mars*, anchored and bowered with her bows facing upstream in roughly the middle of the Tay and half a mile to seaward of the bridge.[4]

The train neared the Fife side of the estuary, passing lower quadrant signals controlled from Tay Bridge South Signal Box. Here the bridge was level again for two spans but just a few yards short of the south bank and still on the bridge, the track split into two directions and actually climbed at 1 in 100 for the last three spans. The left fork was for Newport, the right for Leuchars Junction and the south. Tay Bridge South Signal Box was inside this 'Y' junction and there, with the train slowed to a walking pace, David Mitchell leaned from the cab and passed the Staff to Signalman Barclay with a cheery, 'Good Morning, Bobby!'

Although he had been christened 'Thomas', Barclay found nothing odd about being addressed as 'Bobby'. In the early days of railways, policemen controlled the primitive signalling and ever since the old nickname for a constable persisted for signalmen, as it does to this very day. Barclay was dressed in his uniform of an indigo jacket with a red collar and a cap with a red band. It's quite probable he wasn't wearing his cap, as signalmen down through the years seemed to eschew the donning of headgear, according to their published reminiscences. In an average week with overtime, he might expect 18s in his pay packet. Not a lot considering the huge safety responsibilities inherent with the job.

Mitchell, now with his train back on double track, pulled away from the South Signal Box and accelerated round the curves past Wormit Bay, passing an extensive yard of sidings where on weekdays, goods and coal trains queued up to cross the bridge to Dundee.

Soon after passing Peacehill hamlet and surmounting a small summit on the line, the train coasted down a short 1 in 100 gradient to stop at St Fort station at 7.41 a.m., just over 4½ miles from Dundee. Mitchell brought No 224 and the train to a stand with a single last-minute application of the Westinghouse brake, which he released immediately on stopping. The pump panted away to restore the reservoir air pressure.

Here, David Cunningham, John Fowlis and George Johnston jumped off. They'd meet up on the platform once again to catch the evening 'Edinburgh', George anticipating a canoodle that night with Eliza as they all headed home across the Tay Bridge.

And so the 7.30 wended its way across Fife,[5] the ancient Kingdom of the East Gaels and steeped in the fibres of early Scottish history.

The train would call briefly at poetic-sounding stations like Leuchars and Ladybank, Dairsie and Dysart, Kingskettle, Kinghorn and Kirkcaldy but passengers in mid-Fife on a Scottish Sunday were few and they were getting fewer as the train meandered southwards.

John Sharp had got off at Leuchars Junction at around 7.52 a.m. and was walking the 5 miles to St Andrews as that branch line, like many others, was closed on a Sunday. William Jack alighted at Dairsie (at 7.59 a.m.) on a visit to comfort his mother Jane, as not only had she recently been widowed but also her daughter, William's sister, had been buried the week before. Death had certainly singled out the Jack family at the end of 1879, for by the end of that night, Jane would have no one left when William drowned in the River Tay.

Robert Watson and his two sons detrained at Cupar at 8.06 a.m. By 8.12 a.m. James Smith had left the train at Springfield, where his grandfather lived. At 8.19 a.m., the train arrived at Ladybank Junction, the name curiously derived from 'Our Lady's Bog'. Lindores monks dug peat here in the thirteenth century and the Gaelic version of the name seems to have been bestowed then – 'leathead bog' meaning 'moist slope'. Anyway here, 20 miles and forty-nine minutes away from Dundee, there was quite an exodus of passengers. For waiting at Ladybank was a train for Perth, one of the few branch line connections running on a Sunday. The North British justified this on the grounds that the Caledonian Railway did not operate its Perth to Dundee direct route on the Sabbath which, without the NBR, would leave two important cities with no Sunday train service between them.

Abernethy and Newburgh were stations on this route and destinations for William MacDonald and his son David, Annie Spence, the Robertson brothers and John Lawson. They all clambered aboard the Perth train and were on their way again at 8.35 a.m. But there was no further train ride for 24-year-old Walter Ness. He had a 5-mile trudge to Auchtermuchty, which was on a 'Weekdays Only' branch line.

Meanwhile, the 'Edinburgh' pulled out of Ladybank on time at 8.21 a.m. and headed for Kingskettle, a small village in the Howe of Fife, known locally as 'Kettle', the name of the parish.[6]

The bluish haze of the distant Paps O' Fife (or Lomond Hills) was visible off to the right in the growing daylight. Mitchell opened No 224's regulator wide and lengthened the cut-off with the reversing lever on leaving Kingskettle at 8.25 a.m., in order to climb the steep 1 in 90 gradient up to Falkland Road station and the summit at Lochmuir. Marshall strived to keep up the steam pressure essential for uphill pulling. He maintained a steady round of shovel-shots onto the fire and a constant eye on the pressure gauge. Black smoke appearing briefly at the chimney top gave evidence of each shovel thrown into the firebox and was also a sign of good firing technique.

Suddenly, a mutual greeting of whistle hoots shivered the morning air as their 'opposite number' train – the 7.32 a.m. from Burntisland – whooshed by. Bucketing and swaying down the gradient, it was carrying the morning Edinburgh ferry passengers northwards and would cross the Tay to reach Dundee at 9.25 a.m.

The crew would spend all day there before their return trip at 4.10 p.m. but at least Dundee had more diversions to offer, even on a Sunday, than the town of Burntisland provided for Mitchell, Marshall, McBeath and Murray. The two trains were due to pass each other again that day, going their opposite ways once again between Kirkaldy and Sinclairtown at about 5.45 p.m.

The Gaelic words for a horse meadow are 'marc-innis'. Thus the name 'Markinch' evolved, and was where the train arrived at 8.40 a.m. and where James Crichton got off, on his way to see his father John in Leven. This was yet another destination with no Sunday trains. In fact the Leven branch actually ran from Thornton Junction, the next stop, but it was only a 6-mile walk for Crichton if he started instead from Markinch.

The stop at Thornton Junction, 28½ miles from Dundee, coincided with sunrise at 8.48 a.m., so that the last part of the journey would be lit with watery, winter sunshine.

The line was heading due south now, directly towards the Firth of Forth, and passing through one of the extensive Fifeshire coal-mining areas. Here, a big new pit called The Frances Pit had only recently been opened in 1878 and was known locally as 'The Dubbie', as the mine had been sunk at Dubbie Braes and 'dubby' was a local word for a rock pool. The miles of exchange sidings running alongside the main line were filled with loaded coal wagons, mostly bound for Dundee, where the coal would fuel the jute mills, flax mills and iron foundries. The Tay Bridge carried thousands of tons of coal from Fife every week and had been a vital factor in the boom town economics Dundee was now enjoying.

A couple of miles of uphill running at gradients of 1 in 170 and 1 in 195 brought the train over the hump to Dysart and Fireman Marshall's shovelwork for the outward trip was done. He brushed the footplate clear of loose coal, relaxed back against the tender handbrake standard and sniffed the sharp salt tang of the sea from the broad Firth of Forth which was coming into sight to the left of the engine. It was all downhill to Burntisland now and he could afford to let the fire burn down.

There was a fragile hint of morning gold over everything at Kirkcaldy where the train pulled in at 9.09 a.m. This was the destination of David Neish and daughter Bella. Being a well-read schoolteacher and interested in Scottish history, David explained to his little girl the origins of the town's name, which were several. Kirkcaldy may have been derived from 'calatin', meaning Father of Magicians – or it may have come from the Gaelic 'cala dion' meaning 'harbour of refuge'. Either way, said David to Bella, by the year 1150 the place was already called Kirkcalathin.

The last 6 miles were a delight to the eye as the train ran along a beautiful coastline, passing broad sandy beaches and little rocky coves. Soon the train approached the small town of Kinghorn, named from the Gaelic Ceann Gronna which means 'Blue Headland'. The town had a royal castle, The Kinghorn or Glamis Tower, and had been a royal borough since 1170.[7] Kinghorn in 1879 was a thriving centre for spinning and shipbuilding.

The railway station was (and is) perched high between the town and the firth and sported the original platform lampposts from 1847 which bore cast-iron plates reading 'Edinr & Northn. Raily' (sic), a legacy of the Edinburgh & Northern Railway which had built this section of line. These lampposts actually survived intact until May 1976.

After a pause at 9.17 a.m., when no one either got off or boarded, the train passed through a short 250yd-long tunnel under Witch Hill, so called because of the execution of suspected witches there.[8] To the left of the train and below the station stands the parish church beside the firth. Churches have been built here since the earliest times, new ones being erected on the ruins of the old. The church seen from the train on that Sunday morning was built in 1874. For some reason all the churches in the locality were built without steeples and throughout the ages the town was noted for its lawlessness, these factors begetting a local rhyme: 'Here stands a church without a steeple, a drunken priest and a graceless people.'

In the distance, far across the wide Firth of Forth, Edinburgh was a grey smoky smudge with the stony shoulder of Arthur's Seat rising above it. On this clear still morning, Mitchell and Marshall could see beyond to the Pentland Hills and the distinctive volcanic cone of Berwick Law.

Closer into the foreground of this picturesque panorama lay Inchkeith Island (the Gaelic name *Innse Coit* meaning 'wooded island'), about 2¾ miles out into the Firth of Forth and named after the Keith family, the hereditary Great Marischals of Scotland who once owned Inchkeith.[9]

By 9.24 a.m. the train finally reached journey's end at Burntisland, 39 miles from Dundee. The train approached Burntisland by running in past the Locomotive Works and Roundhouse Engine Shed, built by the Edinburgh & Northern Railway on the seawall.

Looking for all the world like the giant Moroccan cooking pot that is called a 'tagine', with the conical roof and fume escape duct at the top, the engine shed had a turntable in the middle, from which radiated, like the spokes of a wheel, the engine stabling tracks.

Then came the first of Burntisland's signal boxes: East Box. After passing under the wooden-girdered Lammerlaws Bridge, Lammerlaws Signal Box could be seen perched on a convenient rock, controlling the left-hand junction for the lines down to the train ferry docks. Finally, the train ran into Burntisland Terminus itself, which was controlled by the West Box. The terminal building was quite an imposing structure, having a classical arcaded frontage and an overall iron roof of two spans covering the three platform faces. Standing on the quayside was the Forth Hotel, which was originally a manse. This building apparently was not to the minister's liking and the congregation bought him another residence that was away from the harbour. Given that before the Forth and Tay Bridges were built, the passenger travelling from Edinburgh to Dundee went by train from Edinburgh to Granton, then across the Firth of Forth by ferry, train to Tayport and another ferry across the Tay, the early rail service afforded good business opportunities for the town and the ex-manse was rebuilt as a hotel. Next to it were Downie's Stables, which were built for stabling post horses and carriages.

The rails continued through the station to the West Dock, crossing the cobblestone road used by passengers coming up from the ferries.

Off-duty guard David Johnston said goodbye to McBeath and Murray in the guard's van and joined the other Edinburgh passengers, including David Syme and William Threlfell, as they walked down to the ferry pier to board the 9.31 a.m. vessel sailing for Granton. On such a calm morning, the crossing proved to be a pleasure trip. On the other side of the Forth, they caught the 10.12 a.m. train for Edinburgh Waverley. The arrival of this service at 10.36 a.m. gave the day-trippers just five and three-quarter hours to visit their friends and families before starting the homeward trip to Dundee at 4.15 p.m.

At roughly the same time that the Dundonians were stepping down on to the Waverley station platform, Queen Victoria and members of the royal family including Princess Louise, were off to attend Divine Service at Osborne Church on the Isle of Wight, with the Reverend A.L.B. Pelle, MA, Vicar of Holy Trinity, Ventnor, officiating.

After the service, the royal party drove back to Osborne House for lunch, where Queen Victoria no doubt had her favourite aperitif of claret and whisky mixed together.

With the royal family spending Christmas on the Isle of Wight instead of at Balmoral, there would be no further royal trains across the Tay Bridge that year. In fact the one and only time that Queen Victoria crossed Bouch's Tay Bridge was in late June 1879. Royal train journeys to Balmoral were very expensive.[10]

In Burntisland, Marshall and Mitchell prepared for a long dull day. They unhooked No 224 from the carriages, which they were to leave parked up all day at one of the station's platforms. They then took their mount off to Burntisland engine shed, which was a multiple-road roundhouse with a turntable at the centre, as mentioned earlier. They refilled the water in the tender, took the loco into the roundhouse and 'turned her' on the turntable.

'Turning' an engine is a delicate operation. The engine must be driven onto the turntable very slowly and brought to rest gently to avoid straining the mechanism and structure of the turntable. Balance is everything. During the operation of turning, Mitchell and Marshall would have ensured that on the engine, the handbrake was screwed hard on, the reverser in mid-gear and the cylinder drain-cocks open. Being a hand-operated turntable, it was pushed round rather than pulled because when pushing, the man operating the table is behind the pushing bars, so if he should fall or slip the table will move away and leave him clear. A man pulling on the bar, however, might be injured if he slipped or fell, because the bar would pass over him.

Marshall started the injector in order to fill the boiler right up, watching the gauge glass until the water reached the top nut, and then blacked in the fire by shovelling plenty of coal all over the grate, shutting both the dampers and the firebox door. This would slow up the combustion just enough so that the fire would be burnt through by about 5 p.m., when the engine would be needed again.

No 224 was now 'stabled' for the next seven hours. Terminology and phrases such as this were derived from eighteenth-century stagecoach days. The name 'guard' certainly was a throwback from those days as was the phrase 'be in the collar', meaning an engine working hard pulling uphill; this was a comparison to horse-drawn vehicles, where the harness pulled around the horse's neck as a result of the strain. Shouting, 'Whoa, Whoa', to stop an engine and directing 'Engines to take water' are further 'horsey' examples, such as calling an engine your 'mount'. Many of these phrases persist in railway practice to this day.

The men then retired to the crew room for food and tea, but not before they'd had a thorough wash on No 224's footplate. Work on a steam railway engine always entailed getting very dirty indeed and the crew would be covered in oil, coal dust, grease, smuts and grime from even a shortish run like this one from Dundee. Washing facilities at sheds were primitive in those days – for instance having one cold-water tap and using a bucket shared between everyone. At least the engine had hot water laid on. For more personal needs, the shed 'gents' was nothing more than a row of wooden seats with circular holes cut into them and in a situation of minimal privacy. Wads of old newspapers jammed onto a nail masqueraded as toilet paper.

The crew made more tea for their bottles and like comrades-in-arms, shared their food.

The porridge was eaten cold straight from the brown paper wrapping and Mitchell gave John Marshall a big chunk of potted hough from his food bag. They saved their jeely pieces for later and went for a stroll along the seawall, returning to the crew room for a hand or two of cards, a smoke and an afternoon nap on the hard wooden benches.

At that point James Young, the Burntisland Carriage and Wagon Inspector and a man with four years' service with the North British Railway, went to inspect the six carriages of the train.

All passenger-carrying rolling stock was routinely checked over daily and sometimes twice daily, depending on the mileage it was accruing. Wheel failure was an all-too-common cause of some very serious accidents on mid-Victorian railways.

Young used a hammer to clout every wheel and listened carefully to the noise it made. As a 'wheel tapper' he knew that a nice 'ding' would tell him whether a wheel was sound and not about to crack apart. This was a crude method of testing but it was the analogue forerunner of the ultrasonic wheel analysis used today. Because the left side of the train was against the platform edge, he could only access the right-hand side wheels for tapping. The left ones would have to wait until the train reached Leuchars Junction later on the return trip, where the island platform there exposed the left of the train. Young also examined all the carriage springs and checked out the couplings, the brake hoses and the interiors of the vehicles before signing everything off as all correct.

He did, however, miss checking that the Westinghouse brake hose was seated properly on its 'dummy' on the third-class coach before the second-class vehicle abutting the brake or luggage van at the rear.

Back up in Dundee, the day had begun most pleasantly with a clear-skied morning, absolutely no wind and with many of the city's population on its knees inside one kirk (church) or another. These weather conditions persisted through to the early afternoon but people afterwards commented on an eerie stillness to the air. One observer in Dundee noted: 'It was a strange night. From 4 o'clock onwards there were portentous ominous signs seen and heard.'

This became more apparent as the short December afternoon wore on, reinforcing the dour inertia that seemed to permeate Victorian Scotland on the Sabbath.

During the ten minutes after moonrise at 3.31 p.m. and sunset at 3.41 p.m. a small lunar eclipse was observed individually by a number of weather watchers and astronomers.

After sunset, a brilliant rising moon took over the illumination of the Tay valley.

Admiral William Herriot Maitland Dougall RN (Retd) had lived in Scotscraig on the south bank of the Tay near the estuary mouth for many years since his retirement and always kept a meticulous log of all weather conditions. As he noted falling barometric readings, he remarked: 'There's mischief coming.'

Commander Scott, captain of the *Mars*, was also a weather enthusiast, as was Mr Charles Clarke, who had lived at Westfield Cottage, Magdalen Green, hard by the north end of the bridge, for fifty-two years. From their records, a full picture of the onset of the storm can be plotted.

At 9 a.m., the barometer stood at 29.54in of mercury. At 1.15 p.m., the weather was good and the river smooth. However, by dusk at 4.15 p.m., things had freshened up a bit. The 4 p.m. local train from Dundee to Tayport crossed the bridge just as Mr McKinney, the bridge lamplighter, was part-way through his duties. Every day he went out and back across the bridge for 24*s* 6*d* a week, looking after the twenty-eight navigation lights, one per side of each High Girder pier. He lit them at dusk and put them out again at dawn. The piped gas supply for the lamps was actually carried through one of the bridge deck's handrails. Between-times, McKinney undertook odd maintenance jobs on the bridge. That afternoon he pulled his coat more tightly about him as the wind sharpened and hummed eerily through the bridge girder work. He could feel a strong tremor in the decking under his feet as the 4 p.m. clattered past, but there was nothing unusual in that for him. The bridge always vibrated and swayed when a train crossed and he thought nothing of it. Soon afterwards, the 4.15 p.m. 'Edinburgh' from Dundee to Burntisland went by him, the last 'UP' train ever to cross the bridge. Heavier than the 4 p.m. local, it seemed to make the bridge shudder and quiver even more.

Captain Scott aboard *Mars* recorded that the wind was west-south-west and that it had begun to rain quite heavily. At 5 p.m. the wind had veered to westward and was rising, with flurries of sleet from the west. The tide had also begun to ebb. Like the good naval man he was, Scott ordered everything aboard *Mars* to be battened down tight because he could 'sniff' that a gale was coming.

Furious squalls with brief lulls were now attacking Dundee and the Tay estuary. A sharp fall in the barometer was noted by all of the weather enthusiasts, 29.40in to 28.80in by dusk. Seaman Instructor Hugh McMahon kept a careful log aboard the *Mars*, as did Gunnery Instructor Edward Batsworth.

Weather-fan Charles Clarke noted his very lowest barometer reading was at 5 p.m.

The omens were that Dundee, the Tay estuary and, as it proved, most of mid-Scotland could soon expect a very nasty storm indeed. For far out to the west, over the Atlantic Ocean, a huge low-pressure area had been stewing and gathering since earlier in the week. The system spun and gathered strength and, by Saturday night, the harbingers of the whirling lows had crossed Iceland and were reaching Norway.

On Sunday morning, the nascent gale had grown up considerably. The winds were picking up velocity and gusting to 50mph at times. The whole huge vortex, now some 750 miles in diameter, was trailing its coat across central Scotland, Glasgow and the Clyde valley. To the north, one part of the storm was beginning to be forced between the hills forming the Tay valley which, because of its funnel shape, would compress the winds and make them even faster.

By noon the Dundee area, lying at the tightest part of that funnel, was experiencing the classic 'lull before the storm' period of uncanny calm. In the beautiful, quiet early afternoon, only a few weather experts like Captain Scott and Admiral Dougall foresaw a gale in the offing. It crossed no one's mind how the great Tay Bridge might fare in a really big wind. There had been severe gales before and the bridge had stood firm. It was – well, just there – an immovable, indestructible and triumphant piece of work that showed the rest of the world the excellence of British engineering which, of course, was thought to be perfect in every way.

Notes

1   Refer to 2 (i) 'One train at a time' in the chapter note section.
2   Brunel reasoned that the stagecoach driver had had to put up with total exposure for long enough – why should his successor get special treatment? But then Brunel also had this to say about footplate crews: 'I would not give sixpence in hiring an engineman because of his knowing how to read and write. It is impossible that a man that indulges in reading should make a good engine driver: it requires a species of machine, an intelligent man, an honest man, a sober man, a steady man, but I would much rather not have a thinking man.'
3   The bridge deck was actually 14ft wide.
4   *Mars* had been built as an 81-gun three-decker square-rigged ship-of-the-line for the Royal Navy at Chatham in the 1840s and displaced 2,750 tons. After service as a supply ship during the Crimean War, she was converted to screw-and-sail propulsion in 1859 and operated in the Mediterranean for some time. When decommissioned, she languished as a hulk at Sheerness but was saved from the breaker's yard by being brought to moorings on the Tay in August 1869. She hadn't

been painted for eight years and had suffered neglect but was spruced up and converted into a floating school.

Mars's purpose was to train orphan boys for service in the Navy, the Army and the Merchant Marine. The Mars Institution ran the whole enterprise and the ship was captained very competently by Royal Navy Staff Commander Scott, a seaman with years of worldwide experience. He and his officers kept regular weather records which proved vital at the Board of Inquiry into the bridge collapse and gave an idea of the local meteorological picture for that night.

5 Name derived from 'Fib', one of the seven sons of Cruithne, legendary father of the Picts.
6 Kettle is said to take its name from the 'cathel' or battle that took place here between the Scots and the Danes. The village developed in the nineteenth century with the coming of a turnpike road circa 1800 and the opening of the railway in 1847. Linen-weaving and the working of coal and lime were the main sources of employment at the time of our story.
7 It was to this tower on 19 March 1286 that Alexander III, last Scots Celtic King, was riding from Inverkeithing to visit his second wife Yolande, daughter of the French Count de Dreux, when his horse stumbled and fell, pitching Alexander over the clifftop to his death.
8 This tunnel, excavated through an unusual kind of rock called 'Chert y Breccia' (a fragmented black and grey fine-grained siliceous sediment), was an engineering blunder when built by the Edinburgh & Northern Railway because although very short, the tunnellers began from both ends simultaneously yet failed to meet neatly in the middle! Their calculations were way off and to this day, the compensating kink in the middle to get the two halves to join up slows today's Intercity 125s down to a mere 25mph.
9 A strange story connects Inchkeith with King James IV of Scotland. Apparently he could speak eight languages and as an experiment, he placed a dumb woman and two infants on the island to determine which language the children would speak. Some people predicted Hebrew, others Gaelic. Not surprisingly, when they were taken from the island they could not speak at all. In 1497 Inchkeith was used as a quarantine station for Edinburgh victims of 'grandgore' or syphilis in modern parlance. It had a lighthouse opened in 1804 and other construction works included three forts with four 10in rifled muzzle-loading guns. In 1879 these were still being built as a defence of the Forth waterway.
10 Refer to 2 (ii) 'Royal Railway Journeys' in the chapter note section.

3

CROSSING THE FORTH

Tonight the winds begin to rise and roar from yonder dropping day;
The last red leaf is whirl'd away, the rooks are blown about the skies.

Alfred Lord Tennyson, *In Memoriam* (1850)

The very first passengers to start their journey who were to become victims of the Tay Bridge accident were two young ladies from London. We don't have their names, ages or the reasons for their journey to Scotland but we do surmise that on the night of Saturday 27 December 1879 at the Great Northern Railway's King's Cross station, London, they purchased two single third-class tickets for Dundee at 36s 9d each. Anachronistically, the 1879 Fares Table still listed the pricing as 'Gov't 3rd Class', even though the Tory Government Act to improve the lot of third-class travellers had been passed thirty-five years previously.[1]

The ladies then boarded the 9 p.m. overnight train to Edinburgh armed with their green pasteboard tickets, measuring 2¾in long by 1 3/16 in wide. In 1879, on the North British Railway, first-class tickets were white, while second-class and third-class tickets were pink and green respectively.[2]

Departing on a Saturday night meant an early Sunday morning arrival in Edinburgh, but because of the paucity of services on a Scottish Sunday, the young ladies were facing a long day in Edinburgh waiting for their Dundee connecting service.

The nine o'clock train meandered its way up the East Coast route to Scotland, firstly on the Great Northern Railway to York, 188¼ miles from London. Pausing at York from 2 a.m. until 2.10 a.m., the GNR engine was changed for a North Eastern Railway locomotive for the next leg to Newcastle. This very short pause in the journey at least enabled passengers with speedy feet to grab some refreshments from the Royal Station Hotel, which had been opened by the North Eastern Railway a year before, in 1878. But 2.10 a.m. came round very quickly and the train was off and running to Darlington, arriving at 3.15 a.m. and continuing to rattle on through the wee small hours before arriving at Newcastle, with London now 268¼ miles away to the south.

1879 was before the King Edward Bridge across the Tyne had been built so trains to the north had to cross Stephenson's High Level Bridge to the right of Newcastle station in order to enter it from the east end. As a result the new engine from the North Eastern Railway came on at what had been the rear of the train up until that time, and those aboard who had been 'facing the engine' were now pointed the other way round. This probably didn't worry the somnolent passengers until they woke up to the fact many miles further on. Note that these smart and short engine-time changes at York and Newcastle left very little time for passengers to take care of their personal needs at the station facilities, seeing as there were no on-board toilets or refreshments available. The train pulled out of Newcastle at 4.25 a.m. and proceeded northwards on North Eastern Railway metals and up the Northumbrian coast to Berwick-upon-Tweed, arriving at 6.05 a.m., having just crossed Robert Stephenson's Royal Border Bridge, a magnificent twenty-eight-arch stone viaduct some 2,160ft long and 126ft above the River Tweed, and opened by Queen Victoria in 1850.[3]

Here at Berwick, 67 miles north of Newcastle, the route entered North British Railway territory. A final engine change sometimes occurred as a North British Railway locomotive took over for the run across the border and on to Edinburgh but not this night, as the North Eastern engine from Newcastle would work right through. Leaving at 6.10 a.m., the train ran up the NBR main line for the 57½ miles to Edinburgh, calling at Dunbar at 6.53 a.m. About 10 miles short of Edinburgh, the train passed under a small iron girder bridge near the hamlet of Meadowmill and just south of the field where the Battle of Prestonpans (1745) took place. This bridge carried a piece of railway history, to wit, the track of the Tranent-Cockenzie tramway, the very first railway in Scotland, dating from 1722.[4]

Finally the train pulled into Edinburgh Waverley station at 7.40 a.m., ten hours forty minutes and 392¼ miles from London King's Cross.

This arrival time meant that the girls had missed the first of the only two Sunday services to Dundee, which had left Edinburgh Waverley for the Granton ferry connection at 6.20 a.m. At the moment when the ferry connection sailed, they were still aboard their ex-King's Cross train and forging northwards somewhere between Berwick and Dunbar.

So there they were, stuck in Edinburgh with nearly everything shut because it was Sunday and having to wait for nearly nine hours before they could resume their journey to Dundee on the 4.15 p.m. train to the Forth ferry at Granton.

Edinburgh Waverley station was the second largest station in Britain and located very centrally. This was because of the city's geography, with the old medieval town and castle perched on an escarpment to the south and linked via the North Bridge to the new nineteenth-century town on a ridge to the north. Between the two escarpments was a valley, once the site of the Nor'Loch, which had been a fetid open sewer for the old town. The loch was drained in the late eighteenth century and the valley, dry and aired by 1820, was a perfect spot for the city's station when the Railway Age arrived. The site was already a transport centre of sorts, as all the Great North Road stagecoaches to and from England operated from there.[5]

The station arrangement that the two girls saw that Sunday began after 1861, when the North British had already absorbed two other companies. Until the complete rebuild in the early 1890s, the station complex was incredibly cluttered and congested. The main waiting room was only 16ft square and the chief departure platform a mere 4ft wide. Passengers had trouble reaching their trains when they found the platforms piled up with luggage carts, barrels of beer and other things blocking their way. There were some platforms so under-length that trains overlapped them and couldn't be boarded. Often trains didn't arrive at their advertised times and the station staff had no idea when they might appear. The refreshment rooms were hardly *haute cuisine*, the coffee there having been described by the artist William Morris as 'ineffably bad'. At Waverley, the old Booking Offices were originally perched high up on the Waverley Bridge, giving vicarious pleasure to 'persons of a lewd nature' as the winds blew ladies' crinolines far above the level of accepted modesty.

If they didn't know about the custom beforehand, being in Edinburgh at 1 p.m. may have given the girls a bit of a fright. For precisely then, a loud bang accompanied by a jet of whitish-grey smoke emanating from the Half Moon Battery at Edinburgh Castle, signified 'The Edinburgh Time Service', commonly known as the 'One o'clock Gun'. This firing of a blank cartridge from a field gun to denote the time of day was inaugurated in 1861 and the North British Railway contributed £5 towards its installation costs. It continues as an institution to this very day and probably still gives tourists and visitors a jolt if they don't know about it![6]

Meanwhile, the two young ladies from London, stuck in Edinburgh on a Scottish Sabbath with nothing much open in the way of facilities apart from Waverley Refreshment Rooms, were thrown upon their own resources to while away the hours before the 4.15 p.m. train left for Granton and the Forth ferry to Burntisland. They may have wandered around Edinburgh and even partaken of some lunch at Ritchie's Confectionery Rooms and Temperance Restaurant in Cockburn Street, an establishment that was actually open on a Sunday, as was McKinley's Family and Commercial Temperance Hotel, where they may possibly have had some afternoon tea. On their meanderings, they might have speculated with unladylike ribaldry on alternative uses for the items in the shop windows at 4 Brown Square; for these were the premises of G. & J. Leggat, 'Whipmakers to the Queen'. Perhaps they spent a moment gazing through the windows of Adam & Charles Black, fine arts specialists of 6 North Bridge, who were currently displaying original portraits and caricature etchings by the late John Kay.

These window displays would certainly have been of interest to Mr William Henry Beynon, a 40-year-old fine art specialist, photographer, publisher and director of his own company in far-off Cheltenham, Gloucestershire (England). Mr Beynon lived with his wife and three young children at St Alban's Lodge, Hewlett Road in Cheltenham. His offices were in Wellington Street, Cheltenham and he'd been up in Scotland now for about a week on a business trip. Accompanied by his agent, Mr Coulston, he was engaged in assembling an album of lithographic portraits of North British Railway officials. Mr Beynon was well known for this kind of work, having already published, to great acclaim, similar collections entitled *The Bishops of England*, *Our Cathedral Churches*, *The GWR Officials* and *The Midland Railway Servants*. Coulston and Beynon, who was wrapped in a waterproof Ulster overcoat against the wind and cold, now sat in Waverley station refreshment rooms late that Sunday afternoon and were no doubt drinking the awful coffee as they discussed which one of them should go to Dundee that night to continue the research for the projected NBR portrait collection. After a short debate, Mr Beynon elected to go himself and bought a first-class return ticket to Dundee, a piece of white pasteboard which cost him 16s. Mr Beynon had been seriously injured in a railway accident some years before, the result of which caused his left arm to be permanently crippled, but he happily and unknowingly caught the 4.15 p.m. train from Waverley to his death in the Tay.

When Mr Beynon's body[7] was pulled out of the river, he was found to be without his Ulster coat. He'd obviously shrugged this off in the river to help him swim, something which he could apparently do very well. This means that he survived the fall into the Tay and at least managed to get out of his carriage. The Ulster pockets contained a hankie, a pipe, a silver matchbox and gold Masonic scarf pins. A large gold watch with a hefty gold albert strap adorned his waistcoat and his pocketbook contained £18 5s 8d, making him the richest victim on the train that night. Also Mr Beynon was something of an enigma as we'll see, judging by his movements on the doomed train.

Seaman John Scott had just returned from the USA and was travelling home to Dundee, to his mum Margaret who lived at 39 Watson Street. He'd been paid off from his ship the SS *Halcyon* in Hartlepool. He was 30 years old with £2 in gold jingling in his purse, plus 15s and a ha'penny in coin along with his Seaman's Certificate in his pockets. A shortish chap at 5ft 4in, with black hair, he had a few teeth missing in his upper jaw, perhaps a souvenir of dockside brawls. He was travelling to surprise his family who hadn't heard from him since he left Dundee six years ago. William Neilson, 31 years old, was travelling to Dundee from his home at 53 Monk Street, Gateshead to visit his brother George at 31 Step Row Dundee. He was a machine fitter and was leaving his sickly wife Mary at home for this trip. He was 5ft 9in tall, wore a black coat, vest and trousers with a black tie, a muffler and an overcoat. He sported a tattoo of Admiral Nelson on his left forearm.

Robert Culross was a carpenter from Tayport who had recently been employed by the North British Railway to make advertising boards at its stations. In his brown suit and brown Ulster, he was engaged to be married in February 1880. He'd taken a home in Edinburgh but was going to Dundee to invite friends to the wedding. David Graham was a 37-year-old teacher at Dalmary Sessional School in Stirling, and he had red hair and whiskers. In his brown tweed suit and waterproof coat, and standing 5ft 9in tall, he was off to Dundee for Hogmanay (the Scottish word for the final day of the year, synonymous with New Year celebrations).

George McIntosh was an off-duty goods guard travelling home to Dundee. He was 43 years old and married to Isabella, and the couple lived at 25 Hawkhill, Dundee. He was going a bit bald and wore a rupture belt, probably because of the continual humping of sacks and cases that were a part of his job. He'd be joining guards McBeath and Murray in the luggage van at Burntisland. After the accident his personal effects were collected by his mother, Mrs Jesse McIntosh.

From London, going home for Hogmanay to his parents at 1 Thistle Street, was engineer James Murdoch. He was 21, had fair hair and blue eyes and wore a dark tweed suit under his brown Ulster coat.

Including the people we've already met on the 'Up Morning' train from Dundee and who were spending the day in Edinburgh, everyone boarded the 4.15 p.m. train from Waverley to Granton Harbour in order to catch the ferry across the Forth.

The 4.15 p.m. train duly chugged away from the platform on level track and almost immediately plunged into the 398yd-long tunnel under the southern flank of Calton Hill.[8] The gradient fell away steeply at 1 in 78 for about a mile after the tunnel and then the train took a hard left away from the main line at Abbeyhill Junction and ran onto the Leith and Granton branch. The 4.15 train was comprised of a fairly nondescript collection of four-wheel coaches as befitted a short-haul feeder service, and had a couple of noisome fish trucks tacked on to the rear. These were returning as 'empties' to Granton Fish Dock.

The ensemble was tugged along by a Drummond 0-4-2 tank engine. All in all, hardly an auspicious train for the start of a supposedly express journey to Dundee.

It came grinding to a stand at Abbeyhill station, leaving again at 4.18 p.m. Pausing at Leith Walk (4.23 p.m.) and Trinity (4.30 p.m.) it rolled into Granton at 4.35 p.m. The passengers then had a mere eight minutes to collect their luggage, walk down to the ferry dock and board the steamer which was due to set out across the Forth for Burntisland at 4.43 p.m. Also in this short time, all the Edinburgh–Dundee mailbags had to be manhandled from the luggage van, taken down to the ship and loaded on board.

The name Granton was derived from the old English 'Gren Dun' which means Grassy Hill. Around 1835, the Duke of Buccleuch, who owned the land nearby at Wardie, decided to start a bold enterprise by building a brand-new port for Edinburgh, as the existing one at Leith was only able to accept deep-water ships at high tide.

He engaged the services of a most talented young protégé of the Stephensons', namely James Ritson, surveyor and engineer. From 1834 Ritson surveyed the south coast of the Firth of Forth between Granton and Leith, extending inland to Edinburgh, eyeing up all the possibilities for what was later to become the first docking terminus of Thomas Bouch's 'Floating Railway'. His diligence in finishing this work during 1836 meant being outdoors often in ceaselessly pouring rain and getting soaked to the skin for hours on end. These drenchings led to him contracting pleurisy, fever and an untimely death in 1837, aged only 31 years old. Thus was a promising career sadly cut short.

In 1834, he'd surveyed the River Tay from Perth seawards, with a view to improving the navigation of that river from Perth down the estuary and he had also surveyed the site for a new Perth harbour, for which works were eventually started by the middle of the century. Ironically, this gave Perth reason to believe that its status as a seaport would substantially increase. In consequence, the city fought hard when the Tay Bridge designs were being prepared to have the centre girder spans high enough from water level to accommodate the large cargo vessels expected in the future. Of course, this never happened and the irony was exacerbated by the fact that the intransigence of Perth's attitude led to the high-girder section being included in Bouch's final plans. Poor Ritson, in all innocence, had indirectly contributed to the disaster to come.

The Duke of Buccleuch opened the first part of his new facilities on 28 June 1838 which, coincidentally, was Queen Victoria's Coronation Day, a momentous event which must surely have overshadowed his own celebrations. Seven years later, in 1845, the main pier was completed. Granton Harbour had 30ft of water at all tide states, making it accessible to all shipping at all times.

No wonder that the North British Railway chose the port in 1848 for the inauguration of the world's first roll-on roll-off ferry service, instigated by Thomas Bouch, of whom we shall hear a great deal more anon.

With two long breakwaters stretching out into the Forth (Eastern Breakwater 3,170ft and Western Breakwater 3,100ft) the inner harbour was sheltered from rough sea movements in the estuary.

Regardless of the breakwaters' protection however, the swell inside the harbour that night caused by the coming storm was sufficient to cause the paddle steamer (PS) *William Muir* to rise and fall erratically through several feet at the dockside wall, making the midships brow an unsteady bridge for the passengers crossing to get aboard. The fore and aft thick rope springs securing the ship to the dockside chafed and creaked at their bollards with the double effect of wind and tide strain. The wind was blowing hard but as yet there was no rain. Ever increasing white spumes of spray were being whisked across the dark grey waves and onto the ship's deck.

The PS *William Muir* was practically brand new. She was a two-funnelled vessel with oscillating steam engines built by the John Key Company at Kinghorn expressly for the Granton–Burntisland passenger ferry service and delivered for that route in September 1879. The ship had been promised by the end of July and was needed because of the upsurge in traffic after the Tay Bridge opened. The bigger PS *John Stirling*, built in 1874, couldn't cope on its own with the spiralling demand and frequency of the services required, forcing the North British Railway (NBR) to commission the building of another vessel.

With the late delivery of the *William Muir* and the failure on trials of the ship to cross the Forth in a specified time, since rectified by the Key Company, the NBR demanded and obtained £1,000 in compensation from the Key Company. In the unusual custom of the John Key yard at Kinghorn, she was launched fully fitted out and in steam.

She was a very smart looking ship, with her white paddle boxes and two gently raked red funnels, each with a black top and a white band just below it. Her upper works were white and her hull was black with a white-lined boot topping. She carried two lifeboats just abaft (behind) the paddle boxes and the first-class passengers were enclosed at the stern in a wooden saloon with large square windows.

Her gross tonnage was 411¾ tons, she was 174ft 2in long and she had a beam of 24ft 3in and drew a depth of 10ft 9in of water. She could skate across the Forth on a calm day at around 12 knots. The *William Muir* flew a house flag which was a red pennant with a white circle bearing a thistle emblem.

At 4.43 p.m., her captain on the bridge ordered the bow and stern mooring ropes slipped, rang on the engines with the Mechans Limited (of Scotstoun, Glasgow) engine telegraphs and carefully conned the *William Muir* out of the harbour. She flailed her way against the ever-rising swell as she left the lee of Granton and began to beat across the Firth of Forth, steering almost due north as the spray-soaked wind moaned in the rigging and lumpy waves burst over the bulwarks and scantlings, invading the deck spaces and drenching anyone outside the passenger cabin. It was always more difficult to control a paddle steamer as opposed to a screw-driven ship in anything of a seaway but the *William Muir*'s captain had made innumerable crossings of the Forth and was experienced in all the various kinds of weather, wind and tide states that the estuary could throw at him. The voyage to Burntisland from Granton was only 4¾ miles – 4 nautical miles – but the timetable allowed a generous thirty-four minutes for the crossing. The transit that night was in the teeth of a rising gale and this, plus the rolling swell which it was generating, would have been quite upsetting to those passengers who were prone to a touch of *mal de mer*, especially if they elected to remain in the stuffy passenger cabin. Some were spectacularly seasick, losing breakfast, lunch and all pre-journey snacks, the merciless swell acting like a rollercoaster as the ship swooped, buffeted and plummeted.

It would have been like the effect of clear air turbulence in a modern airliner. Some passengers lay on the deck, abject in their misery and oblivious to the freezing seawater which sloshed around them before gurgling out of the scuppers in foamy torrents. A thoroughly miserable voyage for all, except for those natural sailors blessed with 'sea legs'. But at least it was a mercifully short trip to Burntisland.

The fare for the crossing was inclusive in the price of the railway tickets but otherwise the rate from Granton to Burntisland was 10d if you wanted the passenger cabin or 5d if you were happy with steerage, which meant standing on the open well deck forward or being totally exposed to the elements by braving the deckhead of the first-class cabin at the stern. That spot would have been splendid on a fair and calm day but not on a windy wet night with a big sea running.

After 2 miles of chugging, the *William Muir* passed the island of Inchmickery and the two rocks known as Cow and Calf, around 1¾ miles off the port beam and invisible in the Stygian gloom. Around 1 mile further on, plugging northwards, the *William Muir* would pass the large island of Inchcolm and its medieval Augustine monastery, which would have been visible in daylight, around 2½ miles away to port. Inchcolm Abbey was where King Alexander I of Scotland was driven ashore during a storm in 1123 and was fed and sheltered by the hermits there. Between this island and the shore is Mortimer's Deep, named after Sir Alan Mortimer who was a local landowner who'd made gifts to the abbey on condition that he could be buried there. When he died, his lead-lined coffin was ferried by monks to the island but sadly it slipped out of the boat and sank in the firth.

Giving thanks for his deliverance, King Alexander founded a priory so that the monks could pray and care for shipwrecked sailors. But no reassuring thoughts of aid for the ferry passengers were available from the flashes of the Oxcars Lighthouse, because that wasn't opened until 1886.

Still forging north, the island of Inchkeith lay 3½ miles off the starboard side and the crossing was coming to an end, to the relief of all on board.

The *William Muir*'s captain began the process of slowing the ship in preparation for entering Burntisland Docks. He rang down to the engine room via the Mechans telegraphs for HALF AHEAD, then SLOW AHEAD and finally ALL STOP, and so the ship arrived alongside Burntisland harbour at around 5.17 p.m., just about on time. This was a sterling effort given the wind and the waves.

Burntisland possibly derived its name from the burning (Scots word 'brunt') of some fishermen's huts on Black Rocks, a couple of tiny islands to the east of the harbour. It was actually called 'Bruntisland' from 1538 until 1710 and was previously known as 'Western Kinghorne' (sic).

It had been a significant port for many centuries. The Roman name was Portis Gratiae and the town seal shows a three-masted ship. Incidentally, Burntisland's St Columba's parish church of 1592 was the very first church to have been built after the Reformation and it was here in 1601 that King James VI (of Scotland, later to become King James I of England and Scotland at the Union of the Crowns) summoned a General Assembly to discuss a new translation of the Bible, now forever known as the Authorised Version.

It was not until 1844 that properly designed low-water piers were built, to correspond with the Duke of Buccleuch's efforts at Granton. Scotland's railway age was now getting into its stride but the wide estuaries of Tay and Forth appeared as seemingly impossible barriers to any direct route from Edinburgh to the north. So for Fife the railways planned to use ferries. Firstly passenger steamers appeared and then Thomas Bouch, as we'll see, came along with his train ferry scheme.

From their arrival aboard the *William Muir*, the passengers had a scant ten minutes to get themselves and their belongings from the dockside to the railway station platforms. A few had to be actually carried off the ship, such was their sickness. Most had wobbly legs from the bumpy ferry crossing and the solidity of the dockside under their feet must have been both a relief and a reassurance that the world did not consist of only a heaving deck, howling winds and freezing spray. The ten minutes' timing was tight, with the Dundee train scheduled to leave at 5.27 p.m.

Guard McBeath and Mail Guard Murray would have had to work hard to trundle all the mailbags up from the ferry to their train, as well as transporting the various pieces of freight in transit to Dundee in the form of hampers of edibles and other consigned parcels and packages.

Perhaps off-duty guards David Johnston (who had just arrived with the ferry after a day with his wife and children in Edinburgh) and Goods Guard McIntosh would have lent a hand. After all, the 5.27 p.m. departure was officially a mail train with all the rules that the Post Office demanded of it, especially punctuality.[9] On a weekday night, PS *William Muir* would make three more crossings of the firth but, it being a Sunday and no more connections to be made with trains that night, she met the Edinburgh passengers off the 4.10 train from Dundee at Burntisland and plugged back across the Forth, leaving at 6.11 p.m. and arriving back at Granton at 6.45 p.m. After her carriage of the doomed passengers that night, PS *William Muir* continued in service for fifty-eight years with the North British Railway and then served under the auspices of the London and North Eastern Railway when that conglomerate was created in 1923 at the 'grouping' of Britain's railways. She was in service for two years as a minesweeper during the First World War and was finally sold for scrap in 1937.

Notes

1 Interestingly, this fare shows that the railway companies were sticking to the letter of the law. The Railway Act of 1844 set the third-class rate at a penny per mile. 36s 9d equals 441 pennies, exactly the right price for the 441-mile London–Dundee journey.
2 Refer to 3 (i) 'Edmondson's Visiting Cards' in the chapter note section.
3 Refer to 3 (ii) 'The Treaty of Perpetual Peace' in the chapter note section.
4 The tramway had wooden rails and ran from a pithead at Tranent 2½ miles down to Cockenzie harbour with horse-drawn wagons carrying the coal. The track was replaced with iron rails in 1815 and remained operational until 1886. The Battle of Prestonpans (21 September 1745)

during the second Jacobite rebellion was actually fought across the track bed of the tramway, with Sir John Cope's Hanoverian forces lining up their cannon behind a railway embankment! They were overwhelmed by Bonnie Prince Charlie's men in a very short early morning battle.

5   Refer to 3 (iii) 'Edinburgh Waverley Station' in the chapter note section.
6   Refer to 3 (iv) 'The Edinburgh Time Signal' in the chapter note section.
7   The body was identified by a Mr Tweeney and a Dr Schmidt and returned to Cheltenham where undertakers Debenham and Hewett interred the remains in a ceremony conducted by the Reverend J.A. Aston on the Tuesday following 14 February 1880. The coffin was massively built of oak and carried a brass plate on which was inscribed 'William Henry Beynon who lost his life at the Tay Bridge accident December 28 1879 aged 40 years'.
8   Calton Hill is a 355ft-high lump of rock, originally called Dow Craig (from the Gaelic 'Dhu' meaning black). It was (and is) crowned by two monuments. The Athenian Acropolis was an unfinished building initiated in 1816 and originally called The National Monument. It was a replica of the Parthenon in Athens and was erected as a memorial to all those who died during the Napoleonic Wars. The other building was the Nelson Monument which carried the Time Ball. At the eastern end of the hill were 'the quarry holes', a lonely spot famed as a rendezvous for those fighting duels.
9   The era of the mail coach was dying fast. It is easy to see how the Post Office began to rely more upon the railways as they developed their networks to all points of the British Isles. Even in the late nineteenth century a letter posted in London in the early evening would arrive at an address in Dundee the following morning. That is some going for 450 miles in 1879!

4

Duress Non Frango

Pressure Will Not Break Me.

Bouch Family Motto

There is scarcely anything in the world that some man cannot make a little worse and sell a little more cheaply. The person who buys on price alone is this man's lawful prey.

John Ruskin, 1819–1900

It was all about a dream and a dreamer. Thomas Edward Lawrence (of 'Arabia' fame) once said in effect that all men dream but they who dream while awake are the most dangerous. Thomas Bouch was such a man, who dreamt in his waking hours for over twenty years about building a railway bridge across the River Tay and then another over the Firth of Forth. He is the leading player in this story but paradoxically, because of his retiring nature, remains most of the time offstage or just discernible in the wings. However, learning of his earlier career gives insight into the character of the man and hints as to what he did and why regarding 'his' Tay Bridge.

On the evening of 28 December 1879 Sir Thomas Bouch was relaxing at home for Sunday dinner with his family. They lived at 6 Oxford Terrace, Edinburgh, situated high up to the north of the city in the Comely Bank district, commanding panoramic views of the city, the Firth of Forth and distant Fife.

He'd only been 'Sir' Thomas for a few months, receiving the touch of a sword upon his shoulders from his sovereign at Windsor Castle at one o'clock on Thursday 27 June 1879. Also honoured that day was Mr Henry Bessemer, inventor of the Bessemer furnace for manufacturing steel. A subtle irony considering Bouch's choice of materials for his Tay Bridge as we'll see later.

If Sir Thomas had cared to gaze from his upstairs windows during the early evening, he'd have seen the docks at Granton and the northern shore of the Forth, a low dark smudge in the gloaming presided over by the lowering storm clouds that were rapidly gathering. However, by the time the Dundee-bound passengers from Edinburgh were boarding their ferry at Granton, the only scenery that interested Sir Thomas was the spread and scope of his dinner table. He had married Miss Margaret Nelson in 1853 when she was 21 years old and now, twenty-six years later, Lady Margaret Bouch, daughter Ann and son William sat down with him to enjoy the fruits of a supper that was a direct result of the successes of Sir Thomas's life. Bouch was apparently very proud of the fact that his son William had chosen to pursue his father's profession and indeed William had been indentured as an apprentice to his father. He'd been appointed as the Resident Engineer of the North British Railway's Arbroath & Montrose section and was currently busy with the building of a bridge across the South Esk River that had been designed by Bouch senior, of which more in the chapter 'Coda'.

Sir Thomas Bouch, politically a Liberal and religiously a devout Episcopalian, was big-bearded in the fashion of the day and looks older in contemporary pictures than he really was. At the time in question, he was just two months short of his fifty-eighth birthday and could look back on a life as a prosperous and famous engineer in an era of prosperous and famous engineers. The early to middle Victorian age was studded with the likes of Brunel, the Stephensons (father and son), Locke, Brassey, Rennie and Vignoles, who'd all been involved as engineers in the railway boom that swept Britain, revolutionising transport, communications and social history forever. But somehow, almost as if he wasn't 'one of the boys', Thomas seemed excluded from this enviably exclusive club who put up their plates in Westminster, London. From all accounts, this didn't worry him as he always shrank from publicity and held the fourth estate[1] in very low esteem. He preferred to have his own chambers in Edinburgh at 111 George Street and not be one of the 'Westminster Engineers'. The honour of a knighthood for Thomas was, however, not given for his many fine achievements listed here: his long-term beavering that had built 300 miles of railways in Scotland and England, running the Edinburgh & Northern Railway with an iron fist, designing the roll-on roll-off ferries then plying between Granton and Burntisland and which had boosted the North British Railway's goods revenues, the building of the giant cast-iron railway viaduct at Belah in Westmorland and of the beautiful Hownsgill Bridge near Consett. His knighthood had been given for designing and building the Tay Bridge, the longest bridge in the world, perceived as an absolute triumph of British engineering and design skills. There had never been anything like it before anywhere on earth.

Two miles long across the Firth of Tay, it stood as an example of 'British is Best'. For its day, the bridge was outrageous in length, height and spidery impossibility, with every superlative so far expressed in the Golden Age of Engineering rendered inadequate.

Thomas Bouch was born on 25 February 1822 in the small village of Thursby in Cumberland, the youngest of three brothers. His elder brother William, who'd been born in 1813, went on to have a successful career as a locomotive engineer. In 1860, as the Stockton & Darlington Railway's Locomotive Engineer he built the first true class of 4-4-0 engines for the railway, later nicknamed 'Ginx's Babies' after an Edward Jenkins's satire of the time. These engines were built especially for the Stainmore line across the freezing high Pennines, with copious and weatherproof cabs for the severe conditions on that route. William also invented the engine steam brake. He died in Weymouth, Dorset in 1876 and thus never saw his younger brother's magnum opus bridge completed.

The brothers' father, William Bouch, was a retired captain in the merchant navy. 'Bouch' is an old Cumbrian name and the family once bore a coat of arms described thus, 'or on a cross sable five escallop shells apart'.[2] When later placed on a shield, the symbol indicated that the bearer or his ancestor had been a crusader. Thomas Bouch lived up to this 'crusader' mentality for over twenty years as he tried very hard to persuade any powers that be to build railway bridges over the Tay and the Forth, fighting against the doubters and scoffers until he finally succeeded, at least with the Tay Bridge and that albeit only for a while. The collapse of that structure scuppered his plans for the Forth Bridge.

After all, who'd want him as an engineer after the Tay Bridge fell down? As John Prebble put it so lucidly: 'No one would now trust him to build a kitchen wall.'

Bouch's education began at Thursby village school where his teacher, Joseph Hannah, apparently aroused his engineering interest during a lecture on hydraulics. When Joseph Hannah accepted the headship at the Academy School, Carlisle, Thomas Bouch moved with him as a boarder. After his father died in 1838, Bouch, aged 16, became apprenticed to a mechanical engineering firm in Liverpool but he found the position unsuitable and returned home to Thursby.

He then started work as an assistant to George Larmer, who was a railway surveyor. Born in Berkshire, Larmer was fifteen years older than Bouch and was working on surveys for a rail route from Lancaster, through Kendal and Penrith, to Carlisle. This was the original idea for the Lancaster and Carlisle Railway which was eventually superseded by the cheaper route that climbed over Shap Fell in Westmorland and today forms part of the West Coast railway route from London to Scotland. The engineers for the line were Joseph Locke and John Errington. Bouch stayed with George Larmer for four years and then continued to work on in the north of England during this period of enormous railway expansion. He went to Leeds and assisted John Dixon and then moved to Darlington to work on Quaker industrialist Henry Pease's Stockton and Darlington line that had opened in 1825. While Resident Engineer of the Wear Railway, he noticed an advertisement in one of the engineering and railway journals of the day that had been placed by the Edinburgh & Northern Railway (E&NR) in January 1849 under the name of Mr John Balfour, the E&N Chairman.

The Edinburgh and Northern Railway was a route running across the Kingdom of Fife from Burntisland on the Forth to Ferryport-on-Craig on the Firth of Tay.

At Ladybank Junction, part way up this line, a branch struck out in a north-westerly direction to Perth.

Burntisland had ferry connections with Granton, north of Edinburgh. At the top end the line connected with another set of ferries across the Tay to reach Dundee. The route from Burntisland to Ladybank, then via Lindores for Perth and through Cupar for Ferryport-on-Craig was opened in 1847. Another branch ran south-west to Dunfermline, the ancient capital of Scotland, from Thornton Junction.

The recently opened E&NR was already in big financial trouble and the company was looking for a traffic manager to salvage the falling receipts incurred by the difficulties of the company's line from Edinburgh to Dundee. That route, a mere 50 miles, involved any passenger making the journey to use a train from Edinburgh to Granton Harbour, then a ferry across the often-stormy Firth of Forth to Burntisland, followed by a second train journey across Fife to Ferryport-on-Craig on the south bank of the Tay. Then there was another ferry over the river to Broughty Ferry on the north bank. Once arrived, the long-suffering passenger had then to board a horse-drawn omnibus to carry him to Broughty Ferry station on the Dundee & Arbroath Railway, where he caught yet another train for the final 3 miles into Dundee. A passenger seasick from two ferry crossings across often-tempestuous estuaries with a protracted stop-and-start rail journey across Fife thrown in, then had the nuisance of two more modes of transport for the last 3 miles into Dundee. It's no wonder the patronage fell off as travellers deserted this method of reaching Dundee in favour of the rival Caledonian Railway, whose route, although far longer in miles (heading inland to miss the Forth and then a roundabout journey on to Dundee via Stirling and Perth) was at least all by rail, in one carriage and without the traumas of the E&NR route. The Caledonian even advertised their own service on posters and in timetables with the preface 'NO FERRIES', vaunting the easier journey. Then there was the question of goods to be carried between Edinburgh and Dundee, which was even worse than the passenger dilemma, as every wagonload consigned from Edinburgh to Dundee or places north was required to be transhipped onto the ferry at Granton, then manhandled off the ship at Burntisland Docks on the Fife side of the Forth into a train of wagons there, thence to be pulled to Ferryport-on-Craig where the whole time-consuming business of transhipment was perforce repeated and yet again done once more when the ship reached Broughty Ferry on the north bank of the Tay. No wonder the E&NR was losing out big time to the Caledonian in both passenger and goods traffic. The profit and loss accounts books were swimming in red ink.

Thomas Bouch replied to the advertisement and obviously passed whatever interviews were necessary as he gained the Traffic Manager appointment. It was announced on 13 January 1849 at a shareholder's meeting that 'a gentleman of great experience in the working and development of railway traffic' would be the new manager.

This statement was a little free with the truth, as Thomas Bouch, a young 26-year-old civil engineer with no great works as yet behind him, had had absolutely no experience with the day-to-day hands-on task of actually running a railway. An *obiter dictum* here is that given the arduous problems faced by anyone taking the job, the candidates were most probably few and far between. So Thomas may indeed have got the post because no one else wanted it, or because no other candidate had even applied. However, he was in, hired, and he duly moved up to Edinburgh to take up his new position.

On arrival he found that he didn't even have an office from which to work. A room at Waverley station was hastily converted for his use and he attended his first board meeting on 20 February 1849. He reported to his directors that he had already carried out some sanguine and sweeping changes to the staff, having sacked several members for various infractions such as drunkenness, fighting, inattendance to duties and scamming money out of passengers. He outlined his idea to carry out a fact-finding mission across the system which would take a fortnight – this he did with some startling results. At this point in his career, Bouch was exhibiting a diligence and application that would be sadly missing from his activities later in life. After his tour, he decided that the railway was well overstaffed and sacked some seventeen members from the engine works at Burntisland and a further sixty men from the Permanent Way Department. He also hired a lot more inspectors, took personal control of the dock staff at Granton, Burntisland, Ferryport and Broughty Ferry, as well as giving the resident engineer the job of running the Railway Police. This was a serious iron-handed start to his duties which must have impressed the directors, as they next ordered Bouch to inquire into engine-room practices on the ferry boats.

Under the current situation, it was the ferryboats crossing the Forth and Tay which were both the most expensive and the most troublesome items on the E&NR's route from Edinburgh to Dundee. Two freight carriers and one passenger ship worked each of the two firths, requiring a huge staff of about 100 people for the crews and the shore men, making the operating costs per mile six times that of a railway train. The ships were unreliable and far too often were docked for repairs. Bouch discovered that river water was being used in the boilers and the salt and sand in that was having a highly deleterious effect on the boilers and their tubes. Bouch sorted this out immediately he was aware of it by arranging a proper supply of fresh water for the ships' boilers.

He then thought of a solution to the time-consuming and expensive transshipment of goods at all four ferry ports. He reasoned: 'What if loaded wagons could be run directly onto the ferries themselves?', concluding that this would save so much time, effort and running costs. He called his idea 'The Floating Railway'. But in this idea as in so many others, Bouch never quite seemed to invent something that was totally original. History has credited him for inventing the first roll-on-roll-off train ferries but, in fact, the very first wagon ferry appeared in Plymouth,

Devonshire, in March 1812. In 1842 the management of Bedlington Coal Pit at Blyth, Northumberland ordered and took delivery of a twin-screw steamer called *Bedlington* which had rails on its decks and was designed to carry loaded chaldron wagons. This was to circumvent shipment delays deliberately caused by a rival coal company and pre-dated Bouch's train ferries by seven years.[3]

Thomas Bouch may possibly have observed the *Bedlington* going about her ferry duties on Tyneside during his many professional visits to the north-east of England at this time and thus maybe the seeds were sown for his own train ferry idea. Not only was that a possibility, but by his own admission he had heard that Thomas Grainger, who was once the engineer for the Edinburgh, Perth and Dundee Railway (EP&DR), had drawn up designs for a floating 'caisson' (a large cylinder that allowed workers to toil away below water level, which often became part of the construction when all the digging was done) that could ferry wagons across the Tay between Broughty Ferry and Ferryport-on-Craig.

He approached the E&NR board with his idea of 'The Floating Railway'. (In fact the E&NR changed its name to the Edinburgh, Perth and Dundee Railway in 1849, as it was thought that 'Edinburgh & Northern' was too vague a description of where the railway went and the places it served.)

The Board was somewhat tepid in its reception of Bouch's plan, being chary of even more expenditure when it didn't have any spare money to start with. Nevertheless permission was given for the undertaking. This was probably a move motivated by desperation as much as anything else, plus a growing faith in Thomas Bouch, who seemed to be proving himself by his successful activities so far. After all, the Board felt it must embrace any option to fix its railway's woeful performance to its shareholders. A last-ditch chance to mend things had been offered and even though the Board was doubtful, what had it to lose apart from a further investment? Things couldn't get worse for it, or could they?

As Macbeth said in Shakespeare's eponymous play: 'I am in blood stepped in so far that should I wade no more, returning were as tedious as go o'er.' Which really sums up the situation that the EP&DR found itself in 1849. Any solution was worth a try, so Thomas Bouch obtained reluctant permission and went ahead. But how to set about this operation on both firths, which Thomas Bouch had assured the Board might be the salvation of the Edinburgh, Perth & Dundee Railway?

There were two vital interacting engineering elements here. The first was a ship capable of having standard-gauge railway tracks (that is, 4ft 8½in gauge) laid from stem to stern upon its main deck to accept the loaded wagons. Obviously, this would have to be a brand-new ship especially designed for the job – a conversion of an existing vessel was out of the question. Secondly, there had to be some sort of apparatus that enabled the ship, when docked, to take on board those wagons at any state of the tide from the dockside at Granton, Burntisland, Ferryport and Broughty Ferry.

The solution to this second problem is where Thomas Bouch excelled himself. He designed an arrangement of ramps with rails leading up and down, on which were to be hauled the moving platform and cradles that carried the railway vehicles. Given that the spring tidal range in both the Forth and the Tay could be as much as 20ft, this system had to be able to cope with that. Surviving diagrams of this equipment resemble a solution designed by Mr W. Heath Robinson (cartoonist and illustrator, famous for the complicated and outlandish inventions he portrayed) but nevertheless it worked effectively enough.

One could do no better than quote the description of the device used, which was given in an obituary to Bouch, published in 1880 which reads thus:

> The invention embraced three principal features, the inclined plane, the flying bridge connecting the moveable framework with the ship's deck and the means adopted to secure a free space for the shipment of trucks on board. Upon a massive inclined plane of masonry the moveable framework runs on sixteen wheels, the upper part of the frame presenting two lines of rails on the level, while below, the beams and fillings take on the form of a slope. This framework is pulled up or down on the ship to suit the state of the tide. At its centre rise two uprights with a crossbeam, the uprights sustaining heavy weights with chains passing over pulleys and thence to strong cranes or jibs which, hinged at the outer end of the framework, support girders that stretch forward to meet the vessel. These hinged girders allow for the play of the vessel and for the rise and fall of the tide while loading and unloading go on. On board the vessel the difficulty arose that as paddle wheels must be used to give breadth and stability for the rough crossing, the shaft would interfere with the clear run fore and aft. This difficulty was overcome by providing for each paddle a separate engine, with the result that, on the several lines of rails, trucks can be at once run on board over the whole deck space. The first cargo carried across the Forth by the vessel consisted of four hundred tons of turnips.

The specially designed vessel mentioned in the above description was the paddle steamer *Leviathan*. She was designed by Thomas Grainger, who had previously plotted the 1,000yd-long Scotland Street tunnel to carry the Edinburgh, Leith & Granton Railway under Edinburgh New Town to its Canal Street terminus at right angles to the NBR terminus. He was also the man whom Bouch freely admitted had partly given him the idea anyway.

Leviathan had independent steeple engines and paddle wheels to enable them to turn axially and not interrupt the space on the ferry deck, again as described in the obituary. Both the new ferry and Bouch's flying bridges were built by Robert Napier of Glasgow. Services began with the transportation of the turnips on 3 February 1850 and there was a ceremonial opening trip four days later when

Leviathan carried a first-class carriage and twenty wagons. Normally, only road passenger vehicles such as private carriages would be taken (apart from goods and fish wagons) because there was no sheltered accommodation for passengers. There were six other ferries plying the two firths that were just for passengers, their luggage and the Royal Mail.[4]

Full general service across the Forth commenced on 1 March 1850 and was an immediate success, so much so that plans were laid to have a similar arrangement at the Tay crossing between Tayport and Broughty Ferry. When that link was opened on 28 February 1851, it was again PS *Leviathan* which made the inaugural run, another paddle-ferry named PS *Robert Napier* built to the same basic design, having been added during 1850 and that now worked the Granton–Burntisland service.

The EP&DR directors were delighted. At last the railway was able to offer a competitive goods service against that of the Caledonian. Meanwhile, Thomas Bouch, basking in the success of his achievement, felt he could apply to be a member of the Institution of Civil Engineers, which, if granted, would immediately give him professional respectability. Accordingly he did apply and was granted an associate ship – not quite what he may have wanted but it was nevertheless a start down the road to acceptance. On 30 March 1851 Bouch was able to report to the Board on the complete success of the 'floating railway' and its ferries. He noted that 29,000 trucks had been conveyed during the previous six months and over the past thirteen months since commencement of the service not a single working day had been lost due to any shortcomings in the new system.

On this note, a week later, Bouch resigned from the EP&DR, perhaps acting a little prematurely but he was getting ambitious for other things. After all, his reputation was made – he had saved the Edinburgh, Perth and Dundee Railway from financial oblivion and now he could put up his 'plate' as a consultant engineer, ready to go to work for anyone who'd hire him.

There were plenty of would-be clients in Scotland and the north of England. He still nurtured the dream of bridging the Forth and Tay, realising that the EP&DR could never be a completely viable rival of the Caledonian until bridges superseded the ferries across both firths. However, he put these ideas in abeyance until he'd really established himself. The idea in 1851 of huge bridges across the Forth and Tay was still in the realm of dreams. Bouch first proposed the idea of the two great bridges in 1854 but the railway board dismissed it as 'the most insane idea that could ever be propounded'.

Unfortunately, in some jobs that Bouch took on, he was somewhat less than efficient in more ways than his clientele might have expected from such a go-getter. The shortcomings in his handlings of these commissions were pointers to his way of dealing with the Tay Bridge project later, and these inadequacies should have rung alarm bells at the time. However, it is only now that the benefit of hindsight makes this clear and unearths a multitude of sins.

The Kingdom of Fife is a large peninsula between the Forth and Tay estuaries. The Edinburgh & Northern Railway crossed Fife first and then changed its name to the Edinburgh, Perth & Dundee Railway in 1849, as we have seen. The construction of this main line left many viable railway connections out of the loop, as it were. St Andrews, Leven, Largo, Elie, and Crail, among others, were thus affected. Therefore, it was obvious that St Andrews, not wishing to be left out of railway connections, wanted to link itself via a new line with the EP&DR. With Thomas Bouch's reputation flying high, the town asked him to help.

The 'Town Fathers' wanted a connection with the EP&DR at a point along the existing route. They were far-seeing enough not to want to be a marooned as a 'railway island' in the future. St Andrews itself had a university founded in 1411 and golf had arrived in the town in 1754, and by the mid-eighteenth century this pastime was putting St Andrews on the tourist map, so for these reasons the conurbation really wanted to have a connection into the railway network. The construction of this and other new railways in Fife were to give some indications of Bouch's future behaviour. In St Andrews, Provost Playfair and Robert Haig – of whisky distillery fame – set up the company that was to fund and build the railway. The line was to run from St Andrews itself to a junction with the EP&DR at Leuchars, some 4½ miles away.

At the time, as the EP&DR's resident engineer, Thomas Bouch took responsibility for the work but it was at this point, as previously stated, that Bouch resigned from the EP&DR and hung out his own 'Consultant Engineer' sign in Edinburgh when work on the new line had just started. He would soon become known as the engineer who could provide light railways for small local communities who only wished their trains to tootle along at low speeds with lightweight engines on lightweight track. The cheap alternative was always Bouch's *tour de force*, and unfortunately this approach applied later to his work on the Tay Bridge.

The St Andrews line was opened on 1 July 1852 and from the start was operated by the EP&DR and managed on a day-to-day basis by a board in St Andrews. To facilitate interchange, the main line opened a junction station at Milton called Leuchars Junction while its original Leuchars station, a little to the north, became known as Leuchars Old. The St Andrews railway was Thomas Bouch's first ever independent professional commission, and with it he caused a lot of problems and traumas for his clients. To begin with, the junction facilities at Leuchars left a great deal to be desired, with passenger complaints about lengthy delays due to faulty re-marshalling of trains among other reasons. The station itself 'was in a miserable condition with no accommodation or comfort for passengers' according to a board minute. Somehow the short line still managed to turn in a profit, but more trouble was to come.

In 1858, the EP&DR decided to use a heavier engine to cope with the increasing loads that were accruing but the district engineer noted that the track work was not firm enough to carry a weightier locomotive. As the new engine in question was only a small Hawthorn tank locomotive built by the eponymous company at Leith, the St Andrews Permanent Way must indeed have been well below accepted standards.

Mr Barrie, who was the EP&DR engineer, checked out the St Andrews line with care and in much detail. He discovered that the sleeper spacings were at 4ft, instead of the standard gap of 3ft, and that the rail fastenings to those sleepers were of wooden treenails instead of iron spikes. This was evidence of corner-cutting to save money at the expense of safety and reliability of the track.

Mr Barrie noted that two timber bridges crossing rivers were woefully inadequate in structure and design and that the woodwork had never been painted with any preservative such as creosote or tar. Bouch, when approached on the subject, said that 'when these bridges were built, it was his opinion that it would be prejudicial to tar the bridges and they were therefore declared finished'. This was considered to be an incredible statement that flew in the face of what was necessary and prudent.

During the construction period of the St Andrews Railway, another Fife light railway was proposed, this one to run 6 miles from a junction at Thornton with the EP&DR to Leven on the north shore of the Forth and, again, the engineer was to be Thomas Bouch. The project ran into 'Bouch' trouble from the outset. An agreement had been reached with the EP&DR that the Leven Railway would have a junction at Thornton and that the EP&DR would operate the new line. So far, so good. Therefore the Leven Railway contractors arrived to lay in the junction. But on that very day Mr Wilkie, company secretary to the Leven Railway, received a letter from Mr Robertson, the EP&DR's manager, telling him to stop the process at once and threatened all sorts of penalties if the Leven Railway Company proceeded in making the junction.

Wilkie retorted angrily but then apologised when he discovered that the engineer of the Leven, Thomas Bouch, had failed to send in the plans for the proposed junction to the EP&DR.

John Thomas's research on the whole matter of the Leven Railway has thrown up a heap of what we might now call 'Bouchisms'. It was not just for the Tay Bridge collapse that the word 'bouch' or 'botch' has entered the vernacular of the English language!

Mr Wilkie had to write a plethora of letters to Bouch in remonstration of his failure to execute his duties as the engineer in charge. Wilkie pleaded with him to submit plans which were months behind their deadlines and begged him to carry out inspections of supposedly 'finished' sections of the line, and these he conspicuously failed to perform.

Wilkie also was at a loss as to why Bouch had not attended some very important meetings. On one occasion, the secretary sent back a Bouch plan, having noted that all measurements of a single field were in error. He was also distressed enough to inform Bouch that the design for a footbridge was so delayed that it would now cost half as much more in terms of the expense of correspondence, as to build the thing.

Four more letters were sent to Bouch to remind him of a vital meeting, which Bouch still failed to attend. Wilkie had already asked the company solicitor to write to Bouch urging his attendance. The Board of the Leven Railway ordered Bouch on 24 May 1853 to settle immediately the arrangement with the EP&DR regarding Thornton Junction. Eight months later the contract had still not been finalised and the Board sent Bouch an acerbic minute recording its frustration and disapproval.

In October 1853 Bouch was summoned to a meeting at EP&DR headquarters, which he surprisingly actually attended. He heard that to run the Leven Railway, a 'heavy luggage engine' was required but that they, the EP&DR board, were short of the cash required to buy one. There then ensued a boardroom fight because the Leven company was supposed to pass over the money it had kept back for the purchase of its own engine in exchange for the EP&DR promising to give the Leven company a small but suitable engine from its own stock. The Leven Railway didn't like this one bit and said no. The EP&DR was extremely angry at this refusal. The Leven chairman and the engineer went back to Fife realising that they now had to find their own engines and rolling stock and run the line themselves.

Consequently Thomas Bouch ordered a new engine from the Hawthorn Company at Leith. Board of Trade representative Captain Tyler inspected the Leven Railway on 2 August 1854 prior to issuing a certificate. He was accompanied by Thomas Bouch who must have had some trepidation seeing as the completed line bore little resemblance to the plans submitted to parliament and the act that had granted its construction. However, Bouch was lucky in that Tyler's inspection was somewhat cursory. He failed to notice that the curves were too sharp, the gradients too steep and the ballast, supposedly 6in deep, was only 1in in depth in the places where it existed at all.

However, Captain Tyler told the directors that their certificate would be granted on Monday 7 August 1854.

The next trouble was that Bouch had ordered an engine that was fine for the line as described in the parliamentary submission but certainly not fine for the line as he had built it. It consequently arrived and immediately it was obvious that it couldn't negotiate the curves at any speed at all nor attack the steep gradients with any success. How had Bouch missed these elementary facts? Anyone later concerned with the plans or the financing for building the Tay Bridge would certainly have had grave doubts about Thomas Bouch if they had been aware of this information but they were never party to it, nor were they aware of the stories of the debacles to come.

Did Bouch honestly believe that the railway as he had originally designed it could be built with all the corner-cutting and the lax supervision on his part and yet still accept the track loading of a weighty engine obviously unsuited to such a lightly laid line? The Board asked him to find another replacement engine but on 3 October, Mr Wilkie let fly his frustrations when he wrote to Mr Haig that he had neither seen nor heard from Bouch for the two weeks he had promised to find a temporary engine while the new one was being built.

He said: 'Mr Bouch's want of attention to our present interest in the matter is beyond my comprehension.' So, the Leven Board asked Mr Nicholson, Locomotive Superintendent of the EP&DR, to go to England to get an engine 'off the shelf'. He bought one from Cropper & Bell in Chester and also managed to sell the original unsuitable item to the Caledonian Railway. At least the Leven Board got some of its money back. But this temporary engine was also useless in service. Bouch ordered a new engine from the Hawthorn Company in Leith but when it arrived on the line in October there were a lot of problems with steam escaping from places where it shouldn't. A team of Hawthorn engineers came up to work on it immediately but never got it right. The troubles with the original engine had bemused the directors, but they accepted Bouch's word that it was unsuitable for the line. However, it took the Board nearly a year to fully appreciate the extent of the man's incompetence and neglect. The Board sent him letters which were unanswered. The directors also tried to call on him both at his office and at his home, but his staff denied all knowledge of his whereabouts. The main problem was that the chairman wanted the final costs report on the building of the line so that he could pay the contractors, who of course wanted their money. Finally, Bouch delivered the report but the Board was horrified to discover from it that the route had not been constructed in accordance with the parliamentary act which had sanctioned it. This could mean that the Leven Company was in imminent danger of being closed down until the line was deemed fit to carry the travelling public. Secretary Wilkie wrote to Bouch explaining that the directors were upset about the unsuitability of the engine and yet he, Bouch, had said nothing about the defective conditions of the line. Details of the curves, said Wilkie, were totally different from the specifications supplied to the Board of Trade. After further chastisement, Wilkie concluded by saying that the Board of Trade had been misled and that the directors had a very strong case for claims upon Bouch for the consequences. As per normal, Bouch never bothered to reply.[5]

Sadly, the Leven Railway had to endure a catalogue of more 'bouchisms'. The engine shed, which Bouch was building, remained unfinished even after a whole year. The inspection pit was so undersized that the cleaners couldn't get in if the engine happened to be standing over it and it was often flooded to the top, as no drains had been put in.

Cameron Bridge level crossing gates didn't fit when closed for either road or rail, and the Bouch-designed railway signals failed to work and had to be converted to the disc signals of that era. Bouch had the gall to try to get payment for his useless items but Secretary Wilkie would have none of it and with his patience utterly exhausted, got rid of him.

They were glad to be shot of Thomas Bouch as he'd caused nothing but grief and this had not been expected from a supposed 'professional engineer'.

Next, another line with a proposed end-on connection with the Leven Railway was mooted to be built to Kilconquhar. This route had been surveyed by Bouch but after the trials and tribulations of the Leven line under his auspices, the promoters, after learning that most of the measurements of his survey were wrong, gave Bouch the push and appointed as engineer one of Bouch's protégés, a man called Martin.

So much for Thomas Bouch the professional engineer at this stage in his career. His utterances even this early in his life seemed to have become the vapourings of a mountebank. As we now well know, far worse was to follow in the ensuing years. John Prebble described Thomas Bouch as 'a little man on stilts' in that he reached far and away beyond his abilities, perhaps in arrogance, perhaps in ignorance, but probably in both. He was a tragedy in himself, as much as any of the victims who died when his Tay Bridge fell. So he tottered along to the building of that bridge, complacent in his competence to design and build such a thing. Again, to précis Prebble's words, the winds on the night of 28 December 1879 blasted those stilts away from under him as surely as it did the piers holding up his bridge.

In the end, what can we make of the relevance of his family motto Duress Non Frango, translated as 'pressure will not break me'? Perhaps it is not appropriate.

Notes

1 Newspaper journalism.
2 The escallop is the emblem of St James and was originally worn to signify the wearer had made a pilgrimage to the shrine of St James at the church of Santiago de Compostella in Spain. This was the final resting place of St James beneath the site of the present day cathedral in Santiago.
3 Refer to 4 (i) 'Pre Bouch Train Ferries' in the chapter note section.
4 They were *Granton, Burntisland, Auld Reekie, Thane of Fife, Forth* and *Express*. All were paddle-steamers. *William Muir* was added to the fleet in September 1879. The wagon carriers were *Leviathan, Robert Napier* and *Balburnie*. *John Stirling* was added in 1874.
5 Refer to 4 (ii) 'Part of a letter from Wilkie (Company Secretary Leven Railway) to Thomas Bouch' in the chapter note section.

Strangers on a Train

> A person in a railway carriage may be likened to a prisoner of state, who is permitted to indulge in any relaxation and amusement to while away the time but is denied that essential ingredient to human happiness – personal liberty.
>
> *The Railway Traveller's Handbook, 1862*

> Nor should we forget the benefit to rural human genetics brought about by the railway: with less inter-marrying the 'village idiot' has disappeared.
>
> Extract from early twentieth-century essay praising railways

The train of carriages awaiting the Edinburgh passengers trudging up from the quayside to Burntisland station was the product of fifty years of evolution in rail travel.

At the outset of railways in the 1830s and 1840s, passengers were considered an unfortunate problem to be borne by the railway companies. The lines had been built primarily for the conveyance of goods and when the company directors realised they could also make money by carrying human freight, it was only the first-class travellers, paying highly for the privilege, who were encouraged. There was an early decision amongst railway companies to divide passengers into three different classes, to be provided with corresponding drops in comfort levels. A set of engraved plate illustrations appeared soon after the Liverpool and Manchester Railway was opened in 1829. In this series of pictures, the first-class coaches look exactly like three stage-coaches joined together but stuck on the top of a four-wheeled truck, which was just about the truth. The baggage was piled on the roof in the style of stage-coaching days, held in place by the restraining rails and leather straps. Incidentally, the name for a railway apprentice used up until the late twentieth century was a 'strapper', derived from the boys who secured luggage to the roofs of carriages with these leather straps.

The rest of the hoi polloi had to make do with incredibly austere conditions. Trains that conveyed third-class passengers were often shunted off the main line into sidings to let first-class expresses go by. The nicest thing one could say about these vehicles was that they were 'sort of' waterproof and 'sort of' draught proof. They were called, in the vernacular of the day, 'dog boxes'.

Only a short time earlier those third-class folks would often have to stand for the whole journey in roofless, seatless trucks which were open to all the elements, and had to put up with the soot, cinders, smoke and dust kicked up by the passage of the train. These vehicles were called 'horizontal shower-baths' or 'pig-pens'. Clothing, especially that of the ladies with their voluminous crinolines, was often set alight by cinders from the engines, which were then mostly coke-burning. And the sides of the wagons were so low that passengers occasionally fell out.

In 1843, William Ewart Gladstone, then Minister of the Board of Trade and a relatively young man in Sir Robert Peel's Tory government, promoted a bill to improve the rail travel conditions of the poorer classes. The bill, called the Regulation of Railways Act, was enacted in 1844 and ordered all railway companies to provide third-class carriages that had seats and roofs. The act also stipulated that at least one train a day be provided for third-class passengers at the rate of a penny per mile. These trains also had to travel at not less than an average 12mph. Called 'parliamentary' trains because of the act of parliament that had ordered them, these services were nicknamed 'parlys' by railway staff. Of course, the railway companies often got round the inconvenience of running these trains by scheduling the 'parlys' at highly unsociable hours in order to discourage passengers.

The rich upper classes happily went along with this. A first-class traveller, writing to *The Times* newspaper and signing himself 'Justice', said, 'If people could not afford venison and champagne, they should rest content with bread and cheese.' Another correspondent pointed out that it was appropriate that 'the swinish multitude should travel like multitudes of swine'.

But there is a defence to the attitude of the railway companies towards third-class passengers. In those days, the standards of behaviour and personal hygiene were far lower than now and many third-class passengers were people who had exceedingly filthy habits.

The London firm of Keating's frequently advertised its 'Insect Powders' in the pages of railway timetables as 'indispensable to travellers'. This is an indication that many passengers carried fleas and bugs against which more fastidious people needed a defence.

One can understand railway managements, fighting to maintain solvency, not spending a penny more than they were obliged to on carriages carrying people of this kind. If upholstered seats had been provided they might well have been cut to ribbons by hooligans. Leather straps for raising windows were likely to be stolen for razor strops or belts. Vandalism is not a modern phenomenon.

But very gradually, the railway companies began to realise that the third-class clientele represented the principal growth area for the future. Carriage design and construction, although still not that far removed from the stagecoach, improved significantly.

Sir James Allport, General Manager of the Midland Railway, introduced new third-class carriages on his lines in 1872. These vehicles were well designed and comfortable – and all for a penny a mile. Other companies were much slower in catering for the third-class passenger, the North British Railway included.

By 1879, the era of the bogie carriage (and consequently a much smoother ride) had only just dawned, again through the far-sightedness of Sir James Allport.

With a few exceptions, all British railway passenger vehicles were either four or six-wheelers (imported by Allport's Midland Railway from the Pullman Company in the USA), and were consequently bumpy and rocky to travel in. American railways had been using bogie vehicles from very early days because their tracks were very roughly and lightly laid and no other kind of vehicle could be guaranteed to stay on the road. There's no doubt that the early use of bogies in the USA actually retarded their eventual introduction in Britain. In the mid-nineteenth century there was a strong, unreasoning aversion to using anything American. This prejudice arose over the use of the American Westinghouse Braking System. When asked why he didn't fit this system of continuous fail-safe braking to his trains, one engineer remarked, 'Sir, I am an Englishman!' The North British Railway was indeed an exception to this anti-American feeling, being one of the first railways in the UK to adopt the Westinghouse brake. Five out of the six vehicles of the 5.27 p.m. Burntisland to Dundee train were so fitted.

When the advantages of having larger vehicles with bogies became patently obvious, most British railway companies still didn't budge. On many lines designs progressed from four to six-wheelers only but there were other good reasons why the bogie was eschewed. The conditions in Britain were mostly that large numbers of people needed to travel shortish distances and therefore any time standing at stations was a waste of time and money. The principle of the compartment coach with a door on each side of each compartment gave the maximum seats and the quickest passenger ingress and egress times, the opposite to USA requirements. Thus the bogie coach in America far preceded its adoption in the United Kingdom.

At centres of traffic such as busy junctions and city termini, most of the shunting and marshalling of passenger vehicles was done by hand or horse.

It was not merely a case of having carriages small and light enough to be pushed by a couple of men. As a space economy, given the high price of land in big cities, when the stations were built the sidings were not connected with the running lines by points.

Each carriage was taken individually, run onto a very small turntable, swung round at right angles and traversed to the required siding. Shunting like this obviously was impossible with long weighty bogie carriages. To move onwards from the legacy of this infrastructure would require considerable re-investment.

Everyone complained of the draughts and the cold. There was at least one authenticated case of a passenger dying from hypothermia in a railway carriage. More sensible passengers carried rugs and wore caps instead of top hats. The large number of cheese-cutter caps and Tam O'Shanters washed up on the riverbanks after the Tay Bridge Disaster bears pathetic witness to this.

Early second-class compartments were open on both sides and also had rainwater drains drilled in the floor, allowing icy blasts of wind to stab where they may. In winter, even first-class passengers had only the general issue of foot warmers against the cold. These were oval or oblong-shaped tins about 3ft long filled with water, then dropped into vats of boiling water and, just prior to departure time, pushed free of charge into first-class compartments. Second- and third-class passengers were required to pay a fee if they wanted warm feet.

Even though foot warmers were the only source of heat at this time, they were cumbersome and a nuisance to some people. Passengers often tripped over them and one old lady managed to get her train stopped and 'the infernal machine' removed forthwith. Women in the long voluminous dresses of the day were fearful of their clothing being singed. There were complaints that foot warmers gave people colds and made their feet sore.[1]

If passengers were wearing boots, shoes or galoshes with 'gutta-percha' soles, then they needed to be very careful where they put their feet and for how long. Gutta-percha was a whitish rubber substance made from latex and was used to waterproof the soles of boots and shoes. Unfortunately, it had a fairly low melting point and after prolonged contact with foot warmers, tended to soften into a glutinous sticky mess. When a passenger arrived at his station, he might find it impossible to stand and leave the train because his feet would be glued to his foot warmer!

At some stations, porters would reheat the foot warmers by plunging them into boiling cauldrons. But no matter how hot they started out, the pans didn't stay warm for long – about three hours at most. This meant that on long overnight trips they needed changing every now and then, a considerable inconvenience when passengers were trying to sleep.

But the passengers on the two-hour journey aboard the 'Edinburgh' would have found their foot warmers hot enough right until the last moment.

In what was acclaimed as an increasingly enlightened age, railway passengers were cold and often, literally, kept in the dark. For a long time, the carriage lighting was as primitive as the heating arrangements. First attempts were rape-oil lamps let in through holes in the roof. The only way to regulate the oil feed was to knock at the lamp with an umbrella. When the train was in motion the spilled oil, together with rainwater and dead insects, swilled around the glass container and inevitably dripped onto the passengers below.

As late as 1894, a London Chatham and Dover Railway shareholder wrote: 'Then there's the light in the Third Class carriages – that poverty-stricken, timid, retiring, poor-relation kind of illuminant whose chief function is to emphasize the gloom, dirt and misery that lie heavily upon the passengers like a pall.'

But the 'Edinburgh's' passengers on the night of 28 December had the benefit of Mr W.T. Wheatley's idea of lighting carriages with paraffin lamps.[2] Mr Wheatley was, incidentally, the brother of Thomas Wheatley, NBR Locomotive Superintendent and designer of the 'Edinburgh', engine No 224.

W.T. Wheatley ran the NBR Carriage and Wagon Department and in September 1868 he introduced paraffin-oil roof lamps for his carriages on the Burntisland–Tayport service. This route, of course, is almost the same as the one followed by the 'Edinburgh' in 1879 except that with the Tay Bridge as yet unbuilt, the trains ran to Tayport for the ferry to Dundee. Lamp men were employed to keep the lamps properly trimmed but first results were poor. Many travellers crossed Fife in dim or dark compartments and sometimes the lamps exploded when the stores department mixed up naphtha by mistake! But soon things improved dramatically and paraffin lamp use for carriage lighting, headlamps, tail lamps and signal lights was extended across the whole of Fife and the NBR network.

The railway companies paid no heed to the private needs of travellers. *The Railway News* reported that the fitting of lavatories in carriages was not a worthwhile idea because 'they would add too much weight to the train, would earn nothing and would cost too much to maintain'. The article pointed out that it would be necessary to purchase laundry and towels which would probably be stolen by third-class passengers and then there'd be the wages for plumbers to refill and maintain the roof cisterns.

Of the idea to have corridor trains with one or two lavatories under the charge of attendants, *The News* declared: 'The British public do not want it.' It was not until 1892 that corridor trains appeared in Britain, introduced by the Great Western Railway on its Paddington–Birkenhead services, albeit at first only so that ticket collectors could access all parts of the train when on the move.

The Victorians, already a nation of hypochondriacs, were even worse when it came to rail travel. They imagined all kinds of health risks. *The Lancet*, a respected journal of the medical profession, reported that railway tickets would spread infectious diseases and that travelling through tunnels could bring on chills and consumption.

Tunnels were also likely to shock a nervous system unused to 'travelling in the dark in noxious air amid strange noises'. The publication recommended sea biscuits and sherry for warding off fainting fits and that steep gradients could apparently be bad for gout sufferers.

Running to catch a train after a meal, said doctors, would upset the digestion, strain the lungs and might lead to fainting on the platform or even sudden death – at least this idea had an outside chance of actually happening.

Doctor J. Russell Reynolds, a consultant physician at London's University College Hospital, claimed that he suffered more fatigue after a 10-mile journey in a jarring and jolting train than if he had walked the same distance. When people dozed off in a train he said, 'it was not sleep they were experiencing but a stupor brought on by concussion of the brain'.

Other doctors warned that fast-moving trains could induce apoplexy in people with high blood pressure. The magazine *The Lady* stated that many women were ill for days after a rail journey.

In Glasgow, one newspaper reckoned that looking out of carriage windows was fatiguing to the eyes but suggested that serious consequences could be avoided by looking at passing objects in an oblique direction.

A consolation for the poorer third-class traveller was that first-class carriages were the unhealthiest of all. The *British Medical Journal* alleged that the thick upholstery absorbed moisture and thus became perilously damp.

But it seems that the biggest hazard of all was the nature of one's fellow passengers.

From time to time, Victorian trains were filled with disputes and dramas. This was primarily due to the mixing of classes which had hitherto been carefully segregated by the rules of society. Those rules ensured that everyone knew their place, their peers and their betters. But now these divisions had become involuntarily integrated, especially as some of the richer people were penny-pinching enough to travel second class.

Most travellers were totally ignorant of the art of getting along with one another in the confines of a compartment and with no corridors as an escape route, an upset passenger was stuck there until the next station.

There was always a chance that travelling companions may be drunk or might be football fans bent on replaying a match with their fists. Nothing, it seems, has changed! But people did at least get along in one way. Because narrow compartments made leg stretching difficult, by mutual consent one passenger would interlace his feet between those of the passenger opposite, to the comfort of both parties. This was known as 'the treaty of legs'.

Some of the rules imposed by railway companies like the North British were strangely modern by today's standards. In an era long before health considerations arose, it seems that nearly every male in Victorian times smoked or used tobacco products such as pipes, cigars and snuff. The government taxation levied was quite modest but still brought in enough money to build several pre-Dreadnought battleships per year. Yet the railway regulations were very stiff. There was no smoking on any station platforms, waiting rooms or railway property in general. This set of rules predates the modern restrictions by some 130 years! If anyone disobeyed these byelaws, they faced a fine of 40s and a summary removal at the first opportunity from their carriage or the company's premises. There were no such things as smoking compartments in carriages until the Regulation of Railways Act in 1868 decreed their introduction.

Luggage conveyance was reminiscent of modern airline practice – each passenger had a fixed allowance by weight. Anything over and they'd be charged an excess baggage fee.[3] In any event, passengers could only take what we now call 'carry-on' items into their compartments. Everything else went into the luggage van including dogs, which were not allowed into compartments on pain of a 40s fine. Dog tickets were calculated by a sliding scale based on mileage.

Other transgressions of the byelaws brought one of two fines; either £5 or 40s. The larger sum covered such sins as carrying a loaded firearm on railway property or in a compartment, vandalism and improperly pulling the communication cord. The 40s penalty applied to not only smoking and dog-smuggling but also to using obscene or offensive words, annoying other passengers, trespassing or boarding a train while afflicted with a contagious disease.

It is strange how these two standard penalties lasted unchanged for over 100 years without any index linking to inflation. Wrongly pulling the communication cord and trespassing would cost you £5 and 40s respectively, even in the late 1900s, by which time the punishment was risible compared to average incomes in 1879.

A sensible aspect of ticket issuing in Victorian times has disappeared. In those days tickets were only sold if there was room in the train. This prevented overcrowding and ensured that everyone got a seat. In the rare cases of overselling passenger accommodation, preference was given to those persons travelling the longest distances with immediate refunds (providing they were claimed before the train departed) paid to disappointed travellers.

The train parked all day at Burntisland station consisted of six carriages painted in North British Railway dark claret, although possibly one vehicle was finished in varnished teak. They were typical of the NBR stock designed by NBR engineers Dugald Drummond and his predecessor Thomas Wheatley. Although the NBR had a workshop at Cowlairs in Glasgow, manufacturing capacity was never up to the demands and so most new vehicles were outsourced to two contractors. One was the Ashbury Railway Carriage & Iron Works, founded by John Ashbury in 1837 at Knott Mill, Manchester, which then moved to Openshaw, also in Manchester, in 1841. The other contractor was the Metropolitan Carriage & Wagon Company, which started building railway carriages in London in 1840 when its founder, successful stagecoach builder Joseph Wright, realised that road coaches were soon going to be obsolete. The works moved to Saltley, Birmingham in 1847. The train due to leave Burntisland at 5.27 p.m. that night comprised a mixture of these two companies' efforts.

The North British style of carriages was similar to that of many British railway companies with 'recessed' upper panels and 'raised' lower panels on the outside bodywork. First- and second-class vehicles had full-height partitions between compartments, whereas the thirds had divisions only to seat-back height. So the carriage was effectively an open saloon. The basic construction of all the carriages was similar, with the body mounted on the chassis via 1in-thick rubber blocks to deaden noise. The floorboards were arranged so as to be easily renewable. They were of 9in-wide deal tongue-and-groove planks in two layers laid transversely. In second- and third-class vehicles, the flooring was covered with blue linoleum. Seating in third class was of cane, with hardwood backs, although newer carriages had seats covered with some form of 'rep' or hardwearing material covering pads of woven wire.

First-class seats were traditionally sprung using rows of coil springs with horse-hair padding covered with morocco leather, hide or moquettes. Upholstery was dark in colour so as to not show the dirt but the walls and inner door panels were lined with blue cloth. The flooring was waxed.

The window straps were of buffalo hide and those in first class were decorated with stitched patterns. The end walls of the third-class carriages carried advertisements for various products as well as posters for local theatrical productions, auctions, shops and sporting events.[4]

The leading vehicle was No 579, a four-wheeled third-class carriage with five compartments, weighing 8 tons 8cwt empty and 28ft 6in in length measured over the buffers. It had been built in 1877 and was one of the newer batches of third-class carriages fitted with seat cushions and backs. Next to it stood six-wheeler No 414 dating from 1873 and the only first-class vehicle in the train. Weighing 14¼ tons and 38ft 5½in long, it was also the only carriage to have Mansell composite wheels.

A carriage designer's big problem was always the large amount of un-sprung weight of the wheels, axle boxes and spring mountings. If the wheels themselves could be made more resilient, this would mitigate resonance effects. Thus came the Mansell wheel, patented in the 1840s by Richard Mansell, one-time Carriage & Wagon Superintendent of the South Eastern & Chatham Railway. They consisted of sixteen tightly fitting wooden staves made from Moulmein or Rangoon teak. Each stave was 3½in thick, bolted to a wrought-iron hub at the back with a retaining washer at the front. Produced by specialist manufacturers, they were carefully balanced to run true at 60mph, using balance weights bolted to the rims.

Behind No 414 was another third-class carriage, No 629 and identical to No 579 above. Then came four-wheeled third-class carriage No 650, different from the other 'thirds' in that it weighed in at 9 tons 16cwt and was 31ft 5in long.

Last in the line of passenger vehicles was a much older second-class carriage. No 138 had been built in 1865 by the Metropolitan Carriage & Wagon Company and had four spoked wheels. It was also much lighter, smaller and slighter of construction than any other of the vehicles in the train. Weighing empty 5 tons 19cwt, it had only four compartments in its overall length of 25ft 8in, whereas all the other carriages had five.

Because of its age and the fact that second class was soon due to be abolished and the vehicle withdrawn from service, no continuous brake piping had been fitted, which meant that the Westinghouse system down the train effectively stopped with the previous coach, No 650, depriving the final vehicle, the guard's van, of any braking system save the handbrake operated by the guard.

This final vehicle, lettered on both sides LUGGAGE VAN NBR No 146, weighed 8 tons 9cwt and was 26ft 2in long. As well as being a guard's van, it also carried the Royal Mail. The handbrake was operated by a vertically mounted cast-iron hand wheel with S-shaped spokes and stood on a cast-iron pedestal. Turning the wheel operated rod linkages through the floor to pull brake blocks against the wheels.

The legendary fighter pilot Douglas Bader once said that even if he'd been blindfolded, he'd know if he were sitting in a German warplane by its smell alone. There was a special odour that no other aircraft types possessed. It might have been due to a mixture of the smells of Wehrmacht dope, paint and leather – but was nevertheless an indefinable 'Something'.

Opening a door to step into a North British railway carriage produced the same result, a smell peculiar to NB rolling stock alone. Not a dirty smell, not even a coal smell but perhaps the smell of a particular polish or soap. 'Carbolic' was once suggested. It was more subtle than that but nevertheless unforgettable.[5]

After their hours of enforced idleness in Burntisland, Mitchell and Marshall returned to Burntisland engine shed around 4.30 in the afternoon to prepare No 224 for the return trip to Dundee. Mitchell went round all the oiling points with his oilcan, checking the worsted trimmings as he did so. Meanwhile, Marshall was busy on the footplate rousting up the fire. The coal had burned through nicely in the intervening hours and a few quick actions with the long cumbersome pricker very soon whisked it back into life. He opened the dampers and gave the blower a half-turn so that in another half an hour, the 'clock' was reading a healthy steam pressure and continuing to rise. Marshall in his preparations was aiming to achieve just under maximum pressure a minute before departure time without any unnecessary waste of steam from blowing off at the safety valves. Professional firemanship at its best!

So with everything ready, Mitchell and Marshall backed the engine out of the shed and trundled the short distance along the seawall to Burntisland station.

With a gentle clunk of the buffers, No 224 and her train were together again. Marshall did the coupling-up while Mitchell put the Westinghouse brake handle into the 'release' position, which charged the train pipe. He then looked at the Westinghouse pressure gauge which was reading far too low, indicating a leak somewhere. So Marshall jumped off the engine and walked down the length of the train to check all the pipe connections between each carriage. He finally found that the pipe on the fourth vehicle from the engine, which was the third-class carriage No 650, was not properly seated on the 'dummy' and re-secured it. As we've seen, the final two vehicles, the little second-class and the guard's van, were not part of the Westinghouse brake chain. The guard's van was actually fitted with the Westinghouse apparatus but, because the second-class carriage had no piping to reach it, that vehicle was effectively isolated from the system running the length of the rest of the train. This explained the use of the 'dummy' on the last third-class carriage, which blanked off the pipe there.

Marshall stirred the pricker through the fire once more and put eight light shovelfuls of coal around the firebox, watching the steam pressure-gauge needle swing up to near blowing-off point. He'd followed the old maxim –'Fire me light and fire me bright and I will steam with all my might'.

Darkness had fallen like a witch's shroud for over an hour now and the benign afternoon had turned into an evening of rage. The passengers were off the ferry and boarding the train.

Mitchell and Marshall on No 224's footplate got the 'right away' from Guard Davy McBeath at exactly 5.27 p.m. Putting her into full forward gear, Mitchell opened the regulator and she steamed out of the station towards the next stop at Kinghorn, where they were due at 5.34 p.m. and 2½ miles away up rising grades of 1 in 305, steepening to 1 in 128. Mitchell kept the reverser cut-off quite high because of the gradients, so John Marshall plied the shovel to keep the fire bright and steam pressure up, maintaining the footplate crew teamwork which was essential for a good trip. Marshall's job was to supply enough steam and at the right times so that Mitchell could keep time with the train. This involved both the men inextricably and required an intimate knowledge of the road they were traversing. Kinghorn came and went, after negotiating the infamous 'bent' tunnel, with no passengers either boarding or leaving.

All in all, apart from the rough weather, the trip was looking as normal as it ever did. They'd all be home safe in a matter of two more hours. Soon the train was running in to Kirkcaldy station, 3¼ miles on from Kinghorn and up a gentle rising gradient of 1 in 660. Waiting there were schoolmaster David Neish and his daughter Bella, who'd enjoyed a lovely day visiting Mrs Baxter. David pulled his dark tweed topcoat close about him over his check suit against the cold and tightened up his mauve knitted cravat. Here at Kirkcaldy the father of novelist John Buchan was once a Free Church minister and John is supposed to have got the title of his book *The Thirty-Nine Steps* from the number of steps leading from the church down to the beach. Two other famous sons of Kirkcaldy were architect Robert Adam and the economist Adam Smith.

In 1828, William Nairn started a weaving business here and in 1847 his son Michael introduced a method whereby jute was impregnated with linseed oil to make a cheap floor covering known as linoleum. The jute was supplied from Dundee where it was imported in thousands of tons per annum. After the Tay Bridge opened, it was of course far cheaper to transport the jute in bulk by rail and Kirkcaldy boomed with the industry. The town remained the centre of the lino trade for over 100 years. An unfortunate singular drawback was the aroma the linoleum process created. It permeated the whole town and was unavoidable by anyone with a sense of smell.

Perhaps the residents became inured to it over the years but visitors, such as David and Bella Neish, were glad when the train rolled in, so that they could be rid of the miasmic odour emanating from the many linoleum factories and warehouses beside the line.

The 'Edinburgh' duly plugged out of the station at 5.44 p.m. Shortly afterwards, the 4.10 p.m., the 'opposite number' service from Dundee to Burntisland, went hurtling past with much sounding of whistles and waving from the footplate crews. Like the morning exchange, the sister train was running fast down grades of 1 in 105 and 1 in 143. She would reach Burntisland at 6.04 p.m., connecting with the ferry departure at 6.11 p.m. Meanwhile, forging onwards, the 5.27 train reached Sinclairtown, an area now completely absorbed in the expanded conurbation of Kirkcaldy. This was after about 1½ miles of climbing those gradients. Sinclairtown derived its name from the St Clairs, the Earls of Rosslyn.

Waiting to board here was Peter Salmond, a 43-year-old blacksmith from Dundee. He was 5ft 9in tall with salt-and-pepper dark hair and whiskers. He wore a black suit and white tie with a brown tweed topcoat. He was looking forward to getting home out of the cold and wind and to seeing his wife Isabella at their home in Princes Street, Dundee.

The train departed at 5.49 p.m. and headed a further ¾ mile uphill at 1 in 100 to reach Dysart, named from the Gaelic word 'diseart', meaning 'desert place' or sometimes 'hermit's cell', a place for pilgrims and again now part of the Kirkcaldy complex of housing. Pausing there for the lone Dundee-bound passenger, flax-dresser James Millar, the train left for Thornton Junction at 5.54 p.m. Millar lived in Dundee with his wife Elizabeth and their child but had been working in Dysart for the past three months and was only able to visit his family at weekends. This trip, however, was to include Hogmanay. John Marshall's cousin, regardless of the awful weather, was at the platform end to give a cheery wave to the fireman. Neither person would see their relative again. The line now turned sharply to the north, inland and away from the sea through a cutting, past Bogley's Farm to the left and then onto an embankment. Apart from a short stiff rise at 1 in 114, it was all downhill for the 2¾ miles to Thornton Junction, where the train was due at 6.03 p.m. No passengers either joined or disembarked and the train was off again, on time at 6.04pm. The roughly 2½ miles to the next stop, Markinch, were mainly uphill at 1 in 160, 1 in 129 and then level track. The train crossed what is now the A911 main road by a long 50ft-high stone viaduct and then ran up a very short rise at 1 in 104 to arrive at Markinch. Deriving its name from the Gaelic 'marc-innis' meaning a horse meadow, the town, dating back to 3000 BC as a Neolithic settlement, had, by the mid-nineteenth century, become host to thriving weaving and spinning mills, paper mills and a Haig Whisky bottling plant. Waiting impatiently to get out of the cold and wind were three passengers.

Mr William Linskill, carrying a young boy in his arms, was on his way to St Andrews to stay with the Dean and was travelling first class. Linskill was not only to escape the Tay Bridge Disaster by the merest of moments and happenstance, but was to play a role in the enigma of Mr Beynon, whom we've already met at Edinburgh Waverley station. James Crichton had been visiting his father John, a farm servant at Bankhead, Leven. James had trudged the 6 miles from Leven to be aboard the 'Edinburgh' as there was no connecting service on a Sunday from that town. He wore a silver watch and a hair albert strap, plus a steel albert strap, a handkerchief, a bunch of keys and £1 7s 1½d in his purse.

In ones, twos and threes, the 5.27 train was gradually plucking her complement of passengers out of the storm and wind and giving them shelter, warmth and a ride home in apparent safety. The Tay Bridge was getting nearer with every turn of the wheels. On leaving Markinch there were only 23 miles to go.

Notes

1 Francis Webb, Chief Mechanical Engineer of the London and North Western Railway, invented a more efficient type of foot warmer in 1880 just after the Tay Bridge Disaster. It used acetate of soda and the principle of latent heat. Amazingly, this heating source was still in occasional use in Britain at least until 1928 and also during the late 1930s in Victoria and Tasmania, Australia. On the pre-First World War coaching stock used to convey visitors from Sydney to Thirlmere Railway Museum in New South Wales, foot warmers were in use as recently as 1983.
2 Refer to 5 (i) 'Paraffin Oil' in the chapter note section.
3 These allowances were ticket-class related: first-class passengers could have 120lb, second-class 100lb and third-class 60lb.
4 To have a poster placed in a carriage, the advertiser would contact Hugh Paton & Son of 115 Princes Street, Edinburgh, who were the agents with the exclusive rights to display advertisements in trains and on hoardings throughout Scotland and the North of England.
5 Observation by Cuthbert Hamilton Ellis.

6

The Tay and Two Cities

*For never two such kingdoms did contend without much fall of blood;
Whose guiltless drops are every one a woe, a sore complaint.*

William Shakespeare, *Henry V*

*Behold the Tiber! The vain Roman cried,
Viewing the ample Tay from Baiglie's side;
But where's the Scot that would the vaunt repay
And hail the puny Tiber for the Tay?*

Sir Walter Scott

The River Tay was always there. Eons before Dundee and Perth, epochs before the Romans, Kings Duncan and Macbeth and ages before William Wallace. In fact, it had been flowing long before Scotland had human beings inhabiting its banks. Thus the river has many and multitudinous memories if a watercourse could ever be assumed to have anything of the sort. This story is a recent one in the life of the Tay, just over 130 years ago. That's nothing time-wise in the Tay's history. This tale is also a mixture of vanity and vision. Vanity was always mixed up with vision and that is part of this story too.

Later in its life, the river was host to a centuries-old ongoing *contretemps* between Perth and Dundee. These two great cities had arisen upon the banks of the Tay many thousands of years after the river was set in its flow, yet when they did, there were great repercussions for the building of the first Tay Bridge, especially in the need for a large headway for shipping beneath the structure. But it was really the River Tay that was the pertinent factor. After a long gestation mileage as a small stream, then a burn, followed by a full-blown river, it flowed through Perth and then shortly downstream, blossomed and widened into the great estuary of the Firth of Tay upon whose north bank, 20 miles later, grew the city of Dundee. These two cities, Perth and

Dundee, had vied with each other for status and trade for centuries but it was always the Tay that unobtrusively dictated everything. Its upper courses proved perfect for salmon fisheries and provided irrigation for the sheep farming lands, thus ensuring the success of those industries for the hinterlands, while its lower reaches quietly set the best spots for the cities of Perth and Dundee, especially the former's nodal position and the latter's suitability as a deep-sea port for worldwide commerce. It also therefore engendered the rivalry between the two towns that would run on for centuries, the feud indirectly compromising the design and safety of the first Tay Bridge.

So to the beginnings.

Pontius Pilate was said to have been born on the banks of the Tay, although the chronology with the Roman occupation of Britain and Pilate's necessary presence at the trial of Christ would seem to refute this legend utterly. But Methven Woods certainly sheltered William Wallace and Birnam Wood may very well have come to Dunsinane as Shakespeare described in Macbeth. At 120 miles in length, the Tay is the longest river in Scotland and its estuary, or firth, is 25 miles of that length. The river rises on Rannoch Moor, oddly enough on the west side of Scotland. All other rivers rising on the west side empty into the seas to the west but the Tay is an exception, due to geographical and topographical anomalies. From a corrie at the upper end of a great basin which had been cut by a glacier a million years ago, a stream springs from the earth at the western end of Breadalbane and is called first the River Connonish and then Fillan Water. One hundred and ten miles later it reaches Dundee and is called The Firth of Tay. For the first 11 miles of its course, it runs rapidly, dropping 250ft per mile of flow. Flowing south-east through Strath Fillan it becomes the Dochart at Crianlarich, almost as if it can't decide what it should be called. It continues eastwards by way of Loch Dochart and Loch Lubhair in Glen Dochsart to merge with Loch Tay at Killin. From the east of Loch Tay, leaving it at Kenmore (where it can peak 44,000 gallons per second), it finally becomes the Tay proper and has now established its identity. It flows south and east down to Perth and eventually to Dundee. The Tay has the largest catchment area of any Scottish river – some 2,400 sq miles, thus throwing out around 37,400 gallons per second when it passes Perth. The river has always been a premier salmon fishery and its water output is more than the English rivers Severn and Thames combined. In fact, the Tay pushes more water out to the sea than any other British river.

It is convenient to divide the Tay proper into three sections.

The first of these is the Upper Tay which starts from the bridge at Kenmore as it flows out of Loch Tay. Two other major rivers, the Dochart and the Lochay, flow into Loch Tay, so that at birth, the Tay is already a sizeable watercourse about 40yd wide. Then 2 miles downstream from there, it is joined by the River Lyon and becomes about 50yd wide as a result of the extra water influx.

The second section is the Middle Tay – the River Tummel with its own tributaries of Garry and Tilt confluences with the Tay at Ballinluig where the whole watercourse expands to nearly 90yd in width. Step by step, or perhaps gallon by gallon, the Tay is growing into a broad and formidable yet beneficent feature of eastern Scotland, but there is more to come.

At Dunkeld, it is joined by the Braan and then meets the Isla. That river itself has the tributaries of the Ericht, Ardle and Blackwater to add to the water volume and joins the Tay at Meiklour.

On and on goes the list of waters pouring into and augmenting the Tay, with the Almond joining just below Stanley. By Perth, the Tay becomes tidal and its very last tributary, the Earn, floods in just before the Tay River becomes the Firth of Tay and the third subdivision of its course. The Gaelic name for the Tay was 'Tamh', which means rest, quietness and sluggishness. This is an ironic title considering what effect the river would have on Sir Thomas Bouch's Tay Bridge on the night of 28 December 1879.

Three hundred years ago, the Tay gave the east Highlands their prosperity. Tay water is pure and soft and free from dissolved salts: there are apparently no more than three to four dissolved grains per gallon. This made it highly suitable for the dyeing industry, which helped to make Dundee the industrial capital of the north, along with the oft-quoted 'Jute, Jam and Journalism' industries of more recent times thrown in. It is obvious that for such a lengthy watery schism across eastern Scotland that at some time, somewhere, it would have to be bridged for the sake of communications. General George Patton, the controversial high-profile commander of a number of US forces during the Second World War said, during the breakout of the Allied armies in Normandy following D-Day: 'throughout history it has always been fatal not to cross a river.' He was speaking militarily of course, but he was spot on regarding the idea of bridging rivers for communication purposes and indeed to support this principle, Scotland has always been a country of bridges.

Back through the ages, Scotland has always provided opportunities for bridge builders. At Bothwell in Lanarkshire you can still see a bridge dating from the Roman occupation. The Italian invaders obviously presupposed Patton's conclusions from a military viewpoint. Also there are many structures extant from the Middle Ages, for example Stirling Bridge. The eighteenth and nineteenth centuries saw a great number of new road bridges, many originating from General Wade's military road system across the Highlands, built to help troop movements for dealing with the Jacobite Rebellions and later Clan repressions, proving again that Patton was right.

These eighteenth-century bridges were sturdy yet picturesque stone structures crossing many a brawling highland stream. However, the very first and now oldest railway bridge in the world was not Scottish but in County Durham, north-east England. Called originally 'The Dawson Arch' and later 'The Causey Arch', it was built in 1725–26 near the village of Stanley.[1]

The first Tay Bridge, in other words a bridge that actually crossed the non-tidal Tay River, was built in October 1733 at Aberfeldy, another product of the aforementioned works by General Wade. And there have been bridges at Perth since the thirteenth century.

In the middle nineteenth century, Perth and Dundee were two rival cities only 20 miles apart along the River Tay and had been squabbling for supremacy in status and trade for centuries.

Perth, situated at the lowest road bridge point on the Tay, was considered to be the capital of Scotland until the assassination of James I there in 1437.[2] The name derives from the Pictish-Gaelic word for a wood or copse. The Romans knew it as 'Bertha' from the Celtic *aber the* meaning 'mouth of the Tay'.

Actually the settlement at Perth goes back to prehistoric times, the evidence of nearby standing stones and stone circles giving proof of this. However, the Romans built a fort here in AD 83 as a supply base for their occupation of north-east Scotland. The town emerged from a flat wet site at the lowest crossing point on the river and was also the highest point upstream on the Tay, at its confluence with the River Almond, that the Roman ships could reach. This position is about 2 miles north of the current city centre because 1,000 years of silting has moved the highest navigable point downstream. By 1125, King David I had set up a new town on the Tay's west bank. This conurbation was known colloquially by its English-speaking inhabitants as 'St John's Toun' or 'Saint Johnstoun' because the church in the town centre was dedicated to John the Baptist.

King William the Lion granted Royal Burgh status to Perth in the early twelfth century and because of its being a royal residence throughout the Middle Ages, the city is often referred to as the Ancient Capital of Scotland. Enhancing its early importance was the nearby former royal palace of Scone where generations of Scottish kings were crowned sitting on the Stone of Destiny, otherwise known as the Stone of Scone.[3] Soon after his plundering of this treasured Scottish icon, King Edward I of England captured Perth very easily in 1296, as it had no proper defences to speak of but 'Longshanks', as he was nicknamed, had it properly fortified by 1304. These new walls didn't stop Robert Bruce from recapturing Perth in 1312.

Twenty years later it was captured again by Edward Balliol, who was then crowned King of Scotland at Scone but without the benefit of the Stone's blessing. Later still Edward III of England forced six local monasteries to pay for massive city defences in 1336. The place was by now certainly worth defending against the envy of others, as it had become one of the richest burghs in Scotland, with a burgeoning trade as a busy inland port trading with France, the Low Countries and the Baltic. Goods such as Spanish silk and French wine were imported and exports comprised hides, wool, timber and fish. The memories of these times as a successful port would always colour Perth's attitude to Dundee and harden its heart to what it perceived as the parvenu port downstream.

Prior to his restoration in England, Charles II was crowned at Scone in 1651 and Oliver Cromwell, who had executed Charles's father in 1649, came to Perth in 1652, building a citadel to overawe the population and hold down the country. By now, Perth was a manufacturing centre, with successful trades such as wool weaving, tanning and leather goods, blacksmiths, goldsmiths, armourers and gun-makers. The place was really going somewhere!

The Act of Settlement in 1701, enacted by the English parliament and soon extended to Scotland, settled the succession to the crown on the Electress Sophia of Hanover (who was the granddaughter of James I) and her Protestant heirs. No Catholics could now succeed to the throne. The Scots, being staunch Catholics, didn't like this one bit and this fuelled the Jacobite uprisings in 1715 and 1745. When they were all over and defeated finally at Culloden Moor in 1746, with the Jacobite's pretender to the throne Bonnie Prince Charlie only living on in folklore and legend, more industries blossomed in Perth from 1760 onwards. These included linen weaving, bleaching, whisky distilling and a dyeing industry, which utilised the soft Tay water.

During the nineteenth century, Perth's population roughly doubled, but as the population of Britain itself had quadrupled, in consequence Perth grew relatively smaller and less important. Just 20 miles seaward down the Tay, the old rival Dundee was heading for boom town status, its population going from 50,000 in 1840 to 100,000 in 1853. By the time of the Tay Bridge Disaster, 150,000 people lived and worked in Dundee. Perth was envious of its rival and would go to great lengths to maintain a façade of importance. It commissioned surveys to expand its docking facilities and insisted on 88ft headroom under the Tay Bridge (the 'high girders') to allow passage of large seagoing ships. This idea was only a delusion on the part of Perth, as nothing larger than fishing boats and local river traffic ever passed further upstream from Dundee. That city had it all: deep-water moorings for big ships, extensive docks, it was only a short run from the German Ocean (as it was then known; the name North Sea came later) up the wide Firth of Tay to those docks and now in the mid-nineteenth century, it had rail communications from the Caledonian Railway and the North British, with their wagon ferries making it unnecessary to voyage on a further 20 miles of river up to Perth. Perhaps as a sop to its honour, Perth adopted the soubriquet 'The Fair City' in 1828, after the success of Walter Scott's novel *Fair Maid of Perth*.

As an aside, in the ancient game of golf, Perth has always claimed parity with even St Andrews itself, because King James IV became the first golfing King of Scotland. In 1502 he lifted a ban on the playing of golf because he thought that the threat of war with England had receded enough. The original ban on the game was an attempt to encourage archery practice instead. So, at 30 years old, James was the first recorded golfer, and made Perth the oldest-dated golf location in the world where a 'named' golfer is known to have played, probably at the site where North Inch is today.[4]

Where there are the prospects for a fine harbour, a seafaring people will build a port. So it was because of the sea that Dundee was born. Seen from Fife across the

Tay in 1879, the city rose gradually from the north shore to the west and east and much more abruptly to the north. Buildings upon buildings, terraced row upon terraced row, until they reached Balgay Hill and the heights of Craigie and Dundee Law. This conical basalt hill is the remains of an old volcanic lava plug and Dundee Law, at 571ft high dominated the centre of the city, and the buildings nestled around its base like a brood of young children at their grandfather's feet. To the north were the sheltering Sidlaw Hills, to the west, the Carse of Gowrie and to the east, Broughty Ferry and Monifieth.

The immediate hinterland is typical glaciated country, characterised by gentle undulations, occasional knolls and numerous little streams such as the Scouring Burn, Dighty Water, Gelly Burn, Fithie Burn and Dens Burn. The drainage of these is mainly into the Dighty which flows west to east between morainic deposits, before entering the Tay near Broughty Ferry. Indeed the entire Tay estuary was actually scoured out by a glacier, which was what fooled surveyor Jessie Wylie when he undertook his river borings for Thomas Bouch at the early planning stage for the first Tay Bridge.

Wylie thought he'd identified a rock base most of the way across the firth, when in fact the classic glaciated 'U'-shaped valley filled with gravel was the reality. Riverside peat of boreal composition covered by estuarine clays, all lay on crags of old red sandstone to form the site upon which Dundee was originally built. The Romans probably used the place as a supply base during their brief spell in Scotland, but after AD 83 it became known as 'Deeuna'. The original settlement used the natural harbour between Castle Rock to the east and St Nicholas Craig to the west. Then the Picts built a fort on Dundee Law, as it is known today. They called it 'Dun Deagh' which means 'fortress of Daigh', perhaps after an early Pict warrior or maybe the name derived from the Gaelic 'dun de' or 'dun deagh' meaning 'hill of God'.

By 1180 the town was well established and by 1239 a school that William Wallace apparently attended had been set up. Dundee grew up as a small port in the eleventh and twelfth centuries. In 1191 it was given a charter by King William and by the fourteenth century it had become one of Scotland's most important towns. A busy port it was, trading with France, Spain and the Low Countries, importing wine and grain and exporting hides and wool. By the fifteenth century the wool was woven and dyed in Dundee, the dyeing an especially suitable industry, as it was to Perth, because of the soft Tay water. By 1650, the town's population had risen to 11,000 people. This was the start of the eclipse of Perth, 20 miles upstream. The wool industry was definitely on a roll by the sixteenth century and imports included timber, pitch and hemp, and there was also much fishing. In 1564 (after the Reformation) Mary Queen of Scots gave the land once belonging to the Grey Friars to the Dundee townspeople as a cemetery. This area became known as 'The Howff' or 'meeting place' as many craftsmen met there for discussions. To this day, The Howff is the walled heart of medieval Dundee, a spot of quiet in the bustling of the city and allows folk to see the fascinating inscriptions on the gravestones, for example one from 1639 which reads:

> Away vain world! Thou ocean of annoyes
> And com sweet heaven, with thy eternal joyes.

The notorious Provost Riddoch is also interred here at the north-east corner of The Howff. Alexander Riddoch (1745–1822) was an artful, colourful, ambitious and somewhat unpopular man who was, several times between 1787 and 1819, the Provost (the English equivalent of mayor) of Dundee. He lived at 5 Broad Street, now a listed building. Following the French Revolution, he was forced to dance around the Tree of Liberty!

But then the city was almost completely destroyed by General Monck in 1651, fighting on the Parliamentarian side in the English Civil War. The Roundheads pillaged the town and killed 2,000 of the 12,000 inhabitants. Apart from the destruction to the place, over sixty ships were burned. Previously in 1644, Dundee was besieged by the Marquis of Montrose for the Royalists, for which Monck extracted his revenge. For the next 150 years, Dundee's fortunes waned.

The impact of imperialism on Scotland was particularly exemplified by Dundee. The city really was at 'the centre of empire'. In the mid-nineteenth century, it is no exaggeration to say that the city became the 'jute capital' of perhaps all Europe. The fibre, imported from India, was woven into yarn which then produced linoleum, sacks and carpets. This industry was symbiotic to the city's existing involvement in the Arctic whaling trade which was a way of obtaining the oil required for the fibre's treatment before paraffin was discovered. The whaling survey ship *Discovery* (1901) is now preserved at the quayside in Dundee as evidence of the success of this venture. Whale oil was used to soften the jute fibres which was a technology borrowed from the linen industry.

The city, which controlled the coastal route to north-east Scotland, is situated at the point where the Tay estuary narrows before again opening out to the sea. It first rose to importance as a whaling station although by the time of our story this industry was dying off. But Dundee remained one of the chief fishing ports in Britain. The proximity of Dundee to the Fifeshire coalfields, made even more accessible by the Tay Bridge, aided the development of the jute, linen and jam-making industries. Thousands of tons of coal crossed the bridge weekly from these coalfields, each train-load weakening in small increments the fragile and flawed Bouch construction.

We have already learned that the rivalry between the two cities had a crucial effect on the design on the Tay Bridge. Modifications to plans and construction were indirectly responsible for the collapse itself because of the 'high girders' section demanded by the city of Perth.

But let's take a look at the cities, their buildings and life in general as it was for the people who lived there and especially to those who were travelling on the doomed train, who would have been familiar with the city life of Dundee in particular.

Nineteenth-century street life in two cities such as Perth and Dundee would have been much the same. Rag-and-bone men yelling their individual calls, the baker's carts, milkmen's floats and butcher's drays pulled by big straining Clydesdale horses with feathered fetlocks, hides glistening and nosebags tossing. Large Shire-type horses came to Britain after the Norman Invasion in 1066 (originally used as big strong battle horses which could carry an armoured rider) and all the big Clydesdales were descended from them. A horse called Clyde was the very last horse to draw his final load as late as 1966. 'Clydesdales' were the life-blood of the city of Dundee and Perth for several centuries, delivering all kinds of loads. They carried water, meat covered with tarpaulins from the slaughterhouses, and moved sand, stone, jute bales and flour around the docks. They even moved railway wagons when required, as a pair of horses could pull between 3 and 3½ tons. On foot passed frock-coated and bowler-hatted insurance agents, the fruit sellers, the knife grinders, the beggars and main chancers – all the panoply of a thriving city going about its daily business. There were 'buster stalls' on many a street corner in Dundee. For a penny, you could have a portion of mushy peas splodged over pale flabby chips with a dash of vinegar and salt. You ate this delicacy with a spoon whilst sitting on a wooden bench under a makeshift tarpaulin shelter. With only rudimentary hygiene facilities the spoons were dipped in soapy water before the next customer came along. One can imagine the reaction of the European Community Food Regulation Commission today, surely closing all the buster stalls overnight!

Then there were the children of all ages trotting to and from school, sometimes playing their games of hopscotch across the pavement slabs or holding marbles contests. In the parks, the kids ran madly up and down hooting and screaming in fun. Urchins dashed about in typical gamin-like behaviour. Many folks lived in tenement buildings, which proliferated across both cities. In Dundee, building of these started at around 1860 and were nicknamed 'Pletties' which referred to the stone-flagged balconies on narrow iron supports with wrought-iron railings. The Pletties were simple three-storey tenements and consisted of three blocks divided by ridge stacks, giving eighteen flats in all. Although long ago flattened, just one such building survives today. It is at 8 Tait's Lane, just north of Magdalen Green in Dundee, and was listed as a Grade B Building in 1989. Over the years, much of old Dundee has been swept away in the name of progress, such as the spectacular old town house known as 'The Pillars'. Designed by Robert Adam in 1731 it was seen as the most elegant and impressive town house in Scotland and a symbol of the success and flourish of eighteenth-century Dundee. Often used as a meeting place for Dundonians, most of the passengers on the Edinburgh train would have known it well. However, in 1931 it was demolished to make a space for the new City Square. Also demolished in 1970 was St Mary's Roman Catholic church, built in 1851 and a familiar site to our passengers. It was a Romanesque church with twin campaniles, looking somewhat out of place in a Dundee backstreet but there it stood, at the time of our story, in Forebank. The new Overgate Centre begun in 1961 erased yet more buildings which were familiar to 1879 Dundonians. General Monck's Lodging dating from the fifteenth century was one of the first to fall to the bulldozers. Incidentally the excavations disturbed hundreds of skeletons and skulls in the mass grave left after the General's sack of the city in 1651. Lochee High Street lost its beautiful East Church to the demolition gangs in 1960 but the Pavilion in Baxter Park, after years of neglect and vandalism, recently underwent lottery-funded restoration. The 38-acre Baxter Park itself was a gift to the people of the city from jute-baron David Baxter[5] and was opened in 1863 to the joy of 70,000 spectators at a splendid ceremony. Sir Joseph Paxton, he of Crystal Palace fame, had been commissioned to build the park and Prime Minister Lord Russell was the principal attendee on opening day. Onwards through the nineteenth century the park made a wonderful pleasure ground for all Dundonians. It's certain that many of the 'Edinburgh's' passengers would have been regular visitors.

In the nineteenth century, Dundee became famed for its shipbuilding activities. In 1825 the first wet dock was built and was called King William Dock, followed by Earl Grey Dock in 1834, Camperdown Dock in 1865 and finally Victoria Dock in 1875. Up to 1979 at the time of its total demise, the shipyards had built almost 600 great ships – giant tankers, Blue Star liners, Empire cargo ships, ferries and aircraft carriers. They'd all slid down the Dundee slipways since 1874 but international competition and falling demand spelt the end of the industry. However, in 1879, our home passengers would have been all-too-familiar with the sound of banging hammers, riveters' punches clanging and the glare at night from the newfangled arc lamps which had already been used by the Tay Bridge builders during the hours of darkness.

Meanwhile, after digressing about the histories of Perth and Dundee, back to 1879. The 5.27 train had pulled out of Markinch heading almost due north on a stiff upgrade of 1 in 102, which was to last for nearly 2 miles until the summit at Lochmuir was reached. Driver Mitchell left the engine in almost full gear after starting away because of the gradient. After knocking off the injector, as he didn't want cold water rushing into the boiler and cooling it down, John Marshall began to ply his shovel in regular 'eights round the box', keeping the fire fed to maintain the steam Mitchell needed for the climb. Marshall also ran the pricker through the firebed to liven it up as much as possible. The dart or pricker needed careful handling, as it was around 8ft long and to get it in and out of the firebox meant that its length would momentarily foul the loading gauge. Some of it would protrude outside the cab with the attendant danger of hitting a bridge or a line side accessory such as a signal post. This is where a thorough knowledge of the road was needed, especially in the dark. Marshall would have to pick his moment carefully when manhandling the tool to avoid an accident. Part way up the step ascent, Marshall could hear an odd roaring sound above the hard exhaust beats from the chimney. He turned his shovel over, pushing it into the firehole and looked underneath it. Sure enough, he could see a black patch in the grate which indicated a hole in the firebed caused by the fierce exhaust pulling the coals off the firebars. He quickly threw a dozen shovel shots to fill the space and repair the hole. Mitchell nodded approvingly at Marshall's actions. After a deep cutting beside Newton Farm, the summit at Lochmuir Signal Box was passed, the climb was over and Mitchell could shut off the regulator, quieting No 224's chimney barking of the previous 2 miles. A brief stretch of level line followed, which had passing loops laid in on both sides so that expresses could overtake slow-running goods trains. Then they were running down a 1 in 105 gradient towards Falkland Road station. Marshall stopped firing and quickly put the injector on to pull up the boiler water level depleted by the climb they had just finished. He also gave half a turn on the blower valve, in order to avoid a blowback,[6] which could happen when coasting with the regulator off. It was 1½ miles from Lochmuir down to Falkland Road, so Mitchell eased on both the Westinghouse and steam brakes for good stopping power on the downgrade, coming neatly to a stand at the station round at about 6.19 p.m. The tender handbrake was screwed hard on to hold the weight of the train against the falling gradient. In the luggage van at the rear, Guard David McBeath also screwed his own handbrake down. He would release this as he gave the 'Right Away' to the engine crew on starting away. On a sharpish right-hand curve, the platforms nestled in a cutting between two granite overbridges, the second of which carried the roadway to Falkland village itself, over 3 miles away to the north-west.[7]

At Falkland Road station, no one either joined the train or left it, so the pause there was brief. Standing on a down grade of 1 in 95, Mitchell had only to release the handbrake and the Westinghouse for the train to roll onwards under gravity, helped with an ounce or two of steam and passing the 10ft-high granite retaining walls of the cutting on either side. Still on a steep downhill of 1 in 95, the train coasted effortlessly round the right-hand curvature past Forthar Mill Farm to the left and then the line straightened out, but still falling the whole distance to Kingskettle another 2 miles further. There, at 6.24 p.m., the second man called James Crichton who was on the train that night, climbed aboard a carriage.

Crichton was employed as a ploughman at the Mains of Fintry to the north-east of Dundee city and had eight brothers and sisters. He was dressed in mourning clothes and had a double-cased silver watch which had belonged to his father in a waistcoat pocket. Mr Crichton's father, a ploughman at Downfield Farm near Kingskettle, had died on Monday 22 December 1879 and was buried on the following Friday. Apart from coming for the funeral, James Crichton had also arranged with his father's boss to take over his dead parent's job at Downfield. He was going back to Fintry to arrange release from his job there with his own employer, Mr Bell.

However, Bell had told James that given the circumstances of the bereavement, he needn't come back until Monday 29 December. But James Crichton was a diligent and conscientious young man and was now the sole supporter of his mother and two of his sisters who lived in Kettle Village. He therefore decided to catch the train, to expedite his future arrangements. Engine No 224 and her train then tootled off down the last mile of gradient, crossing a high embankment and bridging the River Eden to reach Ladybank Junction at 6.27 p.m. The train was now a scheduled thirty-nine minutes away from the Tay Bridge, which against the rising gale stood out starkly across the river in the fitful moonlight, awaiting its last duty.

Notes

1. Still extant today and a listed Ancient Monument in the care of the County of Durham since 1935, it is a stone single span arch of 105ft which once carried a branch of the wooden-railed and horse drawn Tanfield Waggonway across the Causey Burn (once known as Houghwell Burn) for the cartage of coal from local mines to Newcastle. The line was part of an extensive system constructed by a group of mine-owners known as The Grand Allies. These three men, Sir Thomas Liddell (later Lord Ravensworth), the Earl of Strathmore and Mr Stuart Wortley (later Lord Wharncliffe) made their fortunes controlling most of the collieries in north-east England.
2. Refer to 6 (I) 'Assassination of James I' in the chapter note section.
3. Refer to 6 (ii) 'The Stone of Scone' in the chapter note section.
4. James IV's official accounts for 1502 contain this item: 'Item the xxi Sept to the bowar of Sanct Johnestoun for golf clubs, xiiii s', which means '21 September to the bow maker of St Johnsetoun for golf clubs, 14 shillings'.
5. Sir David Baxter, who died in 1872, lived at Kilmaron Castle near Cupar. In 1879, his widow Lady Baxter still lived there and three lady victims of the Tay Bridge Disaster (two employees plus a niece of Lady Baxter), travelled together from Kilmaron Castle to their doom on the fateful train.
6. A blowback on a steam railway engine could easily occur when the regulator was shut and there was no blast up the blast pipe into the chimney and thus no forward draught through the fire tubes in the boiler into the smokebox. The draught might tend to go the opposite way and exit via the firedoors blasting fiery gusts onto the footplate and severely burning the crew. So turning on the blower a wee bit would obviate that, by squirting live steam into the smokebox and thus maintaining a draught in the right direction through the firegrate.
7. Refer to 6 (iii) 'Falkland Palace' in the chapter note section.

The Rainbow Bridge

> In the case of accident with a heavy passenger train on the bridge, the whole of the passengers will be killed. The eels will come to gloat over in delight the horrible wreck and banquet.
>
> Patrick Matthew, known as 'The Seer of Gourdiehill'

> When we build, let us think that we build forever.
>
> John Ruskin, 1819–1900

Some previous chroniclers of the Tay Bridge story have lightly lampooned Patrick Matthew as some sort of an eccentric Scottish old boy who was a persistent pest when it came to the building of the Tay Bridge. Admittedly, he was strongly averse to the idea and had every right to his opinion but he was far from the rustic apple-tree grower that history has painted him. Born on 20 October 1790, he was an eighteenth-century man from an age past but certainly no fool. In 1831 he published his ideas on the 'Principles of Natural Selection' as propounded later by Charles Darwin, a full twenty-seven years before that luminary brought to the world the same idea in his book *On the Origin of Species* in 1858.

Sadly, Matthew failed to publicise his ideas at the time, inadvertently burying his conclusions in a very obscure tome entitled *Naval Timber and Arboriculture*, wherein he discussed ways of crossbreeding trees to make them more suitable for use in ship construction.[1] The Matthew family estate was at Gourdiehill in the Carse of Gowrie between Perth and Dundee, situated just under 2 miles from the village of Chapelhill, where Patrick Matthew cultivated apple trees.

Apart from that activity, he was very happily married by all accounts and sired five sons and three daughters. Matthew was educated at Perth Academy and then at Edinburgh University, from which seat of learning he admittedly did not graduate. There was nothing supernatural about his predictions which were soundly based upon scientific judgement and not on his being some sort of fortune-teller like Mother Shipton of Knaresborough or even Nostradamus. Nevertheless, he seems to have been tarred with the epithet 'The Seer of Gourdie' (actually 'The Seer of Gourdiehill'), simply because, when he decided to do so, he predicted certain events in the future correctly without any recourse to arcane arts but by the dispassionate dissection of the evidence available to him, plus a little imagination.

All of the above is to firmly establish Mr Matthew's credentials as an erudite man and not a crank. Even so, he described himself as 'a crotchety old man, head stuffed with old world notions, quite obsolete in the present age of progress'. Perhaps he was being too hard on himself or possibly this was true, but he did have an uncanny ability to sieve through facts and come up with sagacious answers. His remarks and prophesies regarding the Tay Bridge project will be quoted many times during this chapter.

No creations of the civil engineer seem to have so great a public appeal as bridges, and the history of their construction and evolution stretches back eons. Therefore Thomas Bouch had, if he'd ever chosen to consult it, a plethora of information on bridges ancient and modern from all over the world to guide him in his planning, the many types of bridges and what might be the best materials to use. This was vital information, especially as he was designing what would become the longest bridge anywhere in the world. Prior to Bouch's first Tay structure, the world's longest bridge was in China and called the Anping Bridge. It was a clapper bridge[2] which crossed (and in fact still does) a tidal estuary in the Fujian Province. There are 331 spans of granite beams supported by stone piers stretching for a little over 1¼ miles. It is of no great height however, only about 12ft above the water. Built between 1138 and 1151 it remained China's longest bridge until 1905. The ironic parallels between the Anping Bridge and the Tay Bridge are the crossing of a wide estuary, the extreme length and the fact that the Anping Bridge deck was 14ft wide, the same width as the first Tay Bridge.

Corbelled arches[3] were used as early as 3,000 BC by the Egyptians and later by civilisations such as the Mayans, the Greeks and by people in India. No record seems to exist of the use of bridges to cross waterways until the ninth century BC. Then, the Assyrians used pontoon bridges to cross rivers. The Greek historian Heroditus described how the Persians crossed the Euphrates in Babylon at about 700 BC. In 480 BC Heroditus told of how Xerxes crossed the Hellespont in that year. The first attempt having been blown away by storms, Xerxes beheaded the engineers responsible. There was a similar result, although not literally, after the inquiry verdict was pronounced by Mr Rothery's report on Sir Thomas Bouch and his bridge.

The Romans built their first bridges using timber. The earliest recorded Roman bridge was built about the sixth century BC, the Pons Sublicus, which became famous as the bridge held by Horatius and two front-line officers against the whole Etruscan army.

By the second century BC, the Roman bridges had developed into stone arch structures, each arch built as a structural entity on piers solid enough to take the side thrusts. That this mode of construction was successful is borne out by the Ponte Milvio, which still carries heavy road traffic across the Tiber in Rome, including 70-ton tanks during the Second World War.

After the Romans, the art of bridge building lapsed until the AD 1100s. In 1177, the famous bridge at Avignon in France was built, some of it still standing today and remembered by the song written in its honour: *Sur Le Pont D'Avignon*. During the Middle Ages, stone arch bridges proliferated across Europe. The cantilever idea and that of the truss arose at this time, probably as a result of the mathematics filtering through from the Arab world. Renaissance men like Leonardo Da Vinci and Palladio drew up plans for the use of these bridge concepts and soon added the suspension bridge idea to their deliberations.[4]

A big step forward was the arrival of iron as a building material. The first iron bridge was built between 1779 and 1781, opening on New Year's Day that year. It crosses the River Severn in Coalbrookdale and is right in the middle of the Shropshire iron industry area. It was made of cast iron but its engineering strategy was such that its ribbed construction was designed so as to use the cast iron 'under compression' and not 'under tension'. Thus it stands today, unlike Bouch's Tay Bridge, which was engineered so that its cast iron was 'in tension'.

Thomas Telford made his first excursion into cast iron with a bridge he built over the Severn at Buildwas. It was only a span of 130ft but turned out to be the precursor to much greater works. When he became the Founder President of the Institution of Civil Engineers he defined civil engineering as 'the art of directing the great forces of power in nature to the use and convenience of Man'. This was an absolute definition of the art of civil engineering, if ever there was one. Telford went on to build the Menai Straits Road Bridge while Brunel was building the Clifton Suspension Bridge and his magnum opus, the Royal Albert Bridge at Saltash.

Thomas Bouch therefore had this long history of successful bridge building laid out before him to draw on for consideration and hard information, should he have chosen to have consulted it, learned from it and implemented all the lessons therein. One would have thought it was guaranteed that with this much data available, Bouch would have been able to build a splendid, well-engineered and safe structure.

The moment of conception for the Tay Bridge could be said to have occurred at the Dundee solicitor's office of Patullo & Thornton on 9 October 1863. Thomas Thornton assembled some far-sighted citizens to discuss bridging the Tay by a railway crossing, since Dundee badly needed a bridge. It was a thriving city with a growing population, and the foundries, jute and flax mills needed coal to power their enterprises. Fife, with its abundant coalfields, was only 2 miles away across the river, yet all the Fife coal had to come to Dundee by ship or by train via Perth, which were long and expensive routes. The next move was a public meeting on 18 October

1864, which was attended by Thomas Bouch bearing his plans. Finally, with everyone in agreement, a prospectus was issued on 4 December 1864.

Patrick Matthew opined that 'the grandeur and difficulty more than the utility and wisdom of the enterprise fascinates the movers of the scheme'. He was rightly commenting upon the hubris surrounding building something this colossal. He was also worried about some other factors. He observed:

> An earthquake would surely bring down the bride [sic]. The sleeping giant whose struggles are felt every season would be quite sufficient to capsize the Wormit Bridge which, being so high and top heavy and so crank like a narrow boat with tall people standing in it would be easily upset.[5]

Bouch stated that to bridge the Tay was 'a very ordinary undertaking and we have several far more stupendous and greater bridges already constructed'. He said he'd estimated the cost at no more than £180,000 and upon this figure would stake his professional reputation. This of course was a completely mad misjudgement of the kind that only Bouch could make. No one asked him where these 'stupendous bridges' were, but it may be inferred that they were the Belah and Hownsgill Viaducts that he'd built already. The Hownsgill Viaduct near Consett, and built of stone, is still there today, albeit now used as a cycle track. It had been built by Bouch for the Stanhope and Tyne Railway in 1858.

The Belah Viaduct is sadly gone now (taken down in 1962) but it did take a fair amount of effort to demolish; this viaduct was a casualty of Dr Beeching's pruning of the British railway network in the 1960s. It was designed by Thomas Bouch and built by Hopkins, Gilkes of Middlesbrough, the same company which was to end up building the Tay Bridge. There are shades of doom here perhaps, but to be fair, Belah was a substantial and long-lasting structure. It was a 'pipe' bridge, its sixteen spans supported by the very same idea as was used at the Tay: cast-iron columns in clusters. That was fine, cast iron being used under compression which was considered good engineering practice. The bridge was on the route from Barnard Castle to Tebay and formed part of the steep climb to Stainmore Summit and was also the highest bridge in England, at an altitude of 1,370ft above sea level. Constructed in just four months it was opened on 4 July 1860 for goods trains and in August for passenger traffic. The 'batter' was far better than that of the Tay Bridge. 'Batter' is the angle or slope of the sides of a bridge or embankment, where the bigger the batter, the more the centre of gravity is lowered, thus giving more stability, very much unlike the Tay Bridge which had hardly any batter at all. The whole thing cost £31,630 and was completed on time, within budget and without the loss of a single life. So, perhaps Bouch was seen, quite rightly on the evidence so far, as the right man for the Tay Bridge job.

However, Patrick Matthew wrote in a letter to the *Dundee Advertiser* that 'The Great Eastern[6] was just such another blunder as the erection of this great bridge will be. They are both steps wide of precedent and beyond experience.' Again he was right, in that he identified the designers of both projects as stepping into the void which exceeded the limits of their competence and experience. Matthew continued to write letters to the *Dundee Advertiser* throughout the early 1870s not only about the recklessness of building the bridge itself, but arguing that the money spent on the bridge would be better used to improve the sanitation of Dundee, which was in itself a moot point.

Not content with the local press Patrick Matthew even wrote to Prime Minister Gladstone with an opinion on the new Houses of Parliament, of which he bitterly disapproved.

He said that 'the man who suggested they proved Britain's power to build anything was patently a fool. The wretched mouldering state of the recently erected Houses of Parliament shows how stupid and careless some of our foremost engineers can be.'

He might have been griping at the Tay Bridge here.

But all Matthew's efforts were in vain since they were totally ignored. No doubt there was great relief among the Dundee businessmen and the bridge builders when Matthews expired in June 1874 aged 84 years. He would carp and annoy them no more.

The bridge having got the 'green light' in modern vernacular, the job was put out to tender. There now ensued a series of difficulties in finding a contractor to actually build the thing. In October 1869 the North British Railway received a letter from John Milroy, representing Thomas Brassey's interest as a builder. Brassey was perhaps the greatest of all the nineteenth-century railway building contractors. By 1847 he'd built one out of every three miles of line in Britain, three out of four in France and one in twenty of the mileage worldwide, a truly enormous series of feats that made Brassey the best qualified company there could possibly be to build Bouch's bridge. Milroy, on Brassey's behalf, quoted a provisional figure of £289,000 but the NBR knocked it back because they'd found another contractor, Butler & Pitts, who would do the job for £229,000. What would have happened if the NBR had agreed to Brassey's offer and had the benefit of the consequent high standard of workmanship in execution is, as John Thomas has put it, 'one of the great imponderables of the Tay Bridge story'.

But before any arrangements could be properly drawn up with Butler & Pitts, the main partner in that firm died and the company withdrew from the project. In May 1871 a new deal was struck with Charles de Bergue's company for the strangely specific sum of £217,099 18*s* 6*d*, a figure which was soon proved to be totally unrealistic and would help send the company bankrupt and unable to continue the job. On the basis of that unrealistic quote, the work began and on Saturday 22 July 1871, the foundation stone was laid at Wormit, Fife by William Paterson, the son of William Paterson who was Resident Engineer of the North British Railway.

The Reverend Mr Thompson, Minister of Forgan, presided because by geographical accident the spot was in his parish and presumably he begged for the Almighty's blessing on the undertaking. No one knows what Paterson Junior actually said as he wielded his little hammer on the first stone laid, because Thomas Bouch had specifically banned any members of the press from attending the ceremony. To the north-west, across the calm River Tay, was the Carse of Gowrie, where Patrick Matthew was at last silent, buried in a churchyard. However, his accurate predictions would continue to haunt the whole venture.

Charles de Bergue was a very successful contractor who knew well what he was about, but he was very ill by the time the Tay Bridge contract was signed. His chief plant manager was a man called Albert Groethe and it was he who led the team in 1871 to start the work. Bouch, meanwhile, began to hire his own staff, including William Paterson Senior and, after consulting with Sir Joseph Bazalgette of the London Metropolitan Board of Works (who had recently rebuilt the entire London sewer system) appointed Henry Noble, who came recommended by Bazalgette as a first-class man in the masonry and brickwork department. A good stonemason was vital to the team because at this time, before Jessie Wylie's hopelessly inaccurate river borings became obvious, Bouch thought that he could build the entire bridge on piers of brick or stone.

On this basis, Cuthbert Hamilton Ellis was of the opinion that Bouch intended to copy the basic idea of the Drogheda Viaduct in Ireland as his plan to bridge the Tay. In the province of Leinster in the County of Louth, the Dublin to Belfast main railway line crossed the River Boyne at Drogheda. The bridge was built between 1851 and 1855 by Welsh engineer William Evans. He dug down and down through unforeseen pockets of deep mud and then went bankrupt! Another engineer, James Barton, took over the works and found a gravel base on the riverbed 43ft below the water level. Shades of the Tay Bridge, one might think – but the idea to use masonry or brick pierage with wrought-iron girders to leap the gaps was sound enough. It was when the brick piers on Thomas Bouch's bridge had to give way, after the first fourteen, to the cast-iron uprights that the horrors of the construction errors really began.

Meanwhile, on 10 April 1873, Charles de Bergue died, which was a complete shock to the enterprise. His company was now controlled by his female relatives: Bergue's widow Sophie Ring de Bergue and his daughter Anne Mary de Bergue. Unfortunately, despite the best of intentions, these ladies were really not up to the job of running a major construction company. It was just after de Bergue's death that the inaccuracy of Wylie's river borings became apparent. But Bouch was undismayed and basically said (paraphrased here): 'Well, we'll redesign the piers using cast-iron columns rather than brick ones. Not only will they be cheaper but it will make them lighter on the compacted gravel base we have available across the river.'

Nobody seems to have asked Bouch why he hadn't done this in the first place if it would indeed save money and be just as strong. But Bouch was radically redesigning the whole bridge concept after the Wylie borings were shown to be a sham. Bouch's mathematical guru, Allan D. Stewart, pronounced Bouch's calculations as unsatisfactory. On the back of this, Bouch proposed that he would redesign the bridge (apart from the first fourteen brick-built piers at the Wormit side) with iron towers, much as he'd done with the Belah Bridge. But Bouch was wrong when he said that iron towers would be cheaper than brick piers. He further redesigned the bridge by cutting the high girders section from fourteen spans to thirteen, thus saving the price of a pier and a span. Each of the thirteen spans to leap the gap that the fourteen would have done was perforce now much longer. Furthermore the new non-brick towers were to have only one caisson, unlike the first fourteen brick towers which had two side-by-side. But a single caisson with its smaller base was not wide enough to carry the eight cast-iron uprights as originally intended. So Bouch settled for only six uprights which, with the narrower base, affected the 'turning moment' and pushed up higher the centre of gravity of each pier. Bouch denied any lessening in stability although it was patently obvious from basic engineering principles and physics that this was so.

Each of the six columns was made up of seven flanged pipes that were of a diameter of 18in. The lowest were bolted through their flange plates to an iron bedplate on top of the caisson. The securing bolts only went down through the plate and into two courses of brickwork, nowhere near deep enough for proper grip and stability. The other uprights were bolted together through their flanges and rigidity was achieved by double wrought-iron channel bars bolted to the lugs already cast in the columns, and these ran diagonally from flange to flange. These cast-in lugs were themselves cast iron and were expected to take all the torsional forces to brace the columns, which the material was inherently incapable of doing. In one of his many written objections to the Tay Bridge, Patrick Matthew correctly predicted that the bridge would suffer from flaws in the use of cast iron and that the foundations themselves would prove very difficult.

Apparently to save even more money, regardless of the fact that there were already extant in Dundee iron foundries which were properly manned by expert iron founders and could probably have done the job cheaper, it was decided to build a foundry on the south bank at Wormit to cater for all the bridge's needs. Ignoring the fact that the De Bergue Company was not a specialist in iron foundry work, this foundry was set up in February 1873 and work proceeded in casting the iron columns and assembling the wrought-iron spans. Caissons were used to get down to the riverbed for each pier, the workmen inside operating in a compressed air environment as they dug away into the mud, gravel and shale.

We humans breathe air, which is 80 per cent nitrogen. Put a human body under pressure and nitrogen is transformed into tiny bubbles that infiltrate blood and tissue. If the pressure on us changes too quickly, such as what happens in a very quick ascent to the surface by a diver, the trapped bubbles in the bloodstream start fizzing like a newly opened bottle of champagne. This clogs the blood vessels, deprives the cells of oxygen and causes such pain that sufferers often bend double in agony, hence the term 'the bends'. This was very relevant to the caisson workers on the Tay Bridge foundation. The caissons were filled with compressed air and when the workers emerged after a day's work under this artificial pressure they often suffered mild 'bends': symptoms such as a tingling sensation on their skin or itchiness. A few felt insistent pains in their joints and, on occasions, some workers would go to bed feeling fine but wake up partly paralysed.[7]

On 26 August 1875 at 2.30 a.m., a violent bang suddenly interrupted the works at Pier 54 when an explosion destroyed the caisson there. This pier was one of many that had no foundation of rock below it and five labourers, working 45ft below the surface in an atmosphere of compressed air, were toiling away to remove the sand and send it topside. Two other men were plastering clay over cracks in the cast-iron caisson higher up. Out in the night air above, and taking a break on the engine platform, were the foreman, the engineman and a boy engine-tender. When the explosion happened, the three standing on the engine platform were blown into the river. The two clay workers managed to scramble up and out, but the engine boiler fell on one and he was killed. As for the five poor souls working at the very bottom, the water rushed in through the ripped air bell plates and drowned them. The cause was never established, although Bouch blamed a coal barge on the river colliding and cracking the upper part of the caisson. Afterwards, malleable iron was used for the caissons, not cast iron.

The De Bergue ladies by now had discovered that their company's finances were in a parlous state and that Charles De Bergue had made a hopelessly unrealistic tender in order to secure the bridge-building job. Bouch, however, went out of his way to render assistance. He checked through the books and figured out what had already been paid for materials, thinking to compensate them. So he then floated the idea with the NBR directors that they may want to think about raising the price of the contract in order to save the firm. At last Bouch pronounced that 'finding the works could not well go under them it was deemed advisable to get the representatives of De Bergue to renounce and give up the contract'. It was clear that they could not go on.

So now Bouch engaged the final contractor, Hopkins, Gilkes and Company, who'd already worked very successfully with him on the Belah Viaduct. The firm took over the Tay Bridge contract in July 1874.[8]

Winning the Tay Bridge contract was a great relief to William Hopkins and Edgar Gilkes as their company was running into severe financial difficulties.[9]

Yet another Patrick Matthew statement came true on the night of 2 February 1877. A sudden storm swept ferociously down the Tay from the west and pounced upon two of the 245ft-high girder spans that had just been raised to their positions on top of their piers but were as yet unsecured on their seatings. Forty workmen were out there, exposed to the gale and trying in vain to shelter among the latticework, which was vibrating madly.

Suddenly the two spans tilted over and crashed into the river with an enormous sound, audible even above the gale. The rescue tug *Excelsior* managed to save all the workmen but one. What Matthew had predicted was that 'the tempestuous impetus of the icy blasts must wrench off the girders as if they were a spider's web or hurl the whole erection before it'.

One of the girders was a write-off but the other, although bent, was straightened out and ended up on the final bridge as the first of the high girders from the south side. Forever afterwards, a slight distortion remained in this girder, making a kink in the rails which guards, maintenance men and drivers described as causing the engines to 'nod' into the girder.

Amongst the luminaries to visit the bridge during its construction, perhaps the biggest superstar in modern terms (discounting Queen Victoria's crossing of the bridge in 1879) was General Ulysses Grant, victor and hero of the American Civil War and up to March 1877 the president of that nation. He came to Dundee in a special train on 1 September 1877 with his wife and his youngest son, Jesse. He was well cheered by everyone. The only reported remark he made about the bridge (and this is apocryphal) was: 'it's a very long bridge for a very small town.' He said nothing about a railway bridge disaster in his own country in northern Ohio just a year before, about which he simply must have known. He kept his own counsel on this topic.

Ironically, the disaster ex-President Grant omitted to mention was paralleled by the Tay Bridge which collapsed just two years after the president's visit. After his apparent remark about the Tay Bridge he went off to enjoy the sumptuous lunch provided by the Dundee City Fathers. It was the Ashtabula Bridge Disaster that he failed to mention even in passing. This accident is little known especially outside the USA, but nevertheless has some uncanny similarities with the Tay Bridge collapse, not the least with the date and the time. Eighty passengers died as the Ashtabula Bridge collapsed in a winter storm on 29 December 1876 at 7.28 p.m., taking a train down with it.[10]

The magnitude of the disaster shocked the entire American nation, which makes it even more odd that Grant made no mention of it. The great Tay Bridge was actually finished soon after Grant's visit in September 1877 and trains began to cross, mostly carrying tons of rubble and stonework destined for the construction of the new Dundee Esplanade and the works required by the North British Railway for their new Dundee Tay Bridge station. Already the cast-iron lugs and bracings in the towers were taking some forceful punishment as these very heavy goods trains lumbered over in great numbers day after day.

In February 1878, Major General Hutchinson inspected the bridge for the Board of Trade. His report, dated 5 March 1878, stated that:

> For the purpose of adequately testing the structure, the North British Company placed at my disposal six new goods engines weighing 73 tons each

and each measuring 48 feet 6 inches over all, the total weight employed being thus 438 tons and the total length of engines 291 feet, or as nearly as possible, 1½ tons to the running foot.

After three days' observations with a theodolite he also found that lateral oscillation was very slight, even with the six engines running over at speed. He noted: 'the ironwork has been well put together both in the columns and girders.' He did suggest that the bridge should be painted white to reduce expansion in hot weather. Far more important was his recommendation of a speed limit of 25mph and that very careful attention should be paid to any scouring actions around the bases of the piers. Subject to all his requirements, Hutchinson saw no reason why the Board of Trade should not allow passenger traffic to use the bridge.

But as a proviso, the final remark in his report was that he'd have liked to see how the bridge behaved in a high wind and intended to return at some time to observe this point. Unfortunately, he was taken ill and never did return. This remark probably saved his professional reputation after the bridge had fallen.

The ceremonial opening was on 31 May 1878 with a special train hauled by Drummond 0-4-2 tank engine No 314 and driven across the bridge from south to north by the great Dugald Drummond himself. The arrival at the new Tay Bridge station was followed by much civic junketing in Dundee.

The bridge had just nineteen months to live.

When the whole thing was open for public passenger traffic, the North British Railway was able to trumpet the achievement in its advertising material. For the year 1879 it crowed on posters, in handbills and on full page advertisements in its timetables that:

> This stupendous bridge spanning the estuary of the Tay at Dundee and connecting with the shores of Fife and Forfar, forms part of the North British Railway system and is now open for passenger traffic. The Bridge is fully Two Miles in length: and the centre of the Estuary, the Railway is carried upon it, at a height of Eighty Feet above high water mark. The view up and down the River when crossing in the Train is unrivalled, and the route to and from Dundee is interesting, varied, and picturesque.

The release went on to say that the express train service from Edinburgh to Dundee via Burntisland was the quickest route between Edinburgh and Dundee, Arbroath, Stonehaven, Aberdeen and the North. At a stroke, the NBR captured 84 per cent of the Edinburgh–Dundee passenger traffic and 63 per cent of the Edinburgh–Aberdeen traffic, to the detriment of the Caledonian Railway. Such was the excited public response to the bridge that folks now didn't seem to mind the Forth ferry crossing if they were going to cross the Tay Bridge!

A whole series of railway excursions were advertised to encourage tourists to roam around the Fife and Dundee area but always with a crossing of the Tay Bridge as part of the journey. These trips were immensely successful, attracting hundreds of sightseers to experience the thrill of travelling over the Firth of Tay on Bouch's much vaunted bridge.[11]

However, the fact remained that the only person in day-to-day care of any sort of this 2-mile bridge of iron was Henry Noble, an inspector of brickwork with no knowledge of iron. Originally, when the bridge opened, James Bell, Chief Engineer of the North British Railway expected to be in charge of it. Instead, the NBR Board retained Thomas Bouch at the derisory sum of £100 a year with Henry Noble as the inspector 'on the spot' as it were. The whole care of the bridge was indeed a leaderless operation. Noble firstly had a crew of seven unskilled men, which comprised the staff of two ordinary miles of railway, not a hugely complex 2-mile iron bridge across an estuary of the North Sea. Noble also had Mr Bell, the boatman who sailed around looking for evidence of scouring of the piers, at the pay rate of 3s 6d a day. McKinney the lamplighter took care of the navigation lights at 21s per week and Neish was the foreman in charge of this small team. James Bell, the North British Railway engineer, had two surfacemen on the bridge's permanent way, tightening fishplate bolts and knocking in the wooden keys between the rails and the chairs. The total wages bill was £14 per week but even that was too much for the NBR, who now began to cheapskate on running the bridge while happily gulping the profits. After September 1878 the staff was reduced to just four men and on 10 January 1879 the Board actually cut the wages of the men by 5s a week! Noble suggested laying off everyone except the lamplighter McKinney after the September 1879 inspections, which pleased the NBR Board no end. So at this stage just Noble and the lamplighter were in sole charge of the longest bridge in the world. Bouch of course, busy with new projects like his Forth Bridge, hardly ever made more than a cursory appearance on site.

During one of his 'inspections' Noble found a 6ft 6in vertical crack in an iron column on Pier 38. Using the stopper-wire from a ginger-beer bottle, he pushed the wire into the crack. It didn't go right in, so after wetting a page of notepaper and placing over the crack, he waited for a train to cross. The paper stuck in place and thus Noble concluded that the bridge was safe!

The trackwork was composed of 24ft lengths of bullhead rail weighing 75lb per yard, fish-plated (plates of metal fixed across) at their joints and held to gauge by oak keys in cast-iron chairs – standard permanent-way practice for the era. Including all the metal and screws, plus the pair of checkrails, the track work weighed about 500 tons. There was an oak deck of 3in planks painted with a waterproof covering to prevent rotting by water and engine firebox embers. Later, the whole bridge deck was given a 3in-deep layer of ballast which did two things – it reduced the fire risk from dropped embers from engine fireboxes, but it also pushed up the bridge's centre of gravity quite a bit more, due to its weight of about 1,000 tons for the 2-mile length, enough to contribute to the collapse on the fatal night by raising the centre of gravity even further than the suspect design had already raised it. But there was no one who was qualified to check out the state of the cast-iron piers nor the fixings of the cross-bracings, whose security depended totally on the lugs cast (in one go) into each column. This, as previously mentioned, meant that cast iron was being employed in its most vulnerable state, that is 'under tension'. In the final stages of the erection of the piers a labourer called Edward McGovern, who was not an engineer, supervised the fixing of the vital tie-bars between the column lugs. But no one had told him how far to tighten the bolts and of course he didn't know himself so he just guessed. But he did notice that the holes in the lugs were mostly too big for the bolts and sometimes the holes were in the wrong places, meaning that the bolts had to be forced in. It must have been hard to get cylindrical bolts to fit into conical holes.

In December 1879, when the bridge had but a week or two to live, Noble found cracks in columns on Piers 73 and 76, one of which was 4ft 6in long, and this time his ginger-beer bottle wire did go right through. On 13 December Noble had each column bound with four iron hoops. He reported this to Bouch who did deign to visit the bridge on 22 December, just six days before its fall. Bouch was not perturbed about the cracks, saying he knew of similar cracks on the Severn and Chepstow bridges. However, on that day, Bouch never went out to the high girders section.

Patrick Matthew called the Tay Bridge 'a rainbow bridge with its disposition to destruction' and none of his foresights were ever mentioned at the Board of Inquiry.

His words were: 'In the case of accident, with a heavy passenger train on the bridge, the whole of the passengers will be killed. The eels will come to gloat over in delight the horrible wreck and banquet.'

Notes

1   His book, published in 1831, was a treatise on how best to grow trees for the needs of HM warship construction and buried at the end, in an appendix, was an examination, based on his evaluations, on how by selective breeding, the quality and certain facets of such trees could be improved. Charles Darwin, coming to the same conclusions as Matthew, had been totally unaware of Patrick's theories when he published his great work on evolution in 1858. When he found out about Matthew's book years later, he apologised publicly and in full in the 3 March 1860 edition of the journal *Gardener's Chronicle* for not recognising the work that Matthew had already done. Furthermore, in subsequent editions of *On the Origin of Species* Darwin freely acknowledged that Matthew had clearly seen the full force of the principle of natural selection.
2   A clapper bridge is one built of straight granite beams resting on stone uprights, only a small step up from the very first bridges which were simply a tree trunk thrown across a small stream. There are several clapper bridges extant today and a good example is at Postbridge on Dartmoor, Devon, which was built somewhere in the thirteenth or fourteenth centuries.
3   A corbelled arch is basically a series of cantilevers where staggered courses of stone project towards the archway's centre, until the courses meet at the apex. An example in modern terms of this technique is the Eskimo igloo.

4   Refer to 7 (i) 'The Art of Bridge Construction' in the chapter note section.
5   He was absolutely correct. About 100 miles north-west of Dundee lay the Great Glen which runs across Scotland at the approximate delineation of N35 degrees E to S35 degrees W. This is one of the major fault lines in Britain and has always been subjected to earthquakes and tremors which have often been felt in Dundee, itself only 20 miles south of the Southern Highland Boundary Fault. 'Earthquake House', containing seismometers, was opened in 1874 to monitor seismic activity in the area. Kessock Bridge near Inverness, opened in 1982 is an 1150yd-long road bridge crossing the strait between the Moray and Beauly Firths and was constructed especially to withstand the kind of disaster that Matthew was predicting for the Tay Bridge. The Kessock crossing actually has two immense hydraulic shock absorbers in the form of a pair of 400-tonne buffers. As for Patrick Matthew's description of the Tay Bridge being top heavy, absolutely right once more.
6   The *Great Eastern* was Brunel's huge steamship designed for transatlantic operations as a passenger liner and when launched in 1858 was the largest ship in the world, being 680ft long and displacing some 12,000 tons, five times larger than anything else afloat. She was a commercial failure and was plagued with accidents. However, she did help lay the first transatlantic cable, her huge holds being capable of carrying the cable mileage required. She languished for twelve years after that and was finally cut up in 1888.
7   Refer to 7 (ii) 'The Bends' in the chapter note section.
8   Refer to 7 (iii) 'William Innes Hopkins' in the chapter note section.
9   After the Tay Bridge Disaster, the Board of Inquiry severely blamed Hopkins Gilkes for the grave irregularities at the Wormit Foundry, which indictment ruined the company. Hopkins went bankrupt in 1880 with his public life in ruins. He tried to sell his grand house Grey Towers Hall for £30,000 but failed to find a buyer. He, his wife and small son moved to Norton, North Yorkshire where nothing was ever heard from them, all further victims of the Tay Bridge Disaster.
10 Refer to 7 (iv) 'The collapse of the Ashtabula Bridge' in the chapter note section.
11 Refer to 7 (v) 'NBR Tay Bridge Excursions' in the chapter note section.

Route of the doomed train: 28 December 1879

Lines closed on Sundays: ----------
Ferry connections: ....
Other lines: ——————

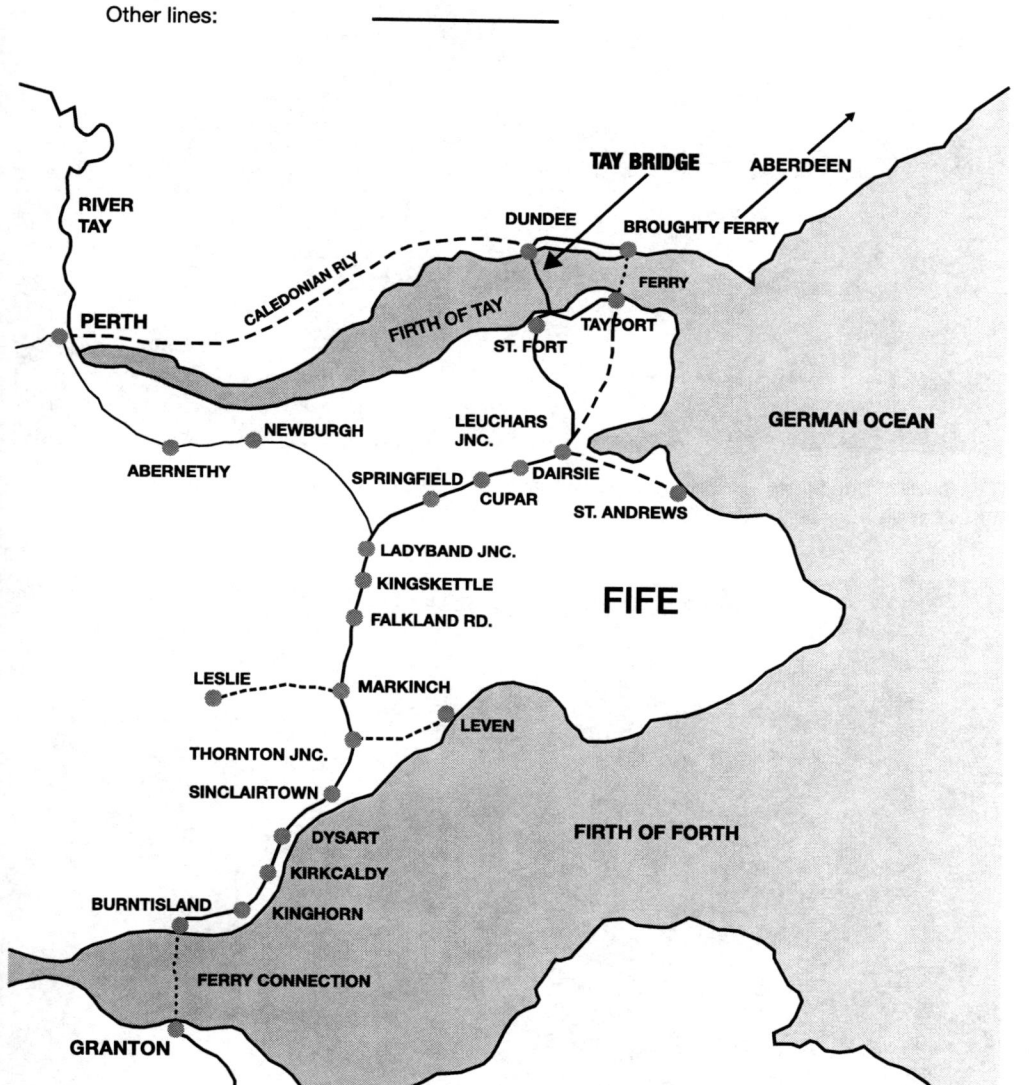

'The Spirit of The Storm' as seen by one newspaper of the time, quoting words attributed to Julius Caesar after he'd invaded Britain: 'I came, I saw, I conquered.' (Alistair Nisbet)

The gap at the southern end of the high girders with steam launches and boats bobbing around in rough waters searching for bodies. The nearest craft seems to be carrying more onlookers than rescuers. (Alistair Nisbet)

Illustrated London News front cover for Saturday 10 January 1880 showing Foreman Roberts' heroic attempt to find out what had happened to the bridge. In reality all was in blackness as the storm raged around him. Note the track ballasting is not shown and why Roberts is wearing a sailor's uniform is a mystery! (Alistair Nisbet)

Front cover of *The Penny Illustrated Paper* in memoriam to Driver Mitchell and Fireman Marshall. The depiction of the accident is erroneous as the engine was inside the cage of the girders. (Alistair Nisbet)

VIEW OF THE TAY BRIDGE BEFORE THE ACCIDENT

Christian Herald newspaper for 7 January 1880 with a spirited, albeit inaccurate version of the disaster moment. The paper is naturally enough suggesting that the accident was God's revenge for running a train on the Sabbath. (Alistair Nisbet)

Illustrated London News engraving of divers exploring the riverbed for the wreckage of the girders and the train. (Alistair Nisbet)

Contemporary engraving, remarkably accurate in detail, of completed first Tay Bridge, looking south. The high girders section is visible in the middle distance with the sharp curve approaching the north riverbank in the foreground. (Alistair Nisbet)

The boys' training ship *Mars*, moored half a mile downstream of the present bridge but in the same relative position to the old structure. It is plain that the Deck Watch (Instructor Hugh McMahon) would have had a very clear view of the train as it crossed. The train and a mile of the bridge disappeared during the instant that McMahon turned his back for protection from the extra-savage wind gust at 7.16 p.m. (R.E. Fraser)

Bouch's bridge looking towards distant Fife. The thirteen high girders are clearly visible in the middle of the picture. Note the nearest five high girder spans are part of the 1 in 73 gradient falling towards the north shore. (Alistair Nisbet)

One of the Tay ferries, nicknamed 'the Fifies', approaching the pier at Newport in rough waters. Many rail passengers went back to using these ferries, having been alarmed by the excess speed of northbound trains and the disturbing oscillations of the bridge itself. (R.E. Fraser)

Illustrated London News engraving of diving and salvage operations some days after the accident. Note lifting sheerlegs erected on the deck of the lighter. (Alistair Nisbet)

The bridge after the collapse looking towards Dundee. Note the mile-long gap where the thirteen high girders and the train disappeared into the river. (Alistair Nisbet)

A line of horsedrawn cabs at Dundee Tay Bridge NBR station east entrance. The track and platforms were (and are) in a deep cutting. Semaphore signals are visible poking up above the Dock Street tunnel through which the lines continued on from Dundee to the north and Aberdeen. The magnificent Caledonian Railway station buildings of Dundee West are in the background. (R.E. Fraser)

Close-up of south end of fallen high girders. The train is inside the girders under the water in gaps 4 and 5 counting from the left. (Alistair Nisbet)

View inside the high girders before ballasting was carried out. Note the checkrails laid inside the running rails. The train's wheels, forced by the wind, ground against the inside of the left-hand guardrail and also against the inner side of the right-hand running rail, causing the sheaves of sparks seen by Guard Shand on the church train and by Barclay and Watt in the south signal box as the 'Edinburgh' crossed the bridge. (Alistair Nisbet)

Looking north from Wormit after the accident. Barclay's signal box can be seen actually on the bridge itself inside the 'Y' of the lines from St Fort (left) and Newport (right). The original signal box, redundant since the opening of the Newport line, is on the left of the approach curve line. The cottages on the left are where Barclay and Watt lived. The gap once bridged by the high girders is visible in the distance. (Alistair Nisbet)

A southbound train of coal empties leaves the present-day bridge in 1964. The scene at the south end of the bridge has changed in some details since 1879 with a new signal box (still in the 'Y' between the Newport line and the main line south through Fife), a water tower and the disappearance on the far left of the railwaymen's cottages. (Alistair Nisbet)

Illustrated London News impression of boatmen searching for survivors by the bridge immediately after the fall. An heroic effort in the raging storm and dark but sadly futile. (Alistair Nisbet)

Barlow's replacement viaduct in 1966 during the last days of steam in Britain. A train of coal empties hauled by a WD 2-8-0 trundles southwards. The stumps of Bouch's bridge are just visible to the right. The downgrade of the bridge towards the north shore, just like Bouch's, can be seen in the far distance. (Alistair Nisbet)

River-level view looking north of the replacement bridge and the forlorn stumps of the Bouch crossing to the right. (Alistair Nisbet)

The angry River Tay surging between the new and old bridge piers with the wind gusting to 40mph. Although nothing like the severity of conditions on the night of 28 December 1879, the picture gives an idea of what river and wind can do. The Tay valley is funnel-shaped and acts like a wind tunnel. Climatic conditions can change very suddenly. The river may appear tranquil and idyllic but suddenly its surface may be transformed into a terrifying Atlantic-type immensity of surging 8ft-waves driven by very strong winds. The Firth of Tay is no place for amateur boatmen or children. Alistair Nisbet notes that when the wind speed reaches 80mph the Tay Road Bridge is closed to traffic. On one day in 2012 both Tay Road and Rail Bridges were closed because of exceptionally high winds. (Alistair Nisbet)

8

Heavy Weather

*I have bedimmed the noontide sun, called forth the mutinous winds
And twixt the green sea and the azured vault, set roaring war.*

William Shakespeare, *The Tempest*

The enigma of Mr William Henry Beynon is furthered at Ladybank Junction where the 5.27 p.m. Edinburgh train pulled in just about on time at 6.27 p.m. It was scheduled to pause there for two minutes, to make a connection with the Perth line, whose incoming train had arrived at 4.57 p.m. carrying twelve passengers for the Dundee connection. That meant a long ninety-minute wait at Ladybank for them all. Annie Spence was travelling home from Newburgh where she'd caught her train for Ladybank at 4.40 p.m. She was a 21-year-old weaver in the jute industry and had been to see her father Andrew. He was 70 years old and had been a weaver himself.

Annie was of medium height with black hair and wore a black satin dress, a velvet hat and white ribbed stockings. She was very glad to see the 'Edinburgh' roll into the platform as it put an end to her tedium and also promised to get her home to 62 Kemback Street, Dundee within the hour.

Walter Ness was 24 years old and a foreman saddler with J.M. Storrar's company in Dundee. Walter lived at 4 Bain Square, Wellgate and was returning home after visiting friends at Auchtermuchty which, with no Sunday train service, had meant the best part of a 4-mile walk in the storm to Ladybank. He was a valued member of the 4th Forfarshire Artillery Volunteers, who were later to bury him with full military honours, providing a funeral party of NCOs and men under Lt Buchanan. He wore a silver watch with a small albert strap, a scarf pin and carried £4 14*s* 2*d* in his purse, along with some foreign coins. There was also his pipe and tobacco pouch, a bunch of keys, some photographs and a few letters in his pockets. He too was glad to see the 5.27 p.m. arrive so that he could get warm and dry after his trek. Dressed well enough for the weather in his tweed topcoat and felt hat, he would have found it still very cold hanging about on a draughty station platform. Coming in on the Perth connection were David Jobson, an oil and colour merchant going home to Dundee, and Thomas Annan, 5ft 6in tall, with dark hair and whiskers. He was an iron turner at the Wallace Works in Dundee. James Foster Henderson was another waiting passenger. Aged 22 years he was a labourer who was stoutly built and had short hair. John Lawson was a 25-year-old plasterer going home (after a visit to his parents in Newburgh) to 39 Lilybank Road, Dundee where lived his wife Mary, their two kids and his sister. He had reddish curly hair and wore a tweed jacket and blue topcoat.

Then there were two young ladies travelling from Newburgh who were both called 'Elizabeth'. The elder of them, at 24 years old, was married and lived at 46 Bell Street, Dundee, while the younger woman was a 21-year-old dressmaker who actually lived in Newburgh and was Dundee-bound – she was clad in a black jacket and dress, black shawl and a fur-trimmed hat.

The Robertson brothers, Alexander (23) and William (21) had been to Abernethy to visit their father. They were both firemen at the Dundee Gasworks. Finally William McDonald (41) and his 11-year-old boy David were coming home to Dundee from Newburgh.

The departing connecting service to Perth was due off Ladybank at 6.32 p.m., just after the 'Edinburgh' plodded on through the storm towards Dundee. The branch connection was timed to arrive in Perth at 7.20 p.m. It appears that Mr Beynon jumped off the 'Edinburgh' on its arrival at Ladybank, seemingly under the impression that he had to change trains. He therefore joined the Perth train waiting across the other side of the platform by mistake. It was only when a porter walked the length of the platform calling out 'Perth train! Perth train!' that Mr Beynon realised his error. Hearing the porter's shouts, Mr Beynon scuttled back out of the train to Perth and frantically rejoined the service he'd abandoned a few moments before. With no time to spare, he jumped into the nearest first-class compartment he came across because Davy McBeath was already blowing his whistle and waving his flag as a signal to Mitchell and Marshall to depart at 6.29 p.m.

In that compartment were Mr Linskill and a young boy, whose identity and relationship with Linskill is unknown, on their way to visit the Dean of St Andrews. Linskill recalled later having a sympathetic chat with Mr Beynon, who was expansive and garrulous about his mistake, as people tend to be when they've just narrowly avoided a blunder.

Mr Beynon and Mr Linskill shared the compartment and nattered away until the train arrived at Leuchars Junction. As we'll see later, it was there that Mr Linskill left the train to be picked up by the Dean of St Andrews's carriage, leaving Mr Beynon to his fate. Meanwhile, the wind, rain and tempest continued to rise in intensity as the train forged on towards Springfield, the next stop. The weather was certainly worsening by the minute. Mitchell and Marshall were finding life pretty uncomfortable now, what with the wind, the rain coming down like stair rods and the biting cold.

They really were not expecting this downturn in the weather on their last lap home; they had anticipated gusty wind maybe and a bit of rain, but not this. Because the storm of 28 December 1879 played such a controversially important part in the Tay Bridge Disaster, it may be wondered why no real notice of its arrival across Scotland was ever forthcoming at the time. After all, in the twenty-first century, we take for granted a reasonable level of accuracy in weather forecasting, especially with extreme conditions such as storms and blizzards (notwithstanding the infamous misreporting of the most destructive storm to hit Britain since 1703 by a hapless BBC weather presenter in 1987).[1]

Meteorology,[2] the study of weather and weather forecasting, is paradoxical in that the science is both ancient and modern, with a gap of over a thousand years between the two eras of its use.

The term 'meteor' was used for anything falling from or crossing the sky other than planets or stars, and is a transliteration from the Greek meaning 'something raised up', thus different from the modern astronomical term. It was the Greeks who started the arcane art of examining what weather actually was and even how to predict what it might do. At around 500 BC there is the first mention of measuring rainfall and 340 BC saw the publication of Aristotle's book Meteorologica which dominated western pre-scientific thought for 2,000 years until the Renaissance. In it, amongst other propositions, Aristotle stated that air has weight. Another Greek philosopher, Theophrastus, was the author of the first weather forecasting manual, which he published in 330 BC, with a follow-up book in 300 BC called *De Ventis* (meaning 'On Winds') which described a basic understanding of air pressure. In relation to Scotland, Aristotle and Greek navigator Pytheas sailed around Britain in 330 BC and reported the North Sea coasts of the island and Europe to be plagued with storms, which surely would have rattled both of them, used as they were to the Mediterranean Sea, which had no tides to speak of and a happy absence of storms apart from exceptional circumstances when local winds, mainly from the vagaries of the North African side to the sea and its particular heat gradient, blew up without warning.

Even the Bible had something to add – Matthew Chapter 16 verses 2 to 3 contain a piece of accurate weather information derived from scientific fact. Jesus says to the Pharisees: 'When it is evening, you say, "it will be fair weather for the sky is red" and in the morning, "It will be stormy today for the sky is red and threatening".' From this has derived the adage: 'Red sky at night, shepherd's delight – red sky in the morning, shepherd's warning.'

This conclusion is true, because the observations are based on the refraction of sunlight through water droplets at different angles at dawn and dusk, causing the red end of the light spectrum to become markedly more visible.

Then there was a big time-gap after the Greeks when science became a lost art in the West. As the Renaissance gathered momentum, René Descartes suggested in 1640 that water vapour was a distinct substance in the air, Torricelli invented the barometer in 1643 and Blaise Pascal, in company with Descartes, carried a barometer up the Puy-de-Dome, a large lava dome in the French Massif Central, and demonstrated by observations at three elevations that atmospheric pressure decreases with increasing altitude. Meanwhile, Robert Hooke invented the anemometer in 1667 – this was a device for judging wind speed.

In 1710 Daniel Gabriel Fahrenheit produced his temperature scale and also a mercury thermometer to record it. Swede Anders Celsius followed in 1742 with his Centigrade thermometer scale.

In the USA, Benjamin Franklin, over a period of years, experimented with lightning, nearly got himself fried a few times, and also deduced the north-easterly movement of a hurricane from eclipse observations. This was the very first time that the progressive movement of a storm system as a whole was ever recorded.

In 1770 Franklin and Timothy Folger actually charted the Gulf Stream, although they didn't discover it. That was done by Ponce de Leon as far back as 1513. However, the Franklin/Folger team went on to use the thermometer as a navigation instrument in 1775. By measuring water temperature they could figure out where they were in the Gulf Stream.

In 1802 an Englishman called Luke Howard sketched and classified cloud formations and just after this in 1805, Admiral Francis Beaufort developed his wind scale without any devices to actually estimate wind speed. By 1841 James Pollard Espy had written a treatise 'Philosophy of Storms' in which he analysed exactly what happens inside a storm front. 1843 saw the first working aneroid barometer (by Lucien Vidie) and in 1849 Joseph Henry of the Smithsonian Institute in the USA established a network of 150 volunteer weather observers, much like the amateur meteorologists spread across the British Isles by the time of the Tay Bridge Disaster. For all its pointlessness and military ineptitude, the Crimean War, fought against Russia by the British, French and Turks in 1854, did throw up by accident a very useful weather observation. In November of that year, a hefty storm sank much of a Franco-British fleet in the Black Sea.

French Emperor Napoleon III assigned astronomer Urbain Jean Joseph Le Verrier the task of forecasting weather. Le Verrier, using synoptic charts[3] (although they were yet to be called that), found that the Black Sea storm had been observed the previous day over the Mediterranean.

He realised that a large network of observation sites could help warn people of imminent storms. Ahead in all matters of weather was the USA. In 1869, with the Western Union telegraph system now nationwide, Cleveland Abbe, of the Cincinnati Chamber of Commerce, proposed daily weather forecasts for newspapers. Abbe's nickname was 'Old Probs' and Mark Twain wrote about him in his usual pithy way: 'Old Probabilities has a mighty reputation for accurate prophecy and thoroughly well deserves it. You take up the newspaper and observe how crisply and confidently he checks off what today's weather is going to be on the Pacific, down South, in the Middle States, in the Wisconsin region.'

In 1870, the USA established its own Weather Bureau and previously in 1855, a Department of Meteorology was set up by Admiral Fitzroy in Britain under the auspices of the Board of Trade. Unfortunately, this new organisation was still not yet sufficiently organised by 1879 to provide a storm warning for Scotland on the night of 28 December 1879.

The North Sea region of Britain, and especially the areas on the Scottish coast, have a long record of storminess, with innumerable shipping disasters and even large coastline alterations. Crossing the mainland of Scotland into the North Sea, these are the most frequented storm tracks in the Northern Hemisphere. The storminess of the North Sea area in particular is known for its succession of flood disasters on its coasts. The written history goes back to the Cymbrian floods of the coasts in the German Bight in 120 BC.

In 1413 a sandstorm completely obliterated the town of Forvie on the northeast coast of Scotland near Aberdeen. Scotland also suffered the Culbin Sands Disaster in 1694 when fifteen farms and a manor house were overwhelmed by a sandstorm that affected 7,000 acres. Clearly, the winds that blow around northeast Scotland are capable of terrible and life-threatening force. The sea area around Muckle Flugga, which is the most northerly of the Shetland Islands and consequently the most northerly part of Great Britain, has recorded at least 500 shipwrecks due to the storms which have raged around this spot. It is where two terrible wind forces meet, one from the east and one from the west. When clashed together and going in opposite directions, the masses of air, not surprisingly, were ever in argument, the collision repercussions of which would be felt hundreds of miles to the south in an area including Dundee and the Tay Bridge. Barra, the most westerly island in Scotland would always be the receiver of the first bad weather and winds as they proceeded towards the mainland. Unfortunately, with the technology of the time, there was no way to report the onset of the huge storm in 1879.

All this data seemed to be unknown to Thomas Bouch as he designed his Tay Bridge. But, in his favour, as we'll see later, he did try to ascertain wind forces in the Tay estuary but unfortunately took the advice of the sources least able to help him with any accuracy.

No one knew about high altitude jet streams until the period of the Second World War in 1941 when pilots, flying westwards from Britain to the USA, encountered headwinds of up to 300mph at around 30,000ft. This effect was also noticed by USAAF B-29 bomber pilots returning from raids on Japan. By 1945, the first quantitative map identifying jet streams was produced. There are billions and billions of tons of air around us on this planet: 25 million tons for every square mile pressing down upon us all. When millions of tons of air rush past at 50mph it is not surprising that trees snap and roofs get ripped away.

Over 100 years ago, Wyville Thompson wrote that:

we sometimes find when we get up in the morning, by a rise of an inch on the barometer, that nearly a half a ton of air has been quietly piled upon us during the night. We don't feel crushed under that extra half-ton of pressure because we're made mostly of incompressible fluids which push back, equalising pressures within and without. At sea level, we tend to think of air as weightless but once air gets in motion, it is obvious it has a great and destructive mass.[4]

A normal or typical weather front may contain 750 million tons of cold air pinned beneath a billion tons of warm air. These figures are almost impossible to comprehend or visualise because of their vastness. The jet streams fuel the velocity of the air masses below them and convection is what moves the air masses around.

Moist warm air from equatorial regions rises until it bumps up against an atmospheric boundary called the tropopause, separating the troposphere from the stratosphere and this is roughly 10 miles high at the equator and about 5 to 8 miles high in temperate zones. The tropopause is the point at which air ceases to cool with height and becomes almost completely dry. The troposphere immediately below it is the lowest of all the Earth's atmospheric layers and is the one in which nearly all 'weather' occurs. The troposphere contains 83 per cent of the atmospheric mass and all the water. The flattening out of the top of a storm cloud into the classic 'anvil' shape is the visible evidence of the tropopause.

The engine that drives all storms is the jet stream. This is a cascading river of cold air at 30,000 to 40,000ft, which hurtles around the earth, pushed by the rotation of the planet. All storms, cold fronts and troughs are pulled to the east by these high-altitude winds. The jet stream, however, is not a steady and regular force because it bounces off the topographical features below it. These irregularities can create huge eddies that come out of the Arctic regions as deep cold fronts. Called anticyclones, the cold air in them flows outwards and clockwise, the complete opposite of a 'low'. Across the leading edge of anticyclones, low-pressure waves can grow and sometimes burgeon into a big storm. Observers can notice this when the wind inches into the south-east, becoming a 'backing wind' going anticlockwise and remembered in the old seafaring rhyme:

> When the wind moves against the sun,
> Trust her not for back she'll run.

This sign is usually the harbinger of bad weather to come. It's the first touch of a low-pressure system going into a cyclonic spin. Admiral Dougall at his home and Commander Scott, Gunnery Instructor Edward Batsworth and Seaman Hugh McMahon aboard the *Mars* all picked up these clues during the afternoon of Sunday 28 December 1879, probably remembering another old sailor's rhyme:

> Mackerel skies and mares' tails,
> Make tall ships carry short sails.

The 'mackerel skies and mares' tails' are those very high teased-out clouds at around 30,000ft that look like fillets of fish with filmy lace-like scrolls.

The moist warm air, having cooled and reached the tropopause, now sinks as it travels away from the equator. When it hits bottom, the sinking air finds an area of low pressure to fill and starts to move back towards the equator. The convection process is stable at the equator but far more random and seasonal in temperate zones. The outcome is that there ensues a fight between systems of low- and high-pressure air. The low-pressure systems carry water into the sky and form the clouds which make rain. The differences in air pressures occur because the heat of the sun's rays is not evenly received across the earth. The air tries to equalise this and rushes from high-pressure areas to low-pressure zones. This, of course, is wind. The bigger the difference in air pressure, the faster and stronger is the wind. Wind speeds grow exponentially.

To explain by example, a wind blasting along at 200mph is not ten times stronger than a 20mph wind; it's a hundred times stronger and a hundred times more damaging.

Gales from the south or south-west were already being reported at most points on the Atlantic coasts of Britain and on the west coast of southern Norway as early as the morning of Saturday 27 December 1879. A severe southerly Force 9 gale was reported that evening at the Scilly Isles, on the west coast of Ireland, the Hebrides and Norway.

By the morning of Sunday 28 December, the storm seemed to ease over most of Britain, especially in Scotland and northern England, where the winds became quite light and generally westerly for a time. However, later in the day, the winds backed and freshened rapidly. After dark the wind was squally and at Aberdeen it was reported to have backed to the south, at Wick and Stornoway to the south-east, before working its way round to west or west-south-west again. In the Firth of Tay, the veer to west-south-west was probably very sudden and squalls were occurring about every ten minutes with the wind at west-south-west force ten. The storm was at its worst between approximately 7 p.m. and 8 p.m., after which conditions began to improve. At the height of the storm people in Scottish towns were loath to go out of doors because of falling trees and masonry, but the severe stages of the storm in Scotland seem mostly to have lasted no more than three to four hours.

Although this account is based on weather observation reports from fifty stations in Britain and neighbouring countries, analysis is still made difficult at this stage in the development of the meteorological observation network by the roughness of wind force estimates at many places – an understandable difficulty at a time when very few observers had experience of instrumental measurements of wind. The instruments themselves were inferior to those used in later times.[5]

In nineteenth-century Britain, weather observations were mostly the work of interested and amateur individuals such as Admiral Dougall at Scotscraig. He was one of many hundreds of retired sea captains and other interested parties such as scientists, doctors, clergymen and gentlemen of leisure who for reasons and enthusiasms of their own, continued to monitor the weather across Britain on a daily basis. The Royal Society was able to pick up a pretty good idea of British weather on any given day, through the encouragement of having these unpaid weather fans across the nation send daily telegrams with details of the wind speed, rainfall, temperature and barometric pressures at each of their locations. It was mooted in one scientific journal that weather forecasting in Britain has not improved by very much in the last 100 years regardless of the billions spent on computers and satellites. Interesting point! But this was a situation peculiar to the British Isles, as all these hundreds of weather fans lived not very far apart individually and their daily reports to the Royal Society enabled highly accurate synoptic charts of the weather across Britain to be drawn up almost every twenty-four hours.

This system of information-gathering would not be possible today as there are no longer the copious numbers of weather fanatics spread across the nation. One might find it surprising in these twenty-first-century days when accurate weather predictions are taken for granted, that no real pre-warning of the great storm on 28 December 1879 was able to be given.

There was no radio or television to disseminate such information in immediacy and newspapers could only carry weather information which was out of date by some hours when they arrived on domestic or other doorsteps. The only instant way was by telegraph. The first cable line was set up between Baltimore and Washington City in May 1844. By 1853, the telegraph mileage in the USA had expanded to 27,000. This greatly facilitated the sending of real-time weather data across the continent. In Britain, although the cable network stood at 4,000 miles, no one knew what to do with it meteorologically. Even though in 1870 in America Mr R. Robinson had introduced the idea of a four-cup anemometer as a way of noting wind speed, this idea was not immediately accepted worldwide. Regarding telegrams, in all fairness, the Royal Society in London with all its information from amateur weather stations, couldn't know where to send the data, and how would any such information help, in time, anyway?

By this time the 5.27 p.m. 'Edinburgh' had arrived at Springfield at 6.34 p.m., having run the 3¼ miles from Ladybank Junction in six minutes, mostly on level track, passing some thick woodland to either side of the line and rattling through no less than four level-crossings over minor roads.

The lone passenger waiting at Springfield station was James Smith, who lived in Dundee and had been visiting his grandfather, Robert Henderson. James worked in Dundee and had little money of his own. Later on, the Relief Fund Chairman sent a donation to the local minister to give to the old man. The minister replied:

I have your favour of this date with two pounds for the old man Henderson, Springfield and beg to thank the Committee on his behalf for the same. I do not think he will be a burden on the fund for long, as he is over eighty years old and very frail and infirm. He would come over to Dundee for the young man's funeral and has been very poorly ever since. His name is not on the list of paupers of the parish and from what I have formerly known of him I believe he would starve before applying for help.

With James Smith aboard, the train then pulled out on its way to Cupar, the next stop and 2¼ miles away down a gradient of 1 in 161 which shallowed out to 1 in 248 for the last fifth of a mile before reaching level track at Cupar station itself. The storm had so far surprisingly little effect on the train's progress across Fife but things would change as the entourage neared the Firth of Tay.

Notes

1 Refer to 8 (i) 'Michael Fish, BBC Weather Presenter' in the chapter note section.
2 The earliest use of the term 'meteorology' as a study is found in the writings of Englishman William Fulke in 1563.
3 Synoptic from the Greek word 'synoptikus' which means an overview of a situation, thus our common English word 'synopsis'. Robert Fitzroy was first person to use the word in relation to a weather map in 1863.
4 Refer to 8 (ii) 'Demonstrate Air Pressure' in the chapter note section.
5 Refer to 8 (iii) 'Historic Storms of the North Sea, British Isles and Northwest Europe, by Hubert Lamb' in the chapter note section.

9

Iron and Cupar

It was not what you'd call terribly bad iron.

Fergus Fergusson, Tay Bridge Wormit Iron Foundry

IRON:
Chemical symbol Fe
Atomic Number 26
Melting Point 1,537°C
Density 7.87g per cubic centimetre
The fourth most abundant element in the Earth's crust
The world's least expensive and most useful metal

Although gold, silver, copper and brass were in common use before iron, it was only when humans discovered how to extract iron from its ores that civilisations really began to develop. The earliest known use of the metal was around 2,000 BC in Egypt, Asia Minor, India and China but this was almost certainly from meteorites and hadn't been extracted from ores. The first processing didn't happen until circa 1,300 BC and was probably accidental as a result of a hot fire built on top of iron-bearing rocks or soil. The rocks would have been reduced to iron by being heated in the presence of charcoal and no air. Over the centuries, the extraction and purification of iron had reached a high degree of sophistication. Thomas Bouch's Tay Bridge was mostly made of it in two forms: cast iron and wrought iron. The difference in the properties and use of these iron types is fundamental as to why the structure collapsed.

Cast iron is an iron/carbon alloy that contains about 4 per cent carbon. It is poured while molten into moulds and takes up the shape of the mould, which is usually packed out with damp sand that follows the shape desired for the moulding.

This kind of iron is inherently very brittle and will break very easily with a tensile force; however, when is is used under compression – for instance in a bridge pier taking a vertical load – it is extremely strong. So Bouch's idea to build his piers from what amounts to a series of cast-iron pipes joined together was quite feasible. Indeed, he'd already built the magnificent Belah Viaduct in Northumberland according to that concept and it stood against all gales and storms for over 100 years without anything going wrong. In fact it took a lot of effort and explosives to demolish the viaduct when the line it carried was closed.

Many other viaducts across the British railway system, such as Meldon Viaduct in Devon, Crumlin Viaduct in South Wales and the Severn Railway Bridge,[1] all contemporaries of Bouch's structure, were also built as 'pipe' bridges and none of them failed either.

Wrought iron is almost pure iron with up to 0.4 per cent carbon and it has very different properties from the cast type. It's malleable, tough and can be forged – ideal material from which to make girder work.

And girder work is indeed what Bouch did with it for the Tay crossing: the huge lattice spans that carried the track and the trains from pier to pier were all made of wrought iron. Referring back to his 1860 structure, the Belah Viaduct (part of the South Durham & Lancashire Railway), stood 190ft high across the valley it spanned. Around 1,000ft long, the piers were made of six 12in diameter cast-iron columns, a system Bouch used on the Tay Bridge. In the Belah Viaduct, he didn't cast the lugs for the cross bracing integrally with the pipes. Instead, and unlike the Tay Bridge construction method, he used wrought-iron straps with properly drilled holes to accept the tie-bar bolts. The contractors for the work were Hopkins, Gilkes & Company who went on to build the Tay Bridge some sixteen years later. When Bouch presented his case for building the Tay Bridge to the Dundee businessmen, the Belah Viaduct was probably the project he was referring to when he said: 'we have far more stupendous bridges already built.'

For the Tay Bridge, so far, so good, one might think – a proven use of the right materials in a proven design.

The fatal design flaw in the construction of the Tay Bridge piers lay in the idea to cast the lugs as an integral part of each pipe section and in one mould. These lugs were the fastenings for the wrought-iron cross-bracings between the pipes, holding the whole thing together and absorbing all the stresses, vibrations and oscillations caused by wind or other dynamic forces. Cast iron is brittle, so when these lugs took the strain from the bracings, they would start to fatigue over time and cracks would form. The problem with any crack in metal is that it becomes a focus site for all the stresses and vibrations which, instead of passing on through the metal, stop there and cause the crack to propagate. Eventually the crack becomes complete across the piece and the metal snaps. Why Bouch decided on this system of casting the lugs is a mystery, as it flew in the face of the technical knowledge available at the time. (Despite some opinions to the contrary, the existence of metal fatigue was actually known. Bouch had not used cast lugs in his previous works such as the

Belah Viaduct. He employed iron straps around the pipe uprights and fixed the cross-bracings to them.)

To compound such failings further, the cast iron that was used, although up to specification when tested by Mr Kirkaldy in London for the Board of Inquiry, was less than satisfactory when certain practices at the Wormit Foundry were employed.

As mentioned before, instead of sub-contracting the pipe-casting work out to any of the reputable foundries operating in Dundee, the bridge contractors decided to build their own foundry on the riverbank at Wormit, almost certainly for reasons of economy.

According to the workmen, the foundry was a benighted place, filled with smoke and fumes from the castings, and suffered from very lax supervision. Certainly Thomas Bouch made extremely infrequent visits when he should have been there regularly as an overseer of his designs, their execution and as the final quality control referee.

But he was preoccupied with the plans for his *magnum opus* – even bigger and more wonderful than the Tay Bridge – the Forth crossing from Edinburgh to Fife.

The cast iron used was 'Cleveland Number Three Pig' and came in the form of ingots from the Cleveland Foundry in Middlesbrough, north-east England.[2]

The iron itself was called 'pig iron' because the molten iron was originally run off from the blast furnace into multiple-branched channels formed in a bed of sand. This was thought reminiscent of a family of piglets feeding from a sow, thus the epithet.

Some of the Wormit moulders called it the worst iron they had ever seen. There were about a dozen or so moulders employed at the built-from-scratch Wormit Foundry and they all said that Cleveland iron was slow and sluggish when poured into the moulds, glowing a dull red and running thickly, instead of the bright crimson and fluidity characteristic of the better grades of Scotch (sic) iron.

So there was constantly the risk of a 'cold shut' – this occurring when the poured iron partly solidifies before getting right around inside the mould and causing an inherent weakness in the casting. The foundry foreman, Fergus Fergusson, described it later as 'not terribly bad iron' – the best he could say about it.

Indeed, Cleveland iron was very poor quality when compared to Scotch iron. The Dundee foundries hardly ever used Cleveland No 3 Pig. To prepare for casting, the moulders 'puddled' or skimmed the molten metal to bring any impurities to the top. Moulder Andrew Forgon, at the Wormit Foundry, said: 'the more you puddled it the worse it was, the rubbish was all through the iron.' Alexander Hampton, another moulder, said: 'You might have puddled the ladle toom!' (Toom meant empty.)

The sand used in the moulds was dampened with salty Tay water instead of fresh water, which caused 'scabbing' (rough irregular projections) on the cast surfaces and other irregularities contributing to uneven facing surfaces when the pipes came to be bolted together. Sloppy placing of the inside patterns or core slippage caused many of the pipes to have uneven metal thicknesses, so that they were asymmetrical.

Some of the pipes came out cracked from the moulds and many of the lugs didn't cast properly. Their bolt-holes were often conical; this was because they were cast and not drilled later, inadvertently causing stress points called 'notches' which would initiate metal fatigue when the bolts were inserted. Such lugs were already doomed to failure before they were even built into the bridge. When any lugs broke off before dressing and painting, the columns were sent back to have the lugs 'burned' back on again. This was done by placing a special localised mould over the column and pouring in molten metal over the fractured lug, thus rejoining it to the column. All the moulders knew very well that a 'burned-on' lug was never as strong as one properly cast with the column.

For cracks and blowholes, the unsupervised workers used a substance called Beaumont's Egg, a corruption of the French words 'beau montage' translating as 'beautiful face', for filler. Made from a mixture of rosin, beeswax, lamp-black and iron filings, it was heated and pasted into cracks in the iron like some nightmarish polyfilla. When rubbed down and painted, the cracks became invisible, so out went the pipes, passed as fit for use to be built into the bridge. The use of Beaumont's Egg was fine for minor pits and blowholes, but at Wormit foundry it was used to cover up major faults. Wilson Winter, the foundry boy, dispensed it to the moulders from a stock in Fergus Ferguson's office with his full approval.

The iron columns were never properly inspected before going out to the bridge, apart from giving them an occasional tap with a hammer, which of course gave no indication whether one side of a column was thicker than the other.

The iron for the bolts that would hold this suspect structure together also came from the Cleveland Iron Works. There is an element of farce in what went wrong here which would be laughable had it not contributed to so many deaths. When ordering, the contractors asked for 'Best Iron' and indeed that is what they got, but the Cleveland Iron Works neglected to mention that they had three grades of iron available: 'Best', 'Best Best' and 'Best Best Best'.

So most of the rivets and bolts for the longest bridge in the world were made from the cheapest grade of iron available. However, by December 1879, the thing had stood for nearly two years and in the minds of the engineering world, railwaymen and most of the passengers who used the bridge daily, it would stand forever.

Blissful in their collective ignorance of such matters, the passengers and staff on board the 'Edinburgh' coasted down the 1 in 161 falling gradient from Springfield towards Cupar, the County Town of Fife. Lying in the rich agricultural lands of the Howe of Fife, it had been the seat of justice and government since 1213. Here it was, if Shakespeare is to be believed, that Macduff, Thane of Fife, had his castle on a rise between the River Eden and the Lady Burn and where were slain, 'all my pretty chickens and their dam at one fell swoop'.

By 1879, the town was thriving, with a spinning mill, a corn and flourmill, two tanneries, three breweries, a foundry and a power mill. The appetite for coal to fuel these industries was borne out by five coal merchants having offices in the station goods yard.

Driver Mitchell kept one hand resting lightly on the Westinghouse handle, ready to brake if the Cupar distant signal was 'on', while Fireman Marshall, with no firing to do when running downhill, leaned out of the cab and caught an early sight of the white light.

You might think that white lights indicating 'all clear' would be confusing, given the lights from house windows and street lighting near the railway. In fact the countryside at night was very much darker in Victorian times than today, much more so than we can imagine these days now that we are accustomed to traffic lights, neon advertising boards plus electric house and street lighting all alongside the line. Modern car drivers may not realise that on the Victorian railway there were no street lights and no bright headlights on the engine. At night the view ahead was pitch black and a driver depended entirely on his knowledge of the road to keep track of his progress.

Marshall called out, 'Alright, it's off', so Mitchell let the train run on, past the meandering River Eden in its marshy water meadows to the right. At night, drivers knew their whereabouts by sound alone, so in the darkness Mitchell waited to hear the wheel-roar as the train crossed the river by a low overbridge. This was his cue to tug the whistle chain for a warning 'toot toot', apply enough Westinghouse brake to slow the train under the Leven Road Bridge, (which was a three-arch stone structure with two small castellated turrets at each end) and come to a stand at Cupar station, which had been opened in 1847 by the Edinburgh & Northern Railway and had a fine set of buildings by Edinburgh architect David Bell. Apart from the double-track main lines, the layout boasted an additional middle road running the length of the station.

The platforms being on level track, Mitchell didn't bother to screw on the tender handbrake. A touch of the steam brake would hold her against any impetus from the wind.

Several little knots of windblown people, plus a few standing alone, were waiting on the platform having been enticed out of the steamy waiting room by the engine's whistle blowing. Spreading only a dim guttering light, the cast-iron gas lamp standards still bore the engraved legend 'EDINr PERTH & DUNDEE RAILy' (sic) beneath their glass lamp-houses, a reminder of the previous owners who had renamed the Edinburgh and Northern Railway as the EP&DR before finally being taken over by the North British Railway in 1862.

Robert Watson stood with his two sons. David was 9 years old and Robert was three years younger. It had been a long day and Dad Watson was no doubt glad to be going home to 12 Lawrence Street, Dundee, where Mrs Watson expected their return at around 7.30 p.m. She'd not been keen on this expedition to visit friends in Fife but the boys had been excited at the idea of crossing the Tay twice in one day. Besides, Mr Watson had promised and didn't wish to disappoint his lads.

All day they'd been full of questions, especially relating to the iron bridge on the Tay. Fortunately Robert Senior was a patient man and well qualified to discuss such matters, as he was an experienced iron moulder and would never have countenanced the use of Cleveland Number Three Pig at his foundry.

Aged 34 years, he'd spent his life dealing with casting and foundry work and had been bombarded with queries from his sons about the great bridge. He'd have told his boys much of what has been discussed at the start of this chapter, although he wouldn't have known of the bridge design faults.

One of the lone passengers was 21-year-old Joseph Anderson, a compositor with the *Dundee Courier and Argus* newspaper, who shared accommodation at 13 South Ellen Street, Dundee with his brother Henry. Joseph had left Dundee to visit friends in Cupar on the preceding day, Saturday 27 December. Another man on his own was Thomas Davidson (28) who was a farm servant wearing a dark tweed coat with a velvet collar. William Veitch (18) was a solo traveller too. He was a Dundee cabinet-maker living at 30 Church Street with Nathaniel his father and sisters Jessie (16) and Maggie (15). He'd left Dundee the previous afternoon to visit his grandfather in Cupar. Against the wind and cold he wore a tweed topcoat, a white muffler and a black felt hat.

The two Bains were brother and sister and had been visiting their uncle Andrew Scott who resided in Cupar. They lived with their father at the Mains of Balgay, a farm to the north of Dundee. There was another brother Henry who had his own farm at The Mains Of Camperdown and it was he who identified and collected personal effects found after the disaster.

Archie Bain was 26 and, as well as being a farmer, he was also the local agent for manure sales. A proud man in a modest way, he was ruddy of face and in good health from his open-air life. Gold sovereigns rattled in the pockets of his Ulster coat along with two hankies, a screw of tobacco and a knife. He wore a silver watch with a gold albert chain. Worsted gloves and a scarf kept the cold out of his hands and neck.

His sister Jessie (22) was by all accounts a very attractive young lady with short brown hair. She was the toast of the young men of Balgay and was apparently pleased with this effusion of admiration but she was 'taken', being paired with a young man whom she wished to marry. In her 'muff' (a tube of fur for keeping the hands warm) was a letter from her boyfriend, along with another she'd written to her father but had forgotten to post. It read: 'My Dear Father, I intend coming home on Sunday night with the 7.30 train. Hoping you are all well and merry. Love to all.'

That night Jessie wore a sealskin hat with a tortoiseshell comb in her hair and carried a silk umbrella. She had 5s 6d in her pocket.

A final group of travellers on the platform comprised three ladies, Eliza Smart, Mrs Easton and Ann Cruickshanks. Ann Cruickshanks, 55 years old, was particularly pleased to see No 224's headlamps coming out of the night for two good reasons.

Firstly, she felt the cold badly and would be happy to be aboard the train and out of the wind. She was wearing thick clothes against the cold with a heavy scarf, black petticoat, skirt and coat and bonnet. Dress-wise, she looked a lot like Queen Victoria, as did many women her age who emulated their sovereign's appearance. Although her home address was Moray Place in Edinburgh, this night she was journeying to allegedly visit a very sick cousin at Broughty Ferry. She was in a petulant and grumpy mood, apparently.

Ann Cruickshanks's second reason to be glad to leave was that she may have been a jewel thief – and in mid-getaway! Now I must stress that the following story concerning Ann is apocryphal but has been heard from several disconnected sources. However, after my correspondence with them, the descendants of the Baxter family most strongly deny that the episode ever happened. Nevertheless it is presented here with proviso of that old Scottish court verdict 'unproven' and furthermore the tale gives some insights into the working lives and conditions of domestic servants in the mid-Victorian era and is valuable for that alone. Despite her dowdy spinster's clothes and unlikely appearance as a criminal, Ann may have just robbed Lady Baxter of her entire collection of valuables.[3]

Kilmaron Castle, now a ruin, was built in 1820 for Sir David Baxter, a respected Dundee 'jute baron' and benefactor. He'd been responsible for the creation of Baxter Park in Dundee as a gift to the people in 1863. Sir David had died in 1872 but his widow, Lady Baxter, continued to maintain the household.[4]

Ann Cruickshanks and Eliza Smart were housemaids to Her Ladyship. Staying over for the Christmas period was the widow Mrs Mary Easton, aged 53 years, and Lady Baxter's niece. She was a short dark-complexioned lady with a turned-up nose and large eyes.

With the festive season done, Mrs Easton planned to return home that Sunday. She was going to 53 Galt Villas, Old Meldrum, north-west of Aberdeen where she had lived with her husband, the Reverend James Easton, so Lady Baxter arranged for a coach and pair to take her to Cupar station. Although actually hailing from Edinburgh, Ann would accompany the widow Easton to Dundee and continue on to Broughty Ferry.

On a Sunday, the only trains from Cupar to Dundee were the two 'Edinburghs'. Ann and Mrs Easton had intended to catch the first one, the 7.32 a.m. from Burntisland, 8.46 a.m. departing Cupar, but Lady Baxter's coachman overslept that morning and they missed it. Which meant that they had to kick their heels all day until they could catch the 'Edinburgh' at 6.41 p.m. to Dundee but Eliza Smart had always intended to catch this later train when she finished work that afternoon. She was going home for a few days' holiday with her parents at 22 Union Mount, Dundee. She was a very tall girl, 22 years old and with a head of dark hair. She was wearing a black corded dress, a black pilot jacket, a black feathered bonnet and white stockings.

Eliza was very much in love with George Johnston, whom we've already met in chapter one, since he travelled to St Fort to see his dad on the outward leg of the fated train. George would be returning to Dundee after the visit and he and Eliza had laid plans to meet on the train when it called at St Fort station. The pair was eagerly looking forward to an unchaperoned trip across the Tay, cosied up in their third-class compartment.

But now they'd be under the disapproving stares of the doughty Miss Cruickshanks and Mrs Easton and would have to stay their passions until reaching Dundee. Eliza giggled to herself at the thought of seeing George's face fall when he opened the carriage door to find the two older women sitting there. But at least they could hold hands beneath his coat.

Ann Cruickshanks had possibly done a very rash thing that day, considering she was about to throw away years of loyal service and reputation, let alone be sent to jail if discovered.

If she did carry out this heist, Ann would have put all the rings, tiaras, earrings and necklaces into her reticule, which was a kind of large purse or bag with drawstrings often carried by Victorian ladies, and one was certainly used by Ann herself. While her body was recovered from the Tay after the disaster, her reticule was never found. If all of the above is true, the Baxter family jewels may still be deep in the mud and silt of the estuary to this day.

Ann's was the very first body the river gave up after the disaster and received what was virtually a state funeral in Dundee as most of the city turned out to witness it.

Through the rising gale, the coachman drove Eliza, Mrs Easton and Ann to the station. Past Easter Balgarvie Farm they went, along the Newburgh Road, turned right into Cupar's main street and down the short lane to the North British Railway station, a distance of only 2 miles, but the wind handled the vehicle quite badly, pushing and heaving the coach body down on its springs.

In the short time at the platform, Fireman Marshall made five quick shovel-shots of coal onto the fire. One he threw right down to the front of the grate, one to each side, one in the middle and a last just under the fire doors at the back. This thickened up the fire bed all over. The next couple of miles were slightly uphill towards the next stop, Dairsie. Although the gradient was only 1 in 400, Marshall didn't want his fire lifted by the exhaust pull and causing another hole if Mitchell opened her out a bit.

The carriage doors slammed as the Watsons, the Kilmaron party and Joseph Anderson climbed into different third-class compartments while the Bains boarded the second-class carriage next to the luggage van where Guard McBeath waved his green flag, blew a peremptory whistle blast and jumped back into the van.

The Tay Bridge was now 12 miles in front of No 224's buffers as Mitchell opened the regulator and started away on time, at 6.41 p.m.

It was a 3-mile run to Dairsie and the timetable allowed eight minutes for the journey. Chugging briefly past the house backs and rear gardens of Cupar the train dived beneath the Pitscottie Road Bridge and re-crossed the River Eden for the last time. About half a mile from Cupar the train passed under Tailabout Bridge, a low single-span stone-built occupation arch.[5]

A couple of miles almost due east, as the line passed Prestonhall and Newmill, lay the valley of the Ceres Burn. One steep-sided double-bend was called Dura Den, where twenty years before there had been an astonishing fossil find. This was of great interest to historian and schoolteacher David Neish. He pointed out of his compartment window into the darkness and began explaining to his daughter Bella how eleven species and more than 1,000 fish had been unearthed in 1858.

Three-foot-long armour-plated fish, with needle-sharp teeth, called *Holoptychius Andersoni* were especially found in abundance. At 5 years old, Bella was somewhat alarmed at this, perhaps imagining that these toothy monsters would suddenly appear out of the night!

Now the train was running on dead level track and curving gently to the left. David Neish heard air rushing through the Westinghouse pipes beneath his feet. Mitchell on the footplate had begun to brake for Dairsie station and Neish, glad of the chance to get his daughter's mind off scary fish, was able to speculate to Bella: 'who do you think will get on the train here?' and proceeded to explain how Dairsie was called Dervesyn back in 1234, a name which meant 'scribe's flourish'. With a 5-year-old daughter, he certainly didn't want to discuss the alternative name source, which were the Gaelic words 'dair bheus' meaning 'oak of fornication'!

There was but a lone passenger on the wind-blown Dairsie platform. Grocer William H. Jack was on his way home to 57 Mains Road, Dundee, after a day comforting his mother Jane on the loss of his sister. William still wore the crêpe black armband in memory of that passing and of his father's just a short time previously. How death did touch the Jack family that December! Driver Mitchell allowed No 224 to coast along the level track leading into the station, with just a whiff of Westinghouse brake needed to bring the train to a halt. Consulting his silver watch, William Jack noted that the train was on time at 6.49 p.m.

Just under 9 miles now to reach the Tay Bridge.

Notes

1 The railway bridge over the River Severn between Sharpness and Lydney had just been opened on 17 October 1879, very much resembling the high girders section of the Tay Bridge. It was 1,387yd long with twenty-two spans 70ft above high water and the piers were of the same cast-iron pipe construction. The bridge lasted until 1960 when in thick fog on 25 October, one of the piers in midstream was struck by two cargo barges which had failed to see the bridge navigation lights. Two spans fell down onto the barges and five lives were lost. It is noteworthy that the bridge's collapse was not because of any design deficiencies. The cast iron had been used properly.

2   In 1850, vast iron ore deposits had been discovered in the Cleveland Hills nearby and, soon after, Middlesbrough became the iron capital of Britain and provided a third of the nation's output. Huge dock complexes were constructed to ship off the thousands of tons of iron produced annually.
3   Refer to 9 (i) 'Life as a Housemaid' in the chapter note section.
4   Built of red brick and with lancet windows and mock crenellations, the castle stood about 2 miles north of Cupar on Kilmaron Hill. The name was derived from 'Church of My Own Ron', Ron being St Ronan, Abbot of Kingarth in the early eighth century.
5   The name is because from a plan view, the approach roads and the bridge form a capital 'S'. The bridge was the site of a sad accident in 1923 when 50-year-old Driver John Thompson was in charge of the 9.05 p.m. goods train from Leith Walk, Edinburgh to Aberdeen. The train passed Cupar Station at 12.30 a.m. Soon the fireman noticed Thompson was missing but he drove on to Leuchars Junction where he reported the matter. A search party went along the line and found Thompson's badly mutilated body about 60yd east of Tailabout Bridge. The police theory was that 'Thompson was standing on his tender oiling the engine and coming into violent collision with Tailabout Bridge was thrown onto the line'.

10

THE LAST ONE ACROSS

I'd not go across the bridge again tonight for 500 pounds.

Guard Robert Shand, on arrival at Dundee with the last
train ever to cross the Tay Bridge

By about five o'clock in the afternoon the strong westerly wind was ever increasing along the Firth of Tay as Admiral Dougall returned home from afternoon church. His house was at Scotscraig on the south bank down near the estuary mouth and about 70ft above sea level. The panorama of views included the Tay itself, the bridge and the German Ocean, now disappearing in the gloaming and spindrift. Noticing a sharp fall in his barometer he remarked to his gardener, 'There's mischief coming!' In truth he was quite worried about his favourite old walnut tree and its ability to stand up against a serious blow of wind. Experience from long service at sea around the world told him that weather-wise, things were going to get considerably worse.

At the same time, aboard the training ship *Mars*, gunnery instructor Edward Batsworth was noting in his log a gale of Force 10 on the Beaufort Scale[1] and Charles Clark, amateur weatherman at Magdalen Green near the north end of the bridge, noticed his barometer showing the lowest pressure all day.

The wind was now coming out of the west-south-west and by 5.30 p.m. it was a full-on gale punctuated by nasty vicious squalls. The city of Dundee began to take a hammering. Chimney cairns, loose window shutters, slates, guttering, garden-shed doors – all were being ripped away as easily as blowing confetti. Pedestrians in the streets were having difficulty in standing upright let alone walking. Around them fell roof-tiles and broken brickwork from chimney cairns, bursting like hand grenades. A row of beach huts on the esplanade was flung against the sea wall, splitting and splintering into shards of wood. The signboard for LAMB'S HOTEL was bowled along the street as if it was made of cardboard. The Dundee streets became a war zone, driving most people indoors to wait things out.

At roughly the same time as the 'Edinburgh' was arriving at Dysart some 30 miles to the south, another train was leaving Tayport for the 8-mile run to Dundee. This was the 5.50 p.m. local service to Dundee, known on Sundays as 'the church train'.

Calling at East Newport and West Newport, the 'church train' was due at Tay Bridge South Signal Box at about 6.05 p.m. Crossing the bridge, it was timetabled to roll into Dundee at 6.10 p.m.

Waiting there in a bay platform while the 'Edinburgh' came in from the south, the train would then make a return trip to Tayport at 8 p.m. Finally, it would return to Dundee at 8.30 p.m., arriving at 8.50 p.m., as it had done every Sunday for the last seven months.

These were the last scheduled train movements across the bridge for a Sunday night. Apart from the weather, everything was so normal and ordinary.

The 5.50 p.m. train duly chugged off from Tayport on time, the two guard's vans and five carriages being hauled by one of the Drummond 0-4-2 tank engines. The driver was Alexander Kennedy and the guard Robert Shand. Like Davy McBeath in the 5.27 p.m. Edinburgh train, Shand had the company of some off-duty railway workers in his van. These were 21-year-old John Black, a parcels office clerk and John Buick, engine fitter. Both were employees of 'the firm across the road' as the rival Caledonian Railway was nicknamed, and both had only just caught the train as it was leaving Tayport. Black was simply late while Buick had gone in an unsuccessful search for a toilet. However, both managed to jump into the guard's van as the train started away.

The North British Railway branch from Newport and Tayport, opened on 13 May 1879, completed a loop from Leuchars Junction. It met the main line from Burntisland actually on the Tay Bridge itself. This had involved building a short new curved section of the bridge to form a 'Y'-shaped junction. A new Tay Bridge South Signal Box was built on the bridge, sitting high and exposed above the river foreshore between the legs of the 'Y'. Which meant that the original South Box, to the left of the line from St Fort, was now redundant as a signal cabin and in use now as a Permanent Way Department store.

The new box was of wooden construction, using timber framing, vertical planking and a slate roof. A set of steps ran down to track level where the signalman could pass and collect the single-line tokens or staffs. The new line to Tayport was single track just like the bridge and therefore had a single-line token of its own.

Thus the signalman was responsible for giving and collecting tokens in both directions for traffic using the new route.

Inside the wind-shuddered cabin, awaiting the arrival of the 5.50 p.m. train, was signalman Thomas Barclay whom I have introduced already. He was 29 years old and had been a signalman on the North British Railway for three years and eight months. He'd been in charge of the South Signal Boxes since the day the bridge opened and had seen it in all its moods and weathers.

He had proudly passed the Opening Day Special Train in May 1878 and stood to attention as the Royal Train carried Queen Victoria past his box in June 1879, the flat thuds of a twenty-one gun salute from *Mars* carrying across the still waters on a glorious summer evening. Since then there'd been no further excitement, just the day-to-day running of a railway. Barclay was a contented man, with a secure job and a cottage to live in just a few minutes' walk from his box. He earned between 18*s* and 25*s* per week for working seven twelve-hour shifts.

Because Driver Kennedy was bringing the 5.50 p.m. Tayport train from the end of one single-line section to the start of another, Barclay had two tokens to deal with when it rolled up to his signal box.

Closing the regulator and gently applying the steam brake on his engine, Kennedy slowed the train down almost to a stop. At around 3mph he passed the token for the Newport section he'd just traversed down to Barclay, who was trying to huddle out of the wind at the bottom of his signal box stairs. Barclay showed Kennedy the Tay Bridge token with a written ticket of authority pushed into a cleft at one end. Before the gale could snatch it away, Kennedy grabbed the ticket from the staff.

These goings-on were because two trains were timetabled to head northwards in succession – the 5.50 from Tayport and, in another hour or so, the 'Edinburgh'. Obviously, if Kennedy took the actual train staff there was no southbound service to bring it back to Barclay.

So a ticket was issued instead. Called the Train Staff Ticket, it was made of thick blue paper and had the following information printed on it:

NORTH BRITISH RAILWAY TRAIN STAFF TICKET TAY BRIDGE

TRAIN No: *(then a space for that information to be filled in by hand)*

DOWN *(meaning issued for a 'down' train. It was standard practice on British railways to refer to trains as either 'up' or 'down'. UP meant travelling towards London and DOWN meant travelling in a direction away from London. For example, all tickets issued by Henry Somerville at the North Box would say UP, as his trains were going south.)*

TO THE ENGINE DRIVER: "You are authorised, after seeing the Train Staff for the section, to proceed from TAY BRIDGE SOUTH Signal Box to TAY BRIDGE NORTH Signal Box, and the Train Staff will follow."

Signature of Person In Charge..

Date:.................................

(These spaces to be filled in by Barclay)

Staff or Token exchanges were normally carried out by the fireman but as the South Box was passed to the left side of the train and his driving position was on the left side of the engine, it was convenient for Kennedy to take care of it.

Being a signalman carried huge responsibilities toward railway safety. It was quite a physical job as well. The semaphore signal levers could be hard to pull depending on how far away the signal was from the box. Some might be up to 1,500yd away but the toughest pulls for Barclay were the pair of 'Up' distants, sited about seventeen spans out from the south bank on the bridge itself.

The wires had to pass round many pulleys and up signal posts, which made for a lot of friction and thus a heavy pull, but it was not just a matter of brute strength. Burly men have been known to struggle a lever about halfway across and then tumble in a heap on the floor as the fat compression springs overcame their efforts.

There was a knack to it. The feet had to be correctly placed with the right foot slightly to one side and the left on the cast-iron treads of the lever quadrant, spine directly in line with the lever. If the pull was a heavy one, the signalman swung backwards from the hips, making use of all available acceleration provided by the spring. Any slack in the wire was used to gather momentum to overcome the increasing friction of the wire. The signalman finished the pull momentarily off balance. This was only for a fraction of a second but could be dangerous for him if he slipped.

However, the levers were easy to replace to 'danger' owing to the tension in the wire. They would often fly back across the lever frame by themselves when the holding latch was released.

The levers were always pulled with a duster in the hands. This prevented sweat from rusting the carefully polished steel handles and made pulling more comfortable because the handle had to move in the hands, which it couldn't do when grasped with bare fists.

The duster was the signalman's unofficial badge of office. In the very rare cases of a signalman having to be removed from a box, for example after an accident when he might be too shocked to continue on duty, his relief might say, 'You'd better give me the duster.' The signals themselves were manufactured for the North British Railway by Stevens & Sons. This company had two factories, one in Southwark, London and another in Glasgow. The firm had been turning out quality signalling gear for railway companies for many years and the North British was a big customer. The signals were all 'lower quadrant', which means that when pulled off to the 'clear' position, the 4ft wooden arms would point downwards from their lattice-metal posts at an angle of about 45 degrees. At night, the distinctive teardrop-shaped spectacle plates were lit by oil-lamps. Originally fuelled by whale oil, these lamps were soon burning a new oil called 'paraffin', which we now know as kerosene and use to power jet aircraft engines. To allow filling and wick trimming, the posts had a pulley mechanism so that the lamps could be winched up and down. This obviated the need for a ladder and the risks of lamp men being knocked off the top of a tall post if a wind was blowing.

By 1879, the design had improved so that a lamp would burn for eight days without attention and yet only use about 8 gallons of paraffin a year. Stevens & Sons also built the lever-frames. The design at both North and South boxes was called 'Glasgow Pattern', in which the levers stood vertically when in normal position so that gravity could assist when they were pulled off. In a Glasgow Pattern frame, the levers were spaced 5¼in apart. A colour code was employed for easy identification of what levers did what. They were painted red for stop signals and distant signals, black for points, blue for point locks and white for 'spare' or out-of-use. The lever number and exact function was engraved on a cast-iron plate fixed to each lever.

Signalmen communicated with each other with speaking instruments, which were fine for general exchanges of information. However, for passing trains between sections from box to box, safety was absolutely paramount and there had to be no chance of any misunderstanding. Consequently, 'block bells' were used. Henry Somerville at the North Box had a bell that could be rung by Barclay at the South Box – and vice versa. Using a bell-code system, they could send each other basic information about the train and its whereabouts.

When for example Barclay wished to send a train across the bridge, he'd send one 'ting' to Somerville as a CALL ATTENTION signal. Somerville would respond by sending one 'ting' back again, meaning he'd acknowledged.

Then Barclay would send a number of beats that described the train he wished to pass over the bridge. In the case of Kennedy's 5.50 train, he'd send four beats, with a gap before the final 'ting' – 3-1. This meant ORDINARY PASSENGER TRAIN (not an express). Somerville would acknowledge by sending 3-1 back again. Just before the train actually set out across the bridge, Barclay would send 'ting-ting' or two beats, denoting TRAIN ENTERING SECTION.

When the train had reached him, Somerville would tell Barclay by sending 2-1 which meant TRAIN OUT OF SECTION. There were many other codes for varying train types and other conditions. You can see that this was a clear and unambiguous means of communicating vital traffic information and although mostly phased out at the end of the twentieth century, remains in use up until the present time on certain lines.

So, with the brakes off, regulator open and a last wave from Kennedy to Barclay, the 5.50 train began the 2-mile crossing of the Tay a few minutes after 6 p.m.

Barclay sent the signal 'TRAIN ENTERING SECTION' to the North Box. Moments later, he heard Somerville's acknowledgement 'ting-ting' on his own block bell. He watched the three red tail-lamps on the back of Shand's guard's van recede into the squalls and dark, then turned to bank up the fire in his stove. Barclay had nothing more to do now until the 'Edinburgh' came up in about an hour, so when he'd received 'TRAIN OUT OF SECTION' from the North Box, he intended to go off to his nearby cottage for a break, returning just before seven o'clock to be ready for the 'Edinburgh'. But before that could happen, the 'church train' had to cross the bridge.

Moving out over the first girders, the train lost the meagre shelter of the south bank and started to take the full force of the gale. It blasted side-on to the engine and carriages, a continuing and steady onslaught with frequent stabbing gusts which could be felt by the three men in the guard's van. A squashy mixture of sleet and rain spattered the left-hand side windows like shotgun pellets. The carriage springs groaned as the wind force pressed the vehicles over and down to the right.

The moon, often obscured by scudding clouds, fitfully lit the seething waters of the estuary far below. The noise of the gale was awesome, deafening and primeval in its roar.

The train plugged doggedly onwards until it was halfway between the South Box and the start of the 'high girders' section. Then John Buick suddenly exclaimed: 'Shand, there is something wrong with the train. Look out!'

He'd been watching forward through a ducket window[2] and seen sheaves of sparks jetting out between the wheels of a carriage further up the train.

Shand's first thought was that a carriage axle had broken. He immediately applied his brake, which was a screw-down handbrake acting only on the guard's van wheels. This train was not fitted with the Westinghouse continuous brake so the only stopping powers available were the engine steam brake and the guard's van handbrake. So Shand needed to attract Driver Kennedy's attention at once. He shone a red hand lamp forward from his van but chose, unfortunately, the wrong side of the train.

As we've seen, Kennedy was driving and keeping a lookout from the left side (the west side) and Shand tried to attract his attention from the east side. The fireman, standing on that side of the engine, may possibly have been in a position to see the alarm signal – but didn't.

By now, the handbrake application was pulling the train almost to a stop. The wheels began to lock as the van was dragged, skidding and screaming along the rails, with steel-on-steel shrieks audible even over the bellowing gale.

Shand unwound the brake until the wheels began to turn once more. He'd realised what was really happening. 'It's not an axle,' he shouted over the wind roar. 'It's the wind pressing the wheel-flanges against the checkrail.' And he let off the brake some more. The train recovered and began to pick up speed again.

Up in front, Kennedy had in fact felt the increased drag from Shand's brake application but put it down to the wind. Trains were always tighter to pull over the bridge when it was windy and this had happened to him before. As he said later: 'I just let her out a bit more', meaning, he opened the regulator further and pushed the reversing lever up another notch, putting on more steam to keep the train speed up.

But now even more sparks were issuing from the wheels on even more carriages, so that the train seemed like a moving fireworks display. The force of the wind was indeed pushing the carriage-wheels over and against the rails – either the checkrail on the left or the running rail to the right. This was like a series of grinding wheels sharpening knives, causing sheaves of sparks to flow aplenty.

Then the train started to pass through the high girders, nodding into that slight kink in the rails and helping to kick off the side-to-side oscillations of the piers. The badly fitting sections of each column ground together, torturing their joining bolts and straining the lugs.

A prancing up-and-down motion of the carriages was becoming more obvious, adding to the tilting-over felt by the men in the guard's van. Invisible below the bridge deck, many of the bolts and lugs holding the column-flanges had had enough. They were starting to give up under the continuous strain of the wind, which was adding its energy to the oscillation and consequent resonance of the bridge.

With the insistent heaving of the gale and the resultant resonance, a lot of the cast-iron lugs had reached their fatigue limit and were cracking apart across their conical bolt-holes, letting the wrought-iron cross-bracings swing wildly from one end or just fall into the river. How many were affected will never be known but obviously not quite enough of them failed to precipitate a collapse.

The bridge was getting into a parlous state, its structural integrity fatally weakening. It wouldn't take much more in this wind to push the exhausted, trembling structure past its limits of endurance.

In the only first-class carriage that was approximately in the middle of the train sat the Reverend George Grubb, an Episcopalian clergyman at St Paul's, Dundee. He was becoming a little annoyed with a passenger who was insisting on demonstrating a pet theory.

Opening a window on the west side of the carriage, Grubb's fellow traveller let the wind pound into the compartment, causing a curious percussive effect on their ears. It was this phenomenon he wished to demonstrate. Grubb described it as 'similar to shocks of electricity felt in the ears, first one ear and then the other'.

The reverend soon tired of that and demanded that the window should be shut. The trip across the river was unsettling enough without the extra mayhem of a gale rampaging around him as he sat.

Then the train was through the 1,000-odd yards of high girders and running down the falling gradient over the last few hundred yards of straight bridge, the sparks spewing from beneath the carriages as thickly as ever. Shand wound on his handbrake once more, to help with the slowing down for the North Box. The train coasted around the sharp right-hand curve, through the bowstring girder spans and rolled to the North Box, where Henry Somerville was waiting to collect the train staff ticket.

The train having changed direction through 90 degrees, the side wind became a tail wind and all the plumes of sparks died away as the wheels were no longer being pressed against the rails.

At 2 or 3mph, Kennedy managed to pass in the ticket to Henry Somerville at the North Box, although the scrap of blue paper was nearly whipped away into the night. Somerville scuttled up his stairs to the warmth of his box and sent the signal TRAIN OUT OF SECTION (2-1 on the block bell) to let Barclay know that the train was over safely. And the train was safe now. The crew and passengers wouldn't know what a narrow escape they'd had for some time afterwards, until the Board of Inquiry published its findings. Privately, Shand, Black and Buick admitted to each other that they'd been badly shaken by the experience of the crossing.

Later, when quizzed by the Board of Inquiry, they adopted a more blasé attitude. This perhaps may have resulted from being 'nobbled' by the North British Railway lawyers and told not to make derogatory comments about the safety of the bridge. The expression 'class action' was yet to be coined but the lawyers could foresee possible suits for damages and were not about to hand legal ammunition to the relatives of victims.

The gale pushed the train down the incline from the bridge, past the goods yards and the engine shed, rumbling to a halt at Dundee Tay Bridge station, five minutes late at 6.15 p.m. With all the dramas, the crossing had taken twice the usual time.

Guard Shand jumped down onto the track and double-checked the carriage wheels and axles for any sign of damage. Finding none, he walked forward to the engine to speak with Driver Kennedy. 'I'd not go across the bridge again tonight for 500 pounds,' he said. 'My carriage was lifted from the rails and streaks of fire came from it.' Driver Kennedy was unmoved and claimed that sparks always came from the wheels on the bridge but Shand insisted the wind had driven the wheels against the rails.

By the time of his appearance at the inquiry, Robert Shand vehemently denied ever making the remark about the £500.

The Stationmaster at Dundee Tay Bridge station was James Smith. He'd been promoted to this prestigious job after twenty-five years' service with the North British, coming to Dundee from Stationmaster postings at Burntisland and Polmont. He was officially off duty that night and, like most Dundonians, was at home sitting out the gale. But off duty or not, a stationmaster's paperwork was never done, and Smith was busy filling out forms for his Superintendent and checking the weekly traffic returns. Office methods in 1879 were still primitive – there were no shorthand clerks to help him, no photocopiers and no typewriters.[3] Everything had to be laboriously handwritten, often in triplicate.

Smith's duties were onerous and make a very lengthy list, which gives a good idea of the sheer workload for someone in his position. Just some of his responsibilities were:

> Totalling up invoices on a daily basis, checking trader's ledger accounts, regularly inspecting all railway premises under his command, visiting goods warehouses and sidings to ensure that wagons weren't being delayed, overseeing the invoices for forwarded traffic, enquiring about goods missing, damaged or received without invoices, attending to correspondence regarding claims about missing luggage,

dealing with traders and their complaints about train delays, signing off the Daily Returns for the Accounts Office, checking the ticket issue for the week, doing a monthly audit of all unpaid accounts and handwriting circular letters.

As if all this wasn't enough, he would attend to the arrival and departure of all important passenger trains and make himself available to the travelling public at large.

No wonder he was peeved when his solitude was disturbed at 6.30 p.m. on a Sunday night when he might have expected some peace before another rigorous week ahead. James Roberts, one of Smith's locomotive foremen, came knocking on his door to say that the gale was blowing loaded coal wagons along the viaduct siding in the goods yard. Smith found this astonishing – so much so that he had trouble believing the story.

Understandably, Smith was loath to go out but this was something he had to see for himself. Reluctantly donning his coat and pulling his hat well down over his ears, he went out into the furies of the night with Roberts and found the unbelievable to be absolutely true. Three wagons, each laden with 10 tons of coal, had been propelled nearly 400yd uphill along the siding by wind force alone. The wagons were of course getting the wind exactly from behind as the siding ran west–east, the direction of the gale. The two men managed to scotch the wagon wheels (wedge them) with hefty wooden pinch bars so that they could move no further. At just about that moment, Henry Somerville at the North Signal Box was shocked as his chimney cairn was blown clean off his building.

After hearing from the foreman that the engine shed doors had nearly been wrenched off, Smith thought he'd better go down to the station to see if all was well there. A buffeted 200yd struggle from the goods yard brought him to the platform ends and there he was appalled at the destruction already wrought by the storm. The glass station roof had been badly damaged, covering the platforms with heaps of shards, which the wind was swirling up and around in razor-sharp crystal eddies.

He issued orders to his inspector, Robert Caird, to close the Union Street station gate to stop any passengers from walking down the stairs into a lethal glass whirlwind. The damage to the station roof was worst in that area and Smith was very worried that it might be blown off altogether. He also got Kennedy and Shand to move their train from the exposed bay platform at the west end of the station to a slightly more sheltered position nearer the main buildings. This train, of course, was scheduled to go back across the bridge to Tayport at eight o'clock after the arrival of the 'Edinburgh' – whether or not Guard Shand got his £500.

The time was now nearly seven o'clock and the Edinburgh train was just reaching Leuchars Junction, a mere 8¼ miles to the south.

In these last minutes of the Tay Bridge's existence, calamity could still have been avoided. There was yet time to stop the 'Edinburgh' from crossing the bridge if anyone had thought of it.

Considering the episode of the coal wagons, the damage to Dundee Tay Bridge station roof and the stories from the crew of the 5.50 p.m. it seems hard to believe, even with the benefit of hindsight, that Stationmaster James Smith didn't take some sort of action to stop the 'Edinburgh' from crossing the river. Disregarding any thought of the bridge collapsing, surely the wind strength alone would have made him think about trying to stop any more crossings, even though such decisions were outside his remit. The storm was worsening further by 7 p.m. and if, as had been reported to him, the carriages of the 5.50 train had been partially lifted off the rails an hour earlier, for all he knew the 'Edinburgh' might now be blown off the bridge completely, especially while crossing the sections before and after the high girders. With only a flimsy handrail as a parapet, there was nothing to stop a derailed carriage plunging off the bridge and into the Tay, taking the rest of the train with it.

But Smith busied himself within his own domain – going into damage control, trying to clear up his station and getting it safe and ready for the arrival of the 'Edinburgh's' passengers. Possibly the ingrained feeling of complete trust in British engineering shared by the public at large made the chance of anything going awry seem so remote, so impossible, that it never entered his or anyone else's head.

With the gale roaring through the girder work, the bridge at this moment was a huge, horrible Aeolian harp.[4] The cacophony produced was satanic, discordant and orchestrated by demons. Broken lugs, disconnected tie-bars, sprung bolts …

Two miles of girders were propped up by eighty-five tortured supports, thrumming in the wind. The ebbing tide, pushed out faster by the gale, smashed and foamed against the brick pier bases. Huge gouts of water jumped high against each pier like packs of wet, maddened dogs barking up iron trees.

And there was another train due, pulled not by a lightweight tank engine like the last one across, but by a big 52-tonner with six carriages.

Notes

1 The Beaufort Scale is a measure of wind strength on a scale of 1 to 12. It was devised in 1805 by Royal Navy Commander (later Admiral) Francis Beaufort to describe the effect of wind on warships at sea. The Royal Navy declared it mandatory in 1838 and it was expanded to include land conditions by the International Meteorological Committee in 1874. The scale was confined to 'effect' rather than speed. Speeds of each number were not agreed until 1926.
2 Ducket windows were small glazed projections from both sides of a guard's van to allow guards to see down the side of a train without having to put their heads out of a window.
3 The first typewriters, the Sholes Gliddon (marketed as the Remington Standard 1) and the Remington Standard 2, were made by the U.S. gun company Remington from 1874–78 and exports to Europe had only just begun by 1879. Carbon paper was available but was too flimsy to be used with an ordinary steel-nibbed pen.
4 As described by Cuthbert Hamilton Ellis.

11

TRAIN OF TUMBRILS

Tumbrils – carts carrying victims to the guillotine during the French Revolution.

From the Gaelic word 'luachair', meaning rushes or reeds, evolved the name Leuchars. In 1879 this was a small Fifeshire farming town to the north of the Eden estuary mudflats. Unusually, for its size, Leuchars boasted two railway stations. The older station, appropriately now called Leuchars Old, was a wayside stop on the original NBR main line from Burntisland to Tayport. Prior to the bridge opening, Tayport was where the Edinburgh trains transferred their passengers to the cross-Tay ferries for Broughty Ferry and Dundee. The second station was the newly built Leuchars Junction, opened on 31 May 1878 at Milton as part of the new main line to Dundee which included the great Tay Bridge itself. This junction was a large island platform with bays let in at either end for St Andrews and Tayport trains.

Two wind-battered men were making their independent ways on foot from St Andrews to Leuchars Junction. Both of them were trying to catch the Edinburgh train to Dundee due to depart at 6.59 p.m. and both were worried about missing it. The gale had been blowing right in their faces which slowed them down considerably throughout the 5 miles they'd been trekking and they were both soaked from the fierce rain squalls which lashed at them constantly.

One man was George Ness. He was a 21-year-old North British Railway engine cleaner and was en route to his night shift at Dundee Engine Shed. Ness actually lived in Ogilvy Street, Tayport, and would normally have caught a local train from there to Dundee. But today, he, his 22-year-old wife Ann (whom he'd married on 29 August 1879) and their 10-week-old baby girl Rachel had been spending time at his in-laws' house in St Andrews. As there were no Sunday trains from there it meant walking to Leuchars to catch the main-line service. No Sunday trains also meant a day off for Ness's father-in-law, John Brand, who was an NBR engine driver of twenty-eight years' seniority, and known locally as one of the 'Tay Bridge Drivers'. Brand and three others, including Alexander Kennedy[1] who'd just driven the last train to cross the Tay Bridge successfully, had been operating the intensive commuter service between Dundee, Newport, Leuchars Junction and St Andrews since the opening of the Newport Railway over seven months ago in mid-May 1879.

Prior to that, Brand had been driving the 'Edinburghs' between Dundee and Burntisland just as David Mitchell did now. Based at St Andrews, he had Sundays off because only the Tayport–Dundee section of the new line ran on the Sabbath. Young George Ness had met his wife-to-be through his friendship with her father at work and they'd married with the enthusiastic blessing of John and his wife, also called Ann.

So George had reluctantly torn himself away from his family, pulled his cheese-cutter cap down over his ears and tugged on a pair of strong gauntlets before braving the stormy darkness and the long walk to Leuchars Junction. Only last week he'd passed the examination for the job as fireman but unless 'firing turns' came his way, he'd have to continue with engine cleaning and shed duties. But work was work and he had a new family to support.[2]

The other man making the wet march from St Andrews was joiner John Sharp who worked for James Keillers, the marmalade and jam makers in Castle Street. When he left Dundee that morning on the 7.30 a.m. train the weather, even in the morning darkness, had showed no signs of turning rough. He'd had a pleasant stroll from Leuchars to visit his friend Robert Brown in Abbey Close, St Andrews. Robert too, was a joiner by trade and the men had enjoyed a happy day together, exchanging carpentry-world gossip and sharing a few drams after lunch. It remained a beautiful wintry Sunday until about 4 p.m., when the weather began to worsen. By late afternoon when Sharp was due to be starting back for Leuchars, darkness was in fast descent and the storm was arriving in force.

Brown urged Sharp not to try to return to Dundee that night. To struggle 5 miles on foot in such wind and rain would be madness, he argued. Why not stay over, let the storm pass and catch the first train back tomorrow morning? There'd be no need to walk to Leuchars with the St Andrews branch line running on a weekday.

Sharp was very tempted. He had a North British Railway timetable in his coat pocket and quickly thumbed through to page 49, table 66, for the Dundee and St Andrews service. He noted the first train out from St Andrews was the 6.20 a.m., which reached Dundee at 7.10 a.m. It was a weekday commuter service and therefore took the more roundabout route via Newport to the Tay Bridge instead of the direct main line through St Fort. He checked to see if he had enough money to pay the difference on the return ticket he already held. Counting out £1 3s 10½d from his pockets, he'd found twenty times more than he needed but it was the subject of money that made up his mind for him.

Sharp was 35 years old and a single man living with his mother and father in Dundee. His aged and infirm parents relied on him totally as their sole means of support. To service this financial load, he worked long hours and begrudged wasted earning time. Even arriving in Dundee at 7.10 a.m. on Monday morning, he'd still have to go home first before starting work, as his parents would be worried about him. It was half a mile walk from Dundee Tay Bridge station to his house at 76 Commercial Street, so by the time he'd got there, explained his overnight absence to his parents, changed into his work clothes and set off again, it would be well past eight o'clock and a slice of his workday gone.

So reluctantly, Sharp decided to leave his friend Robert and head for Dundee that night, regardless of the weather and the windy, wet trudge ahead. He tugged his dark topcoat around himself, pulled his brown sealskin hat down over his ears and set off for Leuchars Junction.

As the 'Edinburgh' rolled down the 1 in 160 bank from Dairsie onto level track, William Linskill, who was travelling to St Andrews, felt the brakes going on under his feet, slowing the train for the Leuchars Junction stop. He stood up in his first-class compartment and began to gather his luggage from the narrow rack above his head, helped by Mr Beynon. Although the St Andrews branch was not open, there'd be no trudging 5 miles through the rain for him. The Dean of St Andrews University, whom Mr Linskill was visiting, had arranged a coach to collect him from the station.[3]

The wheels of the 5.27 train rattled over the points and crossings at Milton Junction where the branch line from St Andrews joined from the south and the train came heavily to a stand at Leuchars Junction, exposed to wind and weather on the flat land by the town. The station was unusual in having a single big island platform in the middle of the Up and Down lines instead of the usual pair of Up and Down platforms.

There were also bay platforms let into the island at each end, which held the connecting train services to St Andrews and Tayport respectively. A long footbridge provided access for passengers. The Edinburgh train was booked to wait here from 6.57 until 6.59 p.m. because even though there was no St Andrews branch connection to be made on a Sunday, Leuchars Junction was a train inspection point.

There had been quite a few accidents on British railways caused by wheel failures. The most recent calamities were at Hatfield on the Great Northern Railway in December 1870 and at Shipton, where a Great Western train came to serious grief on Christmas Eve, 1874. Both of these were cold-weather accidents involving metal wheels and tyres disintegrating. Extreme cold can alter the molecular structure of metal and weaken it, and this effect may have contributed to the sinking of the *Titanic* in 1912, thirty-three years later. Or else the builders, Harland and Wolff in Belfast, may have fallen for the idea of Best/Best Best/Best Best Best iron syndrome and ended up with the worst quality iron rivets. The Board of Trade inspectors at the Courts of Inquiry urged, not for the first time, the introduction of Mansell wheels which, as we have seen, were of wood/metal composite construction and consequently much more resilient. But by 1879, most carriages still weren't fitted with them. However, railway companies took the regular checking of wheels very seriously.

For the second time that day, the 'Edinburgh's' carriages had their springs, wheels and axle boxes checked. Two minutes is not much time to carry out a proper inspection of six carriage under-frames but William Robertson had twenty-eight years' experience as a Carriage and Wagon Inspector for the North British. All the right-hand side wheels had already been tapped by Inspector James Young at Burntisland earlier and now here, with the train standing against the island platform, the left side of the train became accessible. Robertson jumped down onto the track and moved quickly along the train, clonking at every wheel with his hammer and listening carefully above the wind for a healthy 'ding' instead of a sickly 'clunk' which could indicate a crack or a flaw in the wheel.

At the same time he deftly flicked the back of his hand against each axle box to check for any signs of overheating. All was, quite literally, sound.

John Sharp had made it to the platform before the train arrived and tried to dry off in the waiting room. He'd wrung out his sodden woollen mitts and huddled at the fireplace along with the other soaked passengers, two of them children. Amongst the bedraggled group of those waiting were 62-year-old Elizabeth Mann from Forfar and her 14-year-old granddaughter, Lizzie Brown. Red-haired and freckled, Lizzie was a tobacco spinner with the Dundee firm of Fairweather Tobacco Works in Murraygate and lived with her mother and younger brother William in Arbroath Road, Dundee, just east of Albert Street.

Elizabeth wore a crêpe bonnet with a black gown and black stockings while Lizzie had a black chip hat and a black corded dress with light grey stockings. She was 5ft 1in tall.

They'd been visiting Elizabeth's son Charles who lived in Leuchars and Lizzie had gone along for a treat. Her 6-year-old brother should have been with them on this trip but as a punishment for being naughty and throwing tantrums his mum had locked him in his room. He was heartbroken that he couldn't go on the trip. Perhaps this is proof that crime does pay in that William didn't die in the disaster.

Grocer and spirits dealer John Hamilton was 32, had a tweed topcoat with a felt hat and stood disconsolately in his wet clothes next to clerk James Leslie from Baffin Street, Dundee. Margaret Kinnear had been visiting her parents Peter and Janet and was returning to her place of work in Dundee where she was a domestic servant for a Mr Robert Lee. Clad in dark green dress and a black fur-trimmed jacket she also had a rather special and fragile hat.

Everyone moved out under the platform canopy when the train ran in, the raindrops sputtering as they touched the engine's hot boiler barrel.

Immediately after grinding to a halt, the carriages were subjected to a small but determined invasion by the Leuchars passengers, pushing to get aboard out of the weather and stumbling over the knees, feet and foot warmers inside. The only first-class carriage in the train was second back from the engine. It was the six-wheeler No 414, built in 1873 and the sole vehicle in the train to actually have Mansell composite wheels. Inside his compartment in this carriage, Mr William Linskill pulled the leather strap under the door window, causing the droplight to fall open. Head out into the rain and wind, he called to the nearest porter to see if the road carriage sent by his friend the Dean had in fact arrived. Getting the answer, 'No', Mr Linskill assumed there had been some hiccup in the arrangements. He resigned himself to staying on the train, travelling through to Dundee for the night and returning to St Andrews in the morning. Disappointed, he pulled his window up with a snap of the strap and sat back down, sharing the news of his changed plans with Mr Beynon.

George Ness was very nearly too late to catch the train but he shaved off a bit of running time by jumping over the rails to the platform rather than crossing by the footbridge. He also didn't want to risk the station doors being locked against him at the very last moment. For the North British Railway, in its Notice to Passengers, warned that 'At roadside stations the Booking Office doors and the entrances to the Station Platform will be closed on the approach of trains, after which no passenger can be admitted'.

So after crossing the track, Ness ran up the platform ramp, head down against the wind and rain. He was aiming for the nearest shelter, which was the third-class carriage immediately behind the engine and tender. As he passed the engine, a shout from the footplate brought him up short. David Mitchell had recognised him even with his cap about his ears. 'Shame on you George, going for a ride on the cushions,'[4] he said.

'A new fireman passing up a footplate trip even on a night like this?' he added cheekily. 'What would John Brand have to say about that? Come on up and ride with us. Young Marshall here will even let you loose on the shovel!'

Ness knew if he didn't board the engine, he'd never live it down. The story would soon get back to his father-in-law John Brand, which meant endless ribbing and pointed jokes about being frightened of a bit of rain and wind. Anyway, he figured that he couldn't get any wetter than he already was. So up he climbed, greeting his friends and exchanging family news. A grinning John Marshall offered him the shovel but Ness sat down in the meagre shelter of the tender and pulled his coat tighter around himself. Misery loves miserable company, he thought privately.

On the platform, Stationmaster Thomas Robertson held his arm straight up as a signal to David McBeath by the guard's van that the train was ready to go. McBeath blew hard on his whistle and John Marshall on the engine caught sight of the green flag waving. He called 'Right behind, right away' to Mitchell who slipped the reversing lever into full forward gear, yanked the whistle-chain, opened the regulator and let No 224 start away. The big driving wheels had only moved a few turns forward when a porter suddenly rushed along the platform towards the engine, waving his arms and shouting, 'Whoa, whoa, whoa!! Pull up!!' Mitchell slammed the regulator shut and hit up the Westinghouse brake and steam brake handles simultaneously. On the wet rails the engine picked up her feet, the wheels skidding and sliding until the train shuddered abruptly to a stand.

Mitchell was hoping the skid hadn't caused flats on the steel driving-wheel tyres. Inside the train, bags and cases tumbled from the narrow luggage racks[5] and curses flew as people were jolted and bumped together. The three footplatemen craned out of the cab to see what emergency must have occurred but they could only espy the porter gesticulating and banging on Mr Linskill's compartment window. His coach sent by the Dean had arrived after all and, did he but know it, had saved his life. In fact he lived to be 74 years of age and died on 22 November 1929. Apparently all St Andrews mourned his passing, as he was a colourful character and a devout Episcopalian who never tired of telling how he'd escaped the Tay Bridge Disaster. He is perhaps best remembered today for his whimsical St Andrews ghost stories, most of which were flights of fancy from his fertile imagination.

With Mr Linskill off, carrying the young boy in his arms and boarding his coach, the train was finally waved away, apparently leaving Mr William Beynon alone in the first-class compartment.

Stationmaster Robertson and his staff could hear the engine's exhaust noise receding into the battering night as it forged towards St Fort, 3¾ miles distant. It took the left fork at Leuchars Junction, leaving the line to Tayport running northwards through Leuchars Old and past the castle ruins.

As no more services were scheduled that evening, Robertson and his porters began the rounds of closing their station. The waiting room fire was raked out, the offices locked and the lamp room and storerooms secured for the night. Robertson sent his porters home to relax and let the storm blow itself out while they slept, but stayed on himself for a while longer to deal with station paperwork, accompanied by one of his staff.

Thomas Barclay at Tay Bridge South Signal Box had gone home to his nearby cottage after passing the 'church train' over the bridge at 6 p.m. With the sparse Sunday service, there was no need to stay on duty all the time with nothing to do. So, as mentioned before, Barclay was in the habit of going home between trains. Now, at seven o'clock, he was back at his box ready for the 'Edinburgh', due up in a few minutes. With him this time was John Watt, who was a fellow railwayman in the Permanent Way Department. Watt had been working for the North British Railway for twelve years, the first five on the Ladybank to Perth line and in the Dundee district ever since then.

As a surface-man, he was responsible for the maintenance of the railway track but his duties did not include any care of the bridge trackwork, although he did look after the points at the south end junction.

Both living in the same row of railway cottages overlooking the Tay hard by the bridge, Barclay and Watt had become friends and when off-duty, Watt would often spend time with Barclay in his signal box. This evening, both men had had a real fight against the wind after leaving their homes. Once in the box, Barclay stirred up the fire in the stove while Watt took the coal scuttle and put it by the door, intending to fetch more coal from the bunker at the bottom of the steps outside.

The 'Edinburgh', meanwhile, was now well on its way from Leuchars Junction to St Fort. Millions of years ago this region of north Fife was part of the Tay estuary. On leaving Leuchars, the railway passed extensive sand and gravel pits, evidence that this area was once under the sea. Steadying up on a new north-westerly heading, the train met a stiffish 1 in 100 gradient for a mile or so. Mitchell pushed the big reversing lever forward a notch or two nearer full gear and nudged the regulator further open. This sharpened the exhaust bark and Marshall, shovelling to keep pace with the extra demand for steam, noticed how the coal was snatched off the shovel by the increased draught up the chimney. Even still, the pressure gauge started to fall as the cylinders gulped steam faster than the boiler could generate it.

Neither man was worried about that. Marshall was 'mortgaging the boiler'[6] knowing that the remaining couple of miles after the hump were nearly all downhill into St Fort, during which they could shut off the regulator and drift, easily recovering their maximum steam pressure. The train passed St Michael's Wood, looming as a blacker patch in the darkness to the right. At this point the climb ended, allowing Mitchell to ease the regulator back and let No 224 coast downhill through the gentle reverse curves, crossing Motray Water with the dim lights of North Straiton farm just visible half a mile away to the left.

The passengers found little of interest in the Stygian gloom beyond their rain-streaked windows. With nothing to look at and no one to talk to, those travelling alone had miles ago turned to recalling their day, reading a book in the dim light of the paraffin lamps or hoping the storm wouldn't in some way delay their arrival home.

In his third-class compartment, 18-year-old apprentice confectioner William Threlfall was sucking on a sixpenny stick of Edinburgh Rock which he'd bought from Fergusons near the castle. He'd spent the day in Edinburgh with his brother who was a trooper in the Inniskillen Dragoons. William was looking forward to getting home and telling his family all the news of his brother's life as a soldier. He was also musing about the recent discovery by Mr Rudolf Lindt in Switzerland. Apparently Lindt had found a way to make chocolate melt in the mouth. This might very well revolutionise Threlfall's chosen profession.

In the well-filled little second-class carriage next to the guard's van, along with Archie and Jessie Bain, James Leslie was reading a book of poetry by Henry Longfellow and trying not to be distracted by the chatter of his travelling companions. *The Song of Hiawatha* was heavy going for a 22-year-old, even for a lad who'd won a reading prize at Dundee High School when he was 14. Dundee councillor David Jobson who'd joined the train at Ladybank was reading one of the several books he was carrying that night. He was 39 years old and an oil paint and colour merchant by profession. Along with his books, he had £5 1s in cash, two pairs of kid gloves, a gold watch with chain and his pipe and tobacco. No doubt he was looking forward to getting home to his wife Mary and his five children at 3 Airlie Place, Dundee. A model citizen in many ways, David, apart from being a councillor, was a leading member of the Unitarian Church in Constitution Road and had been attending a Mission station in Perth which he had founded at his own expense. He was also a director of the Dundee Society for Prevention of Cruelty to Animals and a member of the Free Library Board.

In the third-class carriage behind the engine, Margaret Kinnear was worried about her hat. On arrival at Dundee station, she had a walk of at least 500yd to her workplace at 6 Shore Terrace, plenty far enough for the wind and rain to tear her Sunday-best bonnet to shreds. A 17-year-old domestic servant earned relatively little and she'd saved long and hard to afford her black straw hat with its blue and mauve feathers, but now the hat seemed doomed. She could of course take it off and try to shelter it beneath her coat but that would squash and bend the fragile feathers and her unprotected hair would be blown into inextricable tangles. Life just wasn't fair, she pouted to herself.

James Murdoch was another third-class passenger wearing headgear unsuitable for the weather. He was a 21-year-old engineer going home to 1 Thistle Street, Dundee and sat quietly pulling on his pipe with, appropriately enough, an embroidered velvet smoking cap on his head.

William Peebles, in his late thirties, was a forester at Corrimony. He was going home to his wife Agnes and their eight children. He carried in his pockets over £4 in cash, his pipe and tobacco, a pocket book and his Gun Licence.

What Thomas Davidson who'd boarded the train at Cupar was doing with an expensive pair of ladies' earrings will probably remain a mystery forever. They were long-drop Czech earrings, made of crystal glass encased in silver. He wore a dark tweed suit under a brown nap topcoat with a velvet collar. Aged 28, Davidson was a farm servant from Linlathen, hardly amongst the high earners. Therefore it was somewhat remarkable that his pockets contained not only the earrings but also a silver watch and not one, but two, silver 'albert' chains. It would be unfair to malign his memory with calumny but his possession of all these valuables is, at the very least, suspicious!

Just after passing under the Kilmany-Newport road bridge at 7.05 p.m., Driver Mitchell closed No 224's regulator and gently applied the Westinghouse for the stop at St Fort. Fireman Marshall threw a quick round of eight shovelfuls into the firebox because there was a mile-long ascent at 1 in 100 on leaving the station which would need a bit of steam to surmount. After that, it was all downhill the last mile to Tay Bridge South Signal Box.

It was common practice for long-distance trains to undergo ticket collection and examination at their penultimate stops. No corridors and inter-vehicle gangways meant no travelling ticket collectors so this was a good way to reduce passenger delays at termini by not having long queues blocking up station exits. But it had to be done in a couple of minutes or the train would be late away. St Fort Station Agent Robert Morris was mildly surprised that the train was on time considering the stormy weather being thrown at it. He had the ticket-collection exercise well organised with himself, porter Alexander Ingles and ticket collector William Friend each checking a third of the train each. The train was due off St Fort at 7.08 p.m. and they had a couple of minutes in hand.

As the men ran along the platform from carriage to carriage, they opened the doors on various little cameos inside that later became set in their minds like snapshots in a photograph album.

William Friend was collecting from the front part of the train and remembered a man with his children in a third-class compartment. A little one was in the man's arms with two more sitting around him and they were all dozy from their long day's outing. Alexander Ingles started at the rear of the train, checking the second-class carriage which had eight passengers in it, then moved to the next one forward. This was a third-class carriage with twenty-one people aboard and a bit of a party going on inside. Seaman John Scott, fortified by occasional swigs from a little brown bottle in his luggage, was regaling his fellow passengers with sea shanties. The two young girls from London were trying hard to stay awake and join in. The lassies had been travelling now for over twenty-two hours and were very tired but happy that they were nearly at their destination.

Robert Morris checked the three compartments of the third-class carriage immediately behind the first. He was teased by some of the twenty passengers with remarks like, 'Is the bridge safe? Will the bridge stand the storm?' These questions were light-hearted; no one really thought there was any danger.

Morris, Friend and Ingles were only collecting tickets from Dundee-bound passengers. Obviously people for destinations further on would keep theirs. Like for example, the three men who were booked to Newport which was on the south bank of the Tay opposite Dundee.

However, in order to get home they first had to cross the bridge to Dundee, change trains and then come back across the bridge once more on the 8 p.m. local, which of course was the return working of the 5.50 p.m. 'church train'. Carpenter Robert Culross, Commission Agent David Watson and 15-year-old apprentice grocer James Peebles were planning to do just that. James was indentured to a Mr Harris in Newport and had been visiting his parents at Boglon, near St Fort.

Ann Cruickshanks, apart from her job with Lady Baxter at Kilmaron Castle, actually lived in Moray Place, Edinburgh. Tonight, however, she was booked to Broughty Ferry, next station on from Dundee and therefore she kept her ticket. As did her travelling companion Mrs Easton, bound for Old Meldrum north-west of Aberdeen. Elizabeth Mann, going home to Prior Road, Forfar, kept hers too. She would say goodbye to granddaughter Lizzie when they reached Dundee. There were travellers who were holding return tickets such as Mr Beynon from England, teacher David Graham from Stirling, flax dresser James Millar from Dysart, 31-year-old William Neilson from Gateshead, mechanic James Patton from Edinburgh and Freemason

Robert Syme, who was a partner in an Edinburgh firm of printers. Mr Syme was quite well off with £12 12s 6d in his purse but no amount of money could buy safety for anyone aboard the train that night. At the extremes of wealth riding the train, William Henry Beynon carried £18 5s 8d in his wallet while George Ness had a mere tuppence. But they were all to become equals in death.

Ingles, Friend and Morris collected two second-class tickets from Edinburgh and one from Glasgow. William Friend noted that the train was unusually full for a Sunday night, which was not that surprising given the fact that Hogmanay was only three days away and Scottish kinfolk loved being together for the New Year's celebrations. Many passengers would have been going home to their family firesides, looking forward to the night of more than a few wee drams, the ringing of bells at twelve midnight, the singing of *Auld Lang Syne* and the fun of the 'first foot' ceremony with the delivery of a lump of coal!

In third class, tickets were collected from the two young ladies who'd come from London King's Cross. Tickets were also collected from passengers who'd come from a variety of places. One ticket was collected from a single passenger travelling from the following places: Burntisland, Hartlepool, St Andrews, Dysart, Kirkaldy, Leslie, Dairsie and St Fort. Other towns had a number of their citizens whose tickets were collected that night: Edinburgh (twelve), Ladybank (two), Perth (seven), Newburgh (five), Abernethy (two), Leuchars (eight) and Cupar (eight).

No first-class tickets were collected. When Alexander Ingles checked the first-class carriage, he found there was nobody in it. Mr Linskill and the boy with him had been in the first-class vehicle since Markinch but as we have seen, got out at Leuchars Junction and were now safely on their way to St Andrews in the Dean's coach. The mystery of Mr Beynon deepens here, as he was certainly a first-class passenger and had, according to Mr Linskill, been in conversation with him in the same compartment – so where was he? He certainly died in the disaster to come, as his body was recovered from the Tay. One can only surmise that when Mr Linskill left to board the Dean's coach at Leuchars Junction, Mr Beynon, deprived of someone to chat with, must have moved to another carriage at the very last moment.

On the engine, the Westinghouse pump panted away to itself while the rain was being blown horizontally along the platform, hosing down the passengers climbing aboard. This and the ticket collecting made for a flurry of activity and the constant opening and slamming of doors.

George Johnston was searching for Eliza Smart, whom he'd arranged to meet on the train. He'd had a fine day with his father at St Fort Estate and now to cap it off perfectly, he was about to meet his sweetheart.

Along the platform he ran with no thought now for the rain and gale, excitedly peering into each compartment window until finally, there she was! But sitting with Eliza were, of course, Ann Cruickshanks and Mrs Easton, whom George had certainly not been expecting to see. Hiding his disappointment with a fixed, almost rictus grin, George climbed in as Ann Cruickshanks glowered disapprovingly at him from beneath her black poke bonnet while holding on firmly to her reticule.

George and Eliza had eyes only for each other and wouldn't have noticed if the roof had blown off, which tragically it was soon to do. With a careful adjustment of his coat to keep off the old biddies' prying eyes, the two managed to clasp hands beneath the folds – not quite the passionate reunion that George had in mind. Still, there was only the bridge to cross now and then the two of them would be alone together.

David Cunningham and Robert Fowlis, who'd been visiting their respective parents, had been waiting at St Fort in the darkness and the ever-rising wind. After a while, 54-year-old Mrs Euphemia Cheape, a domestic cleaner and mother of six children, joined them in their cold and wet vigil. She was on her way to Dundee and must have had a blowy, soaking walk to the station as she'd come from Kilmany, about 2 miles to the south-west of St Fort. Like a mother hen, the train had traversed Fife picking up all her little chicks out of the stormy night. The final ones were now aboard and the last carriage door slammed shut.

The Covenant of Death was complete. It only remained for the train of tumbrils to carry its human sacrifices onto Sir Thomas Bouch's iron altar.

Notes

1. The other two drivers were William Coutts and Ronald Baxter.
2. George Ness had something of a 'shotgun marriage' to Ann Brand although there is nothing to suggest that George's mother and father-in-law were at all unhappy with what had happened. George and Ann were wed on 29 August 1879 and their child Rachel was born on 15 October 1879. So the little girl was only 10 weeks old when her father died in the Tay. His body was recovered on 13 January 1880 but sadly Rachel herself died on 28 March 1880. Father and daughter were buried together in Ferryport-on-Craig churchyard.
3. Mr Linskill preferred to be known as 'Dean of Guild Linskill'. He was the son of Captain Linskill, Mayor of Tynemouth and The Honourable Mrs Linskill, daughter of Viscount Valentia. In his youth, his parents frequently brought him to St Andrews for a holiday and he took so enthusiastically to golf that he eventually settled down in the Home of the Game in 1897.
4. 'On the cushions' is footplatemen's slang for travelling as a passenger.
5. North British Railway compartments had particularly narrow luggage racks above the seating.
6. Putting steam through the cylinders at a greater rate than the boiler could produce it.

12

THE LONG DROP

Why now, blow wind, swell billow and swim bark.
The storm is up and all is on the hazard.

William Shakespeare, *Julius Caesar*

Chances of death in a British railway accident in 1879: 1 in 23,500,000.

As the train pulled uphill away from St Fort and passed Newton Farm, Marshall ran the pricker through the fire for the last time, rousting the incandescent coals to keep them lively enough for the last 4½ miles to Dundee. With the wind blasting, he knew they would need plenty of steam for the hard slog across the bridge. At the same time, the engine was going on shed when it arrived at Dundee and Marshall didn't want to add any more coal to the fire. The shed crew, including George Ness, would definitely not appreciate having to dump out a full firebox of blazing coals. They'd rather have a firebox and ashpan with ashes, cinders, embers and a run-down fire-bed as befits the end of a journey. Marshall, having been a cleaner and shed labourer in his climb up the promotion ladder knew this very well and wouldn't wish the extra work put on his juniors. So he eyed the steam pressure gauge and the boiler water level and, using his judgement and experience as a fireman, decided to leave the injector off and let the boiler water level and the fire run themselves down. He'd done this as a matter of course on many down journeys to Dundee.

All across Fife as the storm worsened, the gale hadn't really slowed up the train's progress. Only a couple of times during the trip had Mitchell looked at his watch and then held out his hand with two fingers pointing downwards. Marshall had nodded, knowing the gesture meant 'two minutes behind'. Overall, the train had been just about on time for the whole journey, having gained some shelter from being inland.

But now, approaching Tay Bridge South Signal Box and reaching the funnel of the Tay valley, all weather protection was rapidly disappearing. Mitchell pondered this as the train passed the Wormit sidings complex, its signal box switched out for Sunday and all boards[1] off in both directions. The gale had started to hit very much harder and if it was like this in the lee of Wormit Bay, what was it going to be like when they were totally exposed on the bridge? He tried to tell Marshall in so many words: 'It's going to be a very rough crossing tonight, John. We'll have to take it steady.' With the wind roar, he had to shout at the top of his lungs before John Marshall understood.

In the signal box, its wooden framing and windows shuddering from the squally blasts, Barclay had received the bell code for TRAIN ON LINE from St Fort at eight minutes past seven. This meant that the train had started its near 2-mile run to his South Box. He therefore sent CALL ATTENTION on his block bell to Henry Somerville at Tay Bridge North Signal Box, received a one-beat acknowledgement and then sent IS LINE CLEAR? Again, Somerville acknowledged at nine minutes past seven. Thomas Barclay pulled off his Down starter signal, followed by his advanced starter out on the bridge, the levers thudding metallically across the frame. He leaned back, duster in hand. The road across the bridge was now set. Three minutes later, the train became visible from the signal box. Fronted by the two red engine headlamps, a string of uncertain flickering carriage lights appeared around the last curve before the bridge. Barclay picked up the single-line staff, heaved on his overcoat and climbed down the steps into the storm to pass the single-line staff to the engine crew.

Mitchell had shut off steam, letting No 224 coast towards the box, slowing down to about 3mph as Marshall leaned out of the cab ready to grab the staff. The wind force took Barclay's breath away as he crouched by the stairs and held up the staff towards Marshall's outstretched arm. There was no chance of an exchange of greetings being heard against the awesome wind noise but the two men managed mutual waves as Marshall snatched the staff and laid it on the tender toolbox lid. Seeing the train's authority for the single line safely aboard, Mitchell pushed the regulator wide open again and set the reversing lever position in full forward gear to get the engine moving against the wind. The big steel coupling rods swung upwards inside the paddlebox splashers and down again in a lazy circle as the train slowly gathered speed. The engine and tender towed the six carriages with their yellow fogged-up windows past Barclay in wind-shredded veils of steam, smoke, rain and sleet. The bright orange firebox glare was reflected high into the savage night sky because Marshall had left the fire doors open even though he wasn't going to shovel more coal. At least there was a bit of light and a trace of warmth and then the train was away out onto the bridge with the uncertain glimmering of the paraffin carriage lights and the three red tail lamps on the guard's van guttering in the blackness to mark its progress.

Barclay fought his way back up the steps into the signal box and gratefully slammed the door shut behind him, cutting off some of the demonic wind moaning. He sent TRAIN ON LINE by bell code to Henry Somerville in the North Signal Box and recorded the time in his Train Register Book. '7.13 p.m.', he noted from the box wall clock, although Somerville wrote '7.14 p.m.' in his own Register Book. The next Sunday night service across the bridge was the 8 p.m. off Dundee, the return working of the 'church train' to Tayport. It wasn't worth going back home for less than an hour so Barclay decided to bank up the signal box stove and chew the fat with John Watt. But first he put his Down signals back to danger behind the 'Edinburgh' and then reset the points on the 'Y' of the bridge in favour of the route to Tayport, ready for the local from Dundee due after crossing the bridge at about ten past eight.

While Barclay clanked his poker through the fire and swept up the ashes, Watt was staring idly out of the box's north-facing windows, watching the train's progress across the bridge.

There was no rain or visible moon at this moment in the storm but the train had to shoulder its way between seemingly solid blocks of wind out onto the first section of the great bridge. These initial spans were carried on fourteen sturdy brick piers, forming the best-designed and most durable supports of the whole bridge. This section never shook or vibrated when trains crossed. If it had all been built this way, it's very likely there'd have been no disaster and the structure might still be there today, no thanks to Mr Jesse Wylie and his inept river borings that is. Beset by frightful winds coming hard and cruelly from the south-west against its left-hand side, No 224 and train plugged away out across the river at a steady 10 to 12mph. Mitchell had lengthened the cut-off by moving the reversing lever to the third notch from centre soon after leaving the South Signal Box and now he and Marshall crouched as low as they could for shelter, given No 224's scant cab. They were not keeping a very good lookout but why would they need to? They were on the bridge, they knew it backwards and no person or object was likely to appear suddenly in front of them.

So it was a case of leaving the controls set with wide-open regulator, plod over the bridge and when they felt the gradient fall away during and after the 'high girders' section, shut off steam and ease on the brakes to pass in the staff at the North Signal Box. Meanwhile, they took what cover they could and meant to hold on tight until reaching the north bank.

'It should only take three or four minutes and we'll all be safe,' thought George Ness as he held his cap down over his ears and stayed bowed down and hunched up in the scant shelter of the tender, sodden and cold. He'd long ago abandoned any attempt to gain comfort from smoking his clay pipe in this wind, which precluded lighting it anyway.

When the train was 200yd out from the South Signal Box, Watt in the South Box noticed sheaves of sparks coming from the right hand side of the carriages, the same phenomenon as had occurred when the 'church train' crossed an hour before. Once again, as with the 'church train' the wind was pushing the right-hand wheels hard against the right-hand running rail and the left-side wheels against the left-hand checkrail.

There were five men in the guard's van now as another off-duty NBR Goods Guard called David Scott had joined the train at St Fort for a lift back home. He was 26 years old and lived with his sister at 7 Yeoman Shore, Dundee, just two minutes walk from Dundee station.[2]

The men could feel the gale forcing the vehicle down onto its right-hand springs and putting a tilt into the floor. Some of the forty-six heaped mailbags slipped off their neat piles and began to slide slowly over the blue linoleum flooring, fetching up against the right side of the van. Mail Guard Donald Murray tried to re-stack them but the bags slithered down again, this time knocking into a hamper containing thirty Leicestershire pies consigned to a bakery in Dundee. Another hamper with a turkey, a brace of partridges and a hare slid across the vehicle in sympathy.

Having crossed the bridge hundreds of times and in all weathers, McBeath, Murray and Goods Guards George McIntosh and David Scott knew what a windy crossing could be like. All the same, David McBeath dug himself a liberal pinch from his silver snuff box and, as if to reassure himself, shouted against the noise of the roaring wind to his companions: 'Safe as the Bank of Scotland, this bridge.' But off-duty guard David Johnston, new to this route and to the bridge, began to feel some misgivings.

His thoughts on his day in Edinburgh with his wife and children were suddenly irrationally tinged with the fear that he may never see his family again, but this dissipated as he looked round at the other four men who seemed completely unconcerned.

Then the train reached the fifteenth span and the last of the brick piers. The first of the cast-iron tubular piers were now supporting the bridge deck. Almost at once, the floor felt slightly 'wobbly', the only word for it – just a feeling under the feet. The van's motion was also a little jelly-like but on the footplate of No 224, the crew felt nothing. After all, the engine and tender weighed 52 tons and that deadweight would tend to mask any oscillating movement of the bridge below.

Some of the passengers riding in the very much lighter carriages did feel a change in the movement. Although George and Eliza sitting opposite Ann Cruickshanks and Mrs Easton in their third-class compartment were oblivious to anything except each other's eyes, the shotgun blasts of windblown salt spray from the river against the windows were certainly rattling the two older ladies, as was the tilt to the right of the whole carriage. They tried to speak to one another but the hellish noises outside defeated them. Surfaceman John Watt in the South Signal Box, having been watching the gouts of sparks, remarked to Signalman Barclay: 'There's something wrong with the train, Thomas!'

Then the train reached the first of the high girders (span No 29 counting from the south bank), which was the distorted span. The first few feet of track were slightly out of true due to the girder having fallen into the river during construction and getting bent. As explained before, it was straightened out and replaced onto the bridge but nevertheless a little distortion was still there. For nineteen months, this slight kink in the rails had caused the northbound trains to 'nod into the girder' as noted by many witnesses. Tonight, the 'Edinburgh' was no exception. The roadbed had recently been ballasted all the way across with some 1,200cu. yd of aggregate to act as a fire retardant. To recap the point made earlier, this added the enormous extra weight of some 1,500 tons very high up right across the bridge, which pushed the centre of gravity of each pier, already too high for a prudent design, even higher. What engineers call 'the turning moment' had become critical and even more so as a train weighing in at about 125 tons was crossing. No 224 and her six carriages plugged onwards through four more high girder spans until the actual instant of collapse, just about when the train was mostly in the fifth high girder. The thirteen high girders forming this part of the bridge formed three sets of continuous girders linked together as five, four and four spans respectively.[3]

The entire bridge, already in deep resonance and fatal oscillation and with the wind's energy adding every second to the swaying motion, finally succumbed to the metal fatigue it had been undergoing for nineteen months, especially the cast-iron lugs holding the tie-bars. It was the camel's back-breaking straw. Below the bridge decking, the tortured ill-fitting iron columns, the fatigued lugs and their tie-bars finally gave up the ghost. Everything simply failed at once. The high girders and the piers below them fell outwards in a truncated arc to the downwind side of the bridge, probably going with the extra vicious gust at around 7.16 p.m. At that moment the train was mostly inside the fifth high girder with just the second-class carriage and the guard's van inside the fourth.

With a shriek of shearing metal, inaudible above the wind noise, the girder work fractured away from the columns beneath, causing violently bright flashes like lightning which were reported later by several witnesses on the riverbanks. Thus the high girders began their fall with a sudden lurch to the right, causing Mitchell, who was on No 224's footplate to be flung sideways.

He tried to recover his footing, reaching vainly to shut the regulator and yank at the brake-handle but skidded on the coal-slack on the footplate boarding before he could grab at anything. Shovels, coal-picks, food boxes and drink bottles all slithered to the right, fetching up against the cab side-sheet in a jumbled heap.

The cant steepened as Mitchell and Marshall shouted incoherently at one another to hang on. Still pulling hard and moving forwards, the engine tipped even further over as the girder slipped off its pier and began to fall in an outwards arc towards the river. Marshall lunged at a cab handrail, missed it and fell hard against the bottom of the hot firebox back plate, the damper control levers cutting two deep gashes in his head.

An avalanche of coal slid forwards from the tender like wet cold black lava, filling the footplate and pouring over Marshall, crushing him face downwards against the open fire hole. Would that he had shut the fire hole doors before crossing the bridge! The heat of 800°F – and the heat – dear God the heat – heat he could taste – coppery, ultra-dry, unbelievably unbearable. As the pain smashed into his brain and roared in his ears, Marshall tried to scream but he needed air to do that.

All he could breathe in were steel-solid bars of white heat, heat and more heat. His facial skin bubbled and blackened and his hair charred and blazed like a Guy Fawkes night sparkler. His eyes felt as if they were being boiled out of their sockets and for a split second Marshall could smell his head being roasted. Insanely, he was a wee bairn again, back in his mother's kitchen as she cooked pork crackling for Christmas dinner. Then he could smell no more as his nose had shrivelled to charcoal. Merciful unconsciousness intervened as the broiled skin on his face began to lift away from the subcutaneous tissue beneath. What was left of his face was baked into a hideous grimace.

The coal slide had missed Mitchell, who'd been hard up against the cab's left side-sheets. As the tilting quickly increased, he grabbed for the edge of the cab side and held on by his fingertips. In a further second, the upright cab side-sheets became horizontal as the cant raced through 45 degrees, 60 degrees and finally 90 degrees. At this point George Ness, crouched in the tender with nothing to hang onto, was probably catapulted along with the train staff into the oblivion of the black screaming spaces between the girder work.

At that angle with adhesion gone, all traction on the rails had ceased and the whole train seemed to stop in mid-air. The engine, with the regulator still wide open, continued to steam hard, pulling at nothing and putting itself into a maniacal wheel-spin like a monstrous fire-breathing dragon trapped in an iron cage.

Mitchell was hanging vertically straight down across the cab, his agonised fingertips on the point of giving way. Oddly, he could hear a man roaring out for God's help. It was only as the black freezing water rushed up at him did he realise that the implorer was himself.

It took another two seconds or so before the entire span, enclosing the engine and four of the six carriages, fell the 88ft and hit the water, along with the last two vehicles in the span behind. All joined together, these two spans took down with them the other eleven high girder spans simultaneously in one cataclysmic collapse.

Behind the engine, the passengers had never travelled in a lift as there were none in Britain until 1901 but now they found out just what it felt like to ride a downward-plunging, out-of-control elevator to the bottom of its shaft.

Hideously burnt, John Marshall wasn't even aware of the cold water that surrounded him and took away the heat of his burns. Amazingly, he was just about alive but another fate awaited him. Completely out of it, he started to drown.

For those among the eighty-five men, women and children who had taken the long drop into the river and survived the fall, there was scant hope of life. Some, like John Marshall, were terribly injured and anyone still alive and kicking was now immersed in very cold tempestuous waters. The average December temperature for the River Tay is a bleak 36°F, only 4 degrees above freezing point, giving an immersion time of only a few minutes before a body's core temperature dropped fatally low. Even for a fit strong swimmer (and Victorians were not known for being enthusiastic or able swimmers), the odds of survival were incredibly low given that the waters were thrashing about under the gale and the tide was ebbing very fast, a racing strong current accelerated by the wind.

The shock factor was total. To be thrown in an instant with no warning whatsoever from a warm railway carriage to fathoms beneath a seething freezing tideway would certainly have caused cardiac arrest amongst some of the older passengers, especially as during the few moments of actual falling, they would all have been piled on top of one another in a confusion of arms, legs and belongings as their carriages turned through 90 degrees. Their screams of extreme distress competed vainly with the roaring horror of the gale and the ripping apart of iron girder work. Then the carriages hit the waters of the Tay, which burst into their compartments, invading in angry cataracts.

Engine No 224 suffered surprisingly little damage from its fall but the front four carriages inside the fifth high girder span were well battered inside and out, not so much from the fall itself but from the ravages of the water pounding at them. The actual carriage body sides were not that seriously damaged as they hit the water right-side on, because their coachwork was mostly protected from the water-collision by the span's girder work. Buoyancy rapidly pulled the vehicles back to a vertical position but not before doors were wrenched open by the impact and the surge in air pressure, caused by the sudden inrush of water, had blown some of the roofs clean off. One of these roofs was noticed by the coaster *Armitus* on the Saturday evening following the disaster (3 January 1880) floating in the North Sea some 5 miles north of Berwick, around 65 miles south of the Tay Bridge. The captain of the ship, on passage from South Shields to Burntisland, of course didn't know about the Tay Bridge Disaster and let the roof float on by, merely noting the fact in the ship's log.

Many passengers would have been 'popped' out of their compartments like corks from a champagne bottle while others were violently washed out by the turbulent water.

The two vehicles inside the fourth high girder span stayed tipped over in line with the rails, although now at right angles to the vertical. The guard's van was badly damaged and its wheels were forced up through the floor but the little second-class carriage was completely destroyed from the solebars up, with no trace of the bodywork remaining.

Those still alive began to drown. Now, the process of drowning is an agonising experience according to the accounts of people who have suffered the process and then been saved at the very last moment. It is not at all like the gentle and peaceful drift into death as suggested by poets and writers. For the passengers wearing their winter coats, jackets, voluminous skirts, hats and boots, the extra water-weight instantly soaked up by such clothing dragged them down even faster and further below the surface no matter how hard they flailed in panic. The pitch black icy water caused complete disorientation – they wouldn't have been able to tell up from down.

A person underwater possesses an inbuilt instinct not to breathe in which, until the very edge of unconsciousness is reached, overrules the torture of having no air. After the initial gasping and possible aspiration of water, the immersion itself stimulates hyperventilation followed by voluntary apnoea, which means deliberate holding of the breath. But eventually, usually after about ninety seconds, so much carbon dioxide is in the bloodstream that the brain triggers an involuntary breath in an attempt to get more oxygen. This moment is called the 'break point' and is the start of the downward slide into death. The first involuntary apnoea usually occurs when the person is still conscious. Spasmodic breaths start to suck water into the mouth and windpipe. If there conceivably could be anything more agonising or worse than not breathing in air, it would be breathing in a lungful of water.

In a small percentage of people when water touches the vocal chords and larynx a muscular contraction called laryngospasm occurs. The windpipe closes down tight like a valve, overcomes the breathing reflex and the victim suffocates without any water getting into the lungs.

But for 90 per cent of people there is no laryngospasm, the water does reach the lungs and ends any further chance of oxygen transfer to the blood. Covering the bronchial tubes and lung alveoli is a surface-active substance made of lipids and proteins. This surfactant, as it is known, lowers surface tension and helps the lung's alveoli to collect oxygen. The influx of water washes it clean away and makes oxygen transfer virtually impossible. Then ventricular fibrillation sets in as the oxygen-starved heart beats very erratically and after several more minutes, stops altogether. The only thing left technically alive is the brain, which tries to do everything to stave off death. It puts the body into a sort of hibernation by cutting back on the metabolic rate and this process is actually helped by cold water hitting the face, which causes impulses to be sent along the trigeminal nerves and is called the mammalian diving reflex. The effect of this reflex, the so-called 'diving reflex' has three factors. Firstly 'Bradycardia' which is a reduction in heart rate of up to 50 per cent, then 'Peripheral Vasoconstriction' which is the restriction of the blood flows to the extremities to increase blood and oxygen supply to the vital organs. Finally, 'Blood Shift' where the movement of blood to the thoracic cavity tries to avoid the collapse of the lungs. Conscious victims will hold their breath (voluntary apnoea) and will try not to access air, often resulting in panic, including rapid body movement. This of course uses up more precious air and the consequent reduction of oxygen in the bloodstream reduces the time to becoming unconscious. The breathing reflex will increase until the victim attempts to inspire. This reflex is not related to the amount of oxygen in the blood but to the amount of carbon dioxide. During voluntary apnoea, the oxygen in the blood is used by the cells and converted into carbon dioxide but oxygen starvation will soon render a victim unconscious. A person with laryngospasm has his airways sealed and stands a good chance, if rescued in time, of surviving with no long-lasting after-effects. Salt water, as in the Tay estuary, is much more saline than blood and due to osmosis, water will leave the lungs and enter the bloodstream. Then there is the fact that water, regardless of its salt content, will damage the inside surface of the lung, collapse the alveoli and cause a reduced ability to exchange air by removing the surfactants, as already discussed above. Due to lack of oxygen, the heart may stop beating altogether. This cardiac arrest stops the flow of blood and thus the transport of oxygen to the brain. Cardiac arrest is known as clinical death – the brain will die after about six minutes in this situation.

So within a very few minutes of the train hitting the water and long before anyone on either riverbank was even certain about the bridge collapsing, all who had been aboard the train had perished.

Over the course of the next few weeks, forty-five corpses were recovered from the river. These were the bodies that by chance remained in the immediate area of the bridge, perhaps by snagging against the smashed girder work or moving only a short distance in the vagaries of local currents and sandbanks. Another thirty-five or forty were never found, undoubtedly swept straight out into the North Sea (or as it was called then, the German Ocean) by the fast-ebbing tide.

The last body found was that of Joseph Anderson, the 21-year-old compositor who'd joined the train at Cupar. His umbrella was washed up on the banks of the Tay a few days after the disaster but his body was carried at the whims of wind and tide to Wick at the very top of Scotland, off Ulbister in Caithness to be exact, and around 200 miles to the north of Dundee. Joseph's remains were brought home to his father, George Anderson, a newsagent in Auchtermuchty and buried in the churchyard there. His gravestone reads:

JOSEPH L. ANDERSON
LOST IN THE TAY BRIDGE DISASTER 28th DECEMBER 1879
BODY FOUND NEAR WICK
FOUR MONTHS AFTER, INTERRED HERE: 28th APRIL 1880

Notes

1 Railway jargon for signal arms.
2 David Scott's sister Janet lived to be 74 years old by 1938 and was the very last person to receive assistance from the Tay Bridge Relief Fund.
3 Refer to 12 (i) 'The "high girders"' in the chapter note section.

WHO SAW WHAT?

> I'm a reliable witness, you're a reliable witness. Practically all God's children are reliable witnesses in their own estimation. Which makes it funny how such different ideas of the same affair get about.
>
> John Wyndham, *The Kraken Wakes*, 1953

With the best will in the world and with complete honesty, people see events as they think they happened. So it was with the fall of the Tay Bridge. No one lied, no one made anything up, they just remembered what they saw – or thought they saw.

Surfaceman John Watt peering north through the windows of Tay Bridge South Signal Box, was the first person other than those aboard to know that something was wrong with the train. He had watched it straining out across the bridge with the three swaying red tail lamps on the rear of the luggage van receding into the blackness. He then saw a spray of sparks from the wheels which grew into a steady flame, pulled eastwards by the wind. He said he watched this phenomenon for about three minutes and then suddenly, there were three distinct flashes and then one final great flash. The train's lights vanished at this moment. Watt turned to Signalman Thomas Barclay and related what he'd seen. Barclay was at first wary of this information and attributed the disappearance of the train to the fact that it had gone through the 'high girders', was running down the gradient out of sight and would re-appear momentarily as it reached the north bank. 'Wait, wait, we'll see her soon,' Watt later alleged Barclay to have said. After a few more minutes, the 'Train Out of Section' bell code should have come through from the North Box but it had not. Mystified, Barclay tried his speaking instrument to contact Henry Somerville but the equipment was dead. The two men, now desperately worried that something was very seriously amiss, decided to leave the shelter of the signal box and trek out across the bridge as far as they could go in order to settle the matter but the wind strength was far too much for them and they could hardly stand up against it. They were fearful, with the wind scything at them from the west, of actually being blown clean over the handrails and into the river. So, after trying to walk against the storm for a few spans, they gave up and retreated to the south bank. They then decided to attempt to view the bridge structure from the side by fighting their way along the riverbank to the east. Only then, as the fitful cloud cover allowed the appearance of the moon, could they see that the high girders, over a thousand yards of the great Tay Bridge, had simply vanished.

On both banks of the Tay that night many other witnesses recounted their experiences.

Mr W.B. Thompson, who was an engineer and shipbuilder at the Caledonian Shipyard, Dundee, had been attending evening service at the Free Church, Broughty Ferry. The congregation was dismissed at 7.06 p.m. (by his watch) and then he walked, or rather lurched and staggered because of the gale, down to the beach to observe the state of the river. He managed to get to the corner of James Place against the fierce wind and there he distinctly saw, as he said:

> Two luminous columns of mist or spray travelling across the river in the direction of the wind. Another one formed in front of me in an instant. It appeared to rise from the centre of the river. I never saw anything like this before and looked around to see if anyone was near me but, seeing no one, thought it better to take shelter. I went inside the railing and held on by one of them, thinking the column of water which was advancing towards me, was to carry everything with it. However, it passed over me, it was spray from the river, not solid water. It struck the house behind me with a hissing noise. The height of these columns I should think was 250 to 300 feet. On the following morning I found that the windows of my house (about 150 feet above the river) were caked with salt. I never saw this before in a westerly wind and can only account for this by one of the columns passing over the house. My theory is that the north end of the bridge gave way first, the failure being caused by one such column rising or passing beneath it.
>
> Such a thing would tend to lift the girders from their piers, so that the wind, which had the effect of lifting the column of spray, had also the effect of raising the girders from the piers. My theory, put briefly, is that there was a heavy upwards pressure as well as a lateral pressure in the wind that night. My opinion is that the spray rising from the plunge of the falling girders and train could not raise to the height at which Provost Robertson saw his columns and that Provost Robertson's columns must have been of the same description as those I saw.

This evidence was sadly never used in the inquiry and the Board never got to hear of it. This is not to say that Mr Thompson's observations were irrelevant. With the knowledge that the 'high girders' were only held to their piers in quite a cursory manner, his evidence could have helped the wind theory propagated by Thomas Bouch and others. It is indeed just, but only just, possible that such an uplift of wind on the high girders could have helped the collapse happen although such an effect would only have been a small contributory cause. The Provost Robertson mentioned by Mr Thompson was at his home in Newport on the south bank of the Tay. He'd been watching out for the Edinburgh train because he knew that his son might very well be aboard, returning to Dundee ready for his work as an apprentice there on the Monday morning. William Robertson, a Provost of the Borough of Newport, not only had some personal serious concerns about the safety of the bridge but also had a very good view of the bridge from his home, a view that was only briefly interrupted by some buildings which obscured some of the first spans. He could see in the otherwise blackness the navigation lights (the ones tended by Mr McKinney the lamplighter) on the high girder piers. He watched the train set out across the bridge and shortly saw two columns of spray illuminated by the navigation lights and then two brilliant flashes of light. He formed the opinion that the bridge had gone over, especially as all the navigation lights were abruptly extinguished. He knew that the gas supply for the lights was carried through the bridge handrails and as the lights had gone out, inferred that the handrail pipes had been fractured by the bridge falling. He timed this as at between 7.15 p.m. and 7.20 p.m. Provost Robertson was to tell this story to the Board of Inquiry a few days later and he was also questioned upon his observations of especially the northbound trains breaking the 25mph speed limit. Of this evidence more later in the Inquiry chapter.

A boy called Jamie Norval was coming home from church on the Dundee side with his father. They reached a low wall at the top of Seabraes and looked out at the bridge. Years later, Jamie recalled saying to his father, 'Was that no lightning?' They'd both seen the flashes reported by many witnesses at the moment of the bridge's collapse. To which his dad replied, 'I don't think so, it was too low down on the water.' Jamie remembered later in life that his father's voice had a strange sound to it.

Mr Smith and two of his children were staying at the newly opened (1878) Queen's Hotel at 160 Nethergate, Dundee. From their room window, the high girders were about 1⅓ miles away in a straight line, with the bridge at an angle of about 45 degrees. The family had an uninterrupted view of the bridge and at just on 7.15 p.m. they saw the train beginning to cross the bridge. A minute or two later there came that extra violent gust which nearly all witnesses seem to remember and Mr Smith's attention was diverted by a door being blown open in the courtyard below. Just as he looked down, one of the children exclaimed that he'd seen flashes of light between the bridge and the river. Then everything seemed to disappear at once – the bridge navigation lights, the twinkling necklace of carriage lamps and the outline of the girders all vanished in an instant. One moment everything was there, the next, nothingness. They neither heard anything above the wind roar and the rattling of their hotel room windows nor saw any columns of spray or splashes out on the river. Although they kept on peering into the blackness, they saw nothing more.

Wine merchant James Black Lawson lived on the eastern perimeter of Magdalen Green and so had a very good view, albeit tightly oblique, of the bridge. He left his house to stand on the embankment by the river and was soon joined by his friend George Clark who had seen three bright flashes as well as the sprays of water reported by Provost Robertson and Mr Thompson. Lawson said, 'There is a train into the river!' The two of them ran as fast as they could the few hundred yards to the North Signal Box which stood high just short of the bridge overlooking the Esplanade. They tried yelling at the box but Henry Somerville could not hear them over the raging wind noise. They struggled partway up the signal box steps just when Somerville came down to meet them. Screaming at the tops of their voices, the three men managed the following exchange: 'Where is the train?' the men asked. Somerville replied, 'It's been a long time on the bridge.' Which was enough for Lawson and Clark to start running the mile to Tay Bridge station with the news where they told Stationmaster James Smith what they'd seen. They reported that they'd seen fire falling from the bridge and expressed their fears that the bridge was down.

Meanwhile, Dundee grocer Mr Phin, in Perth Road, saw the train enter upon the bridge and soon saw 'two fearful volumes of flame'.

Alexander Maxwell was entertaining some friends at his father's house in Magdalen Green quite close to the bridge. One of his guests was William Millar who suggested drawing back the curtains to watch the train cross the river. This was apparently still a novel thing to do amongst Dundee residents who had a view across the river, even though the bridge had been open for nineteen months. They all watched and waited for the train.

At just after 7 p.m., they saw the uncertain glimmering lights of the train as it entered upon the south end of the bridge. Alexander Maxwell was looking at the signal light to the north of the high girders. He noticed it flickering and wondered if it had set fire to its mounting. He then watched the train start going through the high girders and suddenly saw one, two and then three great flashes of light that lasted long enough for him to see the fretwork of the girders. Afterwards, he maintained that the flashes happened in front of the train although William Millar believed that the flashes had come from the train itself. He turned to his other friends and remarked that the fireman was drawing his fire and throwing the coals into the river.[1] Millar's last reported remark was, when he saw a white flash against the bridge: 'They're blowing steam now – the bridge is down!!!'

Peter Barron, a 56-year-old carriage inspector for the Caledonian Railway, was at home in Balgay Lodge, Blackness Road on the Dundee side of the river about half a mile inland from the north end of the bridge just above Magdalen Green. The north end of the high girders were thus about a mile distant from his house. At the height of the storm at about ten past seven he heard a loud crash outside even above the screeching of the wind and went out of his house to investigate. He found the rubble of one of his chimney cairns that had been blown from the roof into his front garden.

He then dealt with some broken glass at the rear of his home but before going back inside, he decided out of curiosity to go across the 20ft-wide Blackness Road to look at the bridge. He knew a train was due any minute and thought he'd observe how it fared in its crossing. To keep himself upright in the fierce wind, he clung onto one of the gateposts at his neighbour Mr Hunter's house. He waited, keeping his eyes on the bridge of which he could see the entire length. At about 7.15 p.m. according to his watch, there was an extra-heavy gust of wind which made him clutch even tighter to the gatepost. It was then that he saw first one high girder and then another break free and fall into the river. Mr Barron described what he saw:

> As far as I could guess in my mind it would have been about the first or second girders of the large ones. I immediately got nervous at once and I rubbed my eyes. In a second or so I saw another lump go. Just at that time, I saw the southernmost part of the high girders. I saw a blink of light and then the blink of light had cleared away. The moon was shining as clear as could be on the river and I saw the large piers from end to end.

Barron then struggled round to Henry Gourlay, a boat-builder and engineer who also resided at Balgay House, to tell what he'd seen. 'I have just come to say that the bridge is down,' said Barron, and his words were received with shock and astonishment. Gourlay initially doubted Barron's observations but because he knew Barron well and considered him very much a reliable man, he agreed that the two of them should go back out for another look. At first Gourlay could see nothing, perhaps because of the fitful moon being covered by scudding clouds. He was very anxious to believe that the bridge was not down and it took a minute's fixed gazing on Gourlay's part before he saw that the high girders were missing.

Brothers George and William Clark were at home at Magdalen Point and were looking at the train as it crossed the bridge. At the actual moment of horror, George had turned away but William cried out that he'd seen fire and feared that the train was over the bridge into the river. He noted three flashes of light and a cloud of spray or steam.

The training ship *Mars* was moored in midstream quite close to the bridge, bows to the west and facing into the gale. As Officer of the Watch, Seaman Instructor Hugh McMahon had the deck from 4 p.m. until 8 p.m. He was an ex-Merchant Service man, not Royal Navy, and held the job of boatswain. His duties were to keep watch generally and make hourly notes in the ship's log pertaining to changes in the weather. The log itself was kept under shelter at the top of a companionway. He later reported that because of Commanding Officer Captain Scott's concerns about a big blow coming along, all the boats and deck fittings aboard *Mars* had been lashed and secured against the danger of loss overboard. At 4 p.m. the wind was blowing WSW and was still doing so at 5 p.m. He recorded a barometer reading of 29.00 and noted it in his log. McMahon had served aboard *Mars* for two years and eight months and had never experienced a worse wind in the Firth of Tay as that on the night of 28 December. He estimated a Beaufort Scale reading of Force 10 to 11, a very strong gale with extra-hard gusts and squalls coming down with a great deal of noise. At around 7.12 p.m., the 'Edinburgh' had started out over the bridge and McMahon watched it battle its way across. When the train was just inside the high girders there was a sudden super-tremendous gust of wind which caused him momentarily to turn his back in defence against it. A few seconds later when he was able to look again, there was nothing but darkness on the river. No bridge, no train, no navigation lights visible – nothing but a black void. He noted by his watch that the time was 7.16 p.m. and entered the event in the ship's log. McMahon raised the alarm and *Mars* went to action stations as it were. Captain Scott called for volunteers to man a boat to row towards the bridge. The boat was duly lowered and conned with great seamanship and courage to avoid crunching into the pier stumps, but nothing and no one was found.

Captain John Greig, 65 years old, was the Superintendent of Lights at Tayport on the south bank near the mouth of the Tay. By then he'd held the job for twenty years and from the 67ft high lighthouse tower just beneath Spears Hill he had a direct sight line to the bridge, some 3¾ miles upstream. He'd come on duty that afternoon at 4 p.m., which was lighting-up time, went home at 5 p.m. and then returned at 7 p.m. The wind was blowing hard in squalls causing a tremulous motion in the tower which made him very uneasy. The whole structure was vibrating and shuddering continuously. Only once ever before had this happened with a westerly gale and that was back in 1859. He reckoned the gusts this Sunday night were far more severe.

Retired businessman Charles Clark lived at Westfield Lodge in Magdalen Green, close to the north end of the bridge. He'd kept a daily weather log for the past fourteen years simply for his own amusement and as a hobby. He had his own private wind-scale from zero to six and he reckoned that tonight's gale was a '6' for sure. The lowest barometer reading he recorded was 29.00 and that was at 5 p.m.

William Robertson had been the Harbourmaster at Dundee for eight years and remembered well how the afternoon had unfolded on 28 December. The high tide that day had been at 2.30 p.m. and the weather was moderate. He was at his office at about 5.45 p.m. when he described the weather as 'blowing fresh'. He intended as usual to go to church that evening but as he left his office and observatory at about five past six to go home and collect his wife for Sunday worship, he remembered how quickly the wind had started to gust up.

He had some difficulty turning the corner at the tidal basin, which was an exposed spot, and when he reached the west end of the Custom House and was clear of the sheds and their shelter, he caught the full force of the gale that had now begun in earnest.

This was at around ten past six. When he got home after a tough struggle against the wind, he told his wife that it was not safe for her to come to church with him and brave the windswept streets with their falling chimney cairns. He accordingly went out again on his own. While in church after he'd got there fighting against the storm, Mr Robertson noted how heavy the squalls had become. Then, a little after 7 p.m., something very strange happened. To him, it seemed like the side of the building or some of the roofing had given way and it sounded as if something was rolling along the roof and was making so much noise that it became impossible to hear what the minister was saying from the pulpit. He feared for the safety of the building. There was a particularly furious gust of wind at that moment, which was 7.16 p.m. by his watch.

Another member of the congregation who glanced at the clock just then was amateur meteorologist William McKelvie. Robertson left the church just as the service was over at around 8 p.m. to find the roads strewn with chimney cairn fragments, doors off their hinges and strips of zinc roofing. He heard from someone outside that something had happened to the Tay Bridge which prompted McKelvie, overhearing this, to return to his own house and to look down on the firth from an upstairs window. When the moonlight was clear against the scudding clouds he could see that the bridge's high girders were gone. Meanwhile, Robertson set out for Dundee Tay Bridge station and found a number of people milling round waiting for the 8 p.m. local service to Newport. It was manned by Guard Shand (the man who stated that he wouldn't cross the bridge again that night for £500), and Driver Alexander Kennedy. There was talk at that time about something being amiss but it didn't seem properly known. Stationmaster Smith and Locomotive Foreman Roberts had already left in an attempt to walk along the bridge to see for themselves. No one at the station at that moment knew that the bridge was down but just then, a since unidentified gentleman ran in to say that the Edinburgh train was 'over the bridge'. He didn't say that the bridge itself was down but implied that the train had gone into the river. At this point William Robertson resolved to return to the observatory above his office and take a good look at the bridge through one of the powerful telescopes there. He took the gentleman witness with him, seeing as he could get no sense from anyone else at the station. The observatory had two very large telescopes and a weatherglass but no anemometer for wind speed. On arrival he shut all the lower doors to prevent the wind roaring through the observatory and causing damage when he opened the west window, which faced in the direction of the bridge. Using one of the telescopes, Robertson commenced a visual sweep of the length of the bridge starting at the north end. He traced the line of the bridge as far as the foremast of a ship lying in the river (which was probably the Pladda) but as he tracked on past the mast he could see there was no more bridge visible and told the gentleman as much. He started another pan, this time from the south end and again came to a gap. Robertson said, 'There is no bridge, the bridge is gone.' He knew then that all the navigation spans or high girders had disappeared. To make absolutely sure, he sent a man back to his house to pick up a pair of night glasses.[2] He and the gentleman then went to the Tay Ferries Superintendent's office to get another look but could see nothing from there. Finally, they went down to the esplanade to look upriver at the bridge. 'Of course,' he said later, 'the thing was very plain. With the night glasses we could see all the stumps standing.'

Stationmaster Smith and Locomotive Foreman James Roberts determined to get to the bottom of the missing train mystery – had it made the crossing part-way and then gone down into the river with the bridge? Or had it stopped just in time before the gap and then reversed back to the south side? Henry Somerville, the North Box signalman, had already managed to report to Roberts that a couple of members of the public had told him that the bridge was gone. Later Somerville said that by 7 p.m., the wind was blowing 'a perfect hurricane. There had been nothing like it since I came to the bridge.' He'd felt the entire cabin shuddering in its exposed position and was alarmed at 6.30 p.m. when his chimney cairn blew off. Nevertheless, he didn't doubt the stability of the bridge.

The 'Edinburgh' was already by now thirty-three minutes late at the North Signal Box and there was still no sign of it whatsoever. All the signals were 'off' ready for its arrival in Dundee and had been so for over half an hour.

There was no way of knowing if the train had in fact stopped in time, not with the telegraph lines cut. The only way to find out, awful as it seemed, was for Smith and Roberts to walk out across the bridge to see for themselves. They managed to reach the North Signal Box against the wind and told Henry Somerville what they were going to do. They heard from Somerville the story as he knew it. He'd received the 'train entering section' signal from South Box signalman Barclay at 7.14 p.m. and expected the 'Edinburgh' to be at his own box in five more minutes. When it hadn't appeared by 7.23 p.m., Somerville tried staring out across the firth to see if he could discern the lights of the train. Nothing.

He then tried to use his 'speaking instrument' to call Barclay and also the telegraphic instrument. No result, nothing worked. Smith and Roberts then set out southwards across the bridge, an act of great bravery on both of their parts, seeing as they were walking into the unknown and the gale was still rampaging and threatening to throw them both over the bridge's side at any instant. This was all too much for Smith who collapsed, giddy and gasping with his arms around a handrail post. He simply couldn't go on. Roberts resolutely persisted alone into the nightmare of the storm. Eventually, although it must have seemed to him like forever and more, he reached the end of the low spans. He should have been able to see the high girders looming above him into the night sky but there was nothing. Crawling to within about 8yd of the last standing span he saw the gap. There were no high girders left, just nothingness.

This moment was wonderfully captured for the front page of the *Illustrated London News* edition of Saturday 10 January 1880, where the artist has drawn what Roberts must have seen.[3]

Roberts could see that the broken-off rails weren't twisted, just bent downwards. A huge jet of water was spurting from the severed end of the Newport water main and the ebbing tide was certainly swirling on something just below the water. More than that, he did not stay to discover. He crawled back northwards and reached Smith just where he'd left him, reporting that there was not a sign of the train except a red light in the far distance which might suggest that it had miraculously stopped just in time before reaching the gap. They both regained the north bank of the firth safely and Roberts went to the Harbour Office to try and get a boat out. Smith meanwhile went back to his station to telegraph what news there was to the NBR Head Office in Edinburgh using the Post Office telegraph, as the railway's own cable running across the bridge was severed.

Meanwhile, Harbourmaster William Robertson tried to arrange for the Dundee harbour tug to go up to the bridge. Unfortunately the tide had ebbed too far by now to get her afloat and the tug sat beached immovably upon her bottom. She couldn't move again until the incoming tide refloated her.

With that option gone for now, Robertson then made for the Tay Ferries office to see if the passenger ferry *Dundee* could do the job. Again he was thwarted as Captain Methven, the Ferry Superintendent, had just left aboard the *Dundee* to make a crossing of the Tay to Newport, having been stormbound since 6 p.m. There was nothing to do but wait for her return.

Considerable crowds had amassed both at Dundee station and the ferry pier, distraughtly eager for news, some news, any news. Reports of the events out on the bridge had raced around the city regardless of the storm still raging, and those with relatives on the train were amongst the first to gather. Wild speculation was rife: the train was in the river – the train had safely backed off the bridge and returned to Wormit – the bridge wasn't down at all and the train had simply been held at the South Signal Box because of the gale-force wind. There was some consolation from the passengers who'd crossed on the 'church train' who told of mighty wind gusts and sheaves of sparks from the wheels. But they had arrived safely, so maybe the 'Edinburgh' would so as well. Hope against hope rose, fell and rose again. Disaster is hard to accept because the human mind will always have an optimistic disbelief that shields it from the cold truth. So the crowds milled around in a state of denial, still hoping that the train would miraculously steam intact into Dundee station. The railway authorities at Dundee played somewhat cruelly on this, albeit only to prevent a possible surging panic, by suggesting that everyone went home because the 5.27 Edinburgh train's crossing had been held back until the gale moderated. Few in the crowd swallowed this line and the ranks were hardly diminished. Nearly everyone preferred to stay on the spot and wait – and wait.

At just about 9 p.m., the watching crowd at the ferry pier made out a boat approaching from the darkness. It was from the training ship *Mars* and everyone hoped for some concrete news. But the boat's crew had nothing to report from its perilous visit to the bridge at around 7.30 p.m. However, as Hugh McMahon on deck duty had actually seen the train crossing the bridge at 7.15 and then momentarily turned his back to shelter from the extra-strong gust, the fact that he then saw nothing more whatsoever proved finally that the train was lost. If it had not fallen into the river or had set back to the Fife side, McMahon would surely have seen its lights. After all the waiting and speculation, despair set in and the awful facts finally accepted. There was, however, the faint hope of survivors out there clinging to the pier stumps. While waiting for the ferry *Dundee* to return from Newport, *Dundee*'s Provost Brownlie organised a supply of blankets and food to be brought down to the quayside, ready to be put aboard the ferry when she arrived. *Dundee* appeared there at 10 p.m., having had to make considerable detours from the usual route of passage because of the wind and tidal currents. What's more, the ferry had not been able to approach the bridge during this crossing.

With the stores of materials for rescue and comfort quickly put aboard, Captain Methven took the *Dundee* out again, this time to head directly upstream for the long gap in the bridge. Harbourmaster Robertson was aboard now as she got herself round the middle bank and closed in as tightly as possible to the stumps. Robertson was the first man jumping into a lowered boat, which also had as crew two hands, a master rigger and one of *Dundee*'s captains. The river was running very heavily and the waves were littered with pieces of wood of all sizes, mostly planking from the bridge deck. No bodies or luggage were seen. The boat managed to pull along the entire length of the gap and Robertson could see the bare stumps with just two of them trailing broken iron columns. The crew called out desperately against the wind and water noise but were answered by silence, not survivors.

Meanwhile, back at the South Signal Box, Barclay and Watt by now knew what had happened. They determined that the dire news should be broken somehow to somebody in authority. Barclay decided to stay at his post while Watt ran back 2 miles down the line to St Fort to try and raise the alarm. Stumbling along the track into the teeth of the gale and endlessly stubbing his toes against the wooden sleepers he finally reached St Fort station and ran up the platform ramp towards the station building, but all was in darkness. Stationmaster Morris, porter Ingles and ticket collector Friend, with no more train services that night after the 'Edinburgh', had wasted no time in closing up the station and scuttling home out of the weather. Running to Stationmaster Morris's house hard by St Fort station, Watt managed to knock up Mrs Morris but she told him that her husband was out. (Goodness knows where Morris had gone in the storm and at that time of night.)

Forlornly now, Watt realised he must now run another 3½ miles further onwards to Leuchars Junction with his news. It must have been well after 8 p.m. by the time he arrived there. Watt was in a very sorry state, soaked through with rain and exhausted from the effort of pounding against the gale in the Stygian gloom but luckily Leuchars Stationmaster Thomas Robertson was just finishing up his paperwork with one of his staff and hadn't yet gone home. He was about to take his boots off when Watt gushed out his story to an incredulous Robertson who flatly disbelieved him, putting the tale down to the ranting of a madman. He was so convinced that Watt was rambling and talking nonsense that Robertson sent his porter out for the local doctor. After the GP had arrived and with further quizzing of Watt, Robertson was at last convinced that what he'd heard from the distraught man was in fact true. They all bundled themselves into the doctor's gig and set out the 5 miles to St Andrews, where the news had already been confirmed by the Caledonian Railway's telegraph from Dundee, the NBR's own line, of course, being severed when the bridge fell. So they turned around and went back to Leuchars where Robertson was sure he'd be needed soon when the news had reached Edinburgh. Thinking ahead, he reasoned that some sort of special train carrying NBR officials would turn up in a few hours, needing his presence. Around now, when the water remaining in their pipes had run out, many residents of Newport turned on their cold water taps for kettle-filling and expected the usual cascade. Instead, there was a mere dribble and a gurgle because the water main across the bridge had been severed by the fall. The water spraying in torrents from the broken pipe may have accounted for the 'blowing steam' noted by William Millar. Accordingly there were more than a few puzzled raised eyebrows from Newport householders wanting their evening cup of tea.

Although not a direct witness, seeing as he'd escaped death by getting off the train at Leuchars Junction, Mr William Linskill, on his visit to the Dean of St Andrews and travelling in the carriage sent for him, said later that 'during the journey the great gale seemed to gather itself for one mighty effort and bore down on us with a tremendous roar and crash. It seemed to surround us and get under our cab and lift it across the road.' The time, he noted, was 7.16 p.m. Most of the witnesses to the fall, although differing in their various opinions as to what they saw, seem to agree on one major point. There was an especially vicious gust of wind at 7.16 p.m., just when the train fell down with the bridge and at the time observed by many witnesses. Many of the passengers' watches stopped at that time or just after.

It was about 11 p.m. that a frantic knock on his front door at 6 Oxford Terrace in Edinburgh awoke Sir Thomas Bouch. A North British Railway messenger from Waverley station had run all the way with some appalling news – the great Tay Bridge had fallen and no one knew why or how at this moment. Bouch, with his son William, procured a cab to Waverley station, paying the standard charge from Oxford Terrace to the station of 1s 6d.

An emergency train had indeed been cobbled together just as Leuchars Junction Stationmaster Robertson had surmised. It carried Bouch, his son William and three North British Railway officials,[4] northwards to the scene. They'd all been unceremoniously sprung from their firesides and beds and arrived at Waverley station where they huddled together bemusedly and saying little. They were taken from Waverley to Granton, there to embark on the wagon ferry *Leviathan*. Being larger than the passenger ferry *William Muir* she would be more stable in the unruly waters of the Forth because, although the storm had now mostly passed, the river would still be seething for some hours to come. The ship was ballasted by a load of empty goods wagons which were trundled aboard to lower the waterline and to make her heavier in the water and less likely to be tossed around.

On arrival at Burntisland, the luminaries of the NBR joined a hotchpotch train to take them to Tayport and the ferry thence to Dundee. The previous train to have crossed Fife northwards was of course the doomed 5.27 p.m. from Burntisland so therefore, after her passage with no further traffic scheduled until the following morning, all the signal boxes were 'switched out' with their signals showing 'clear' in both directions. The signalmen had all sent their 'box switched out' message to each other after the passage of the 'Edinburgh' by dinging '7-5-5' on the block bells. When they reopened on the Monday morning, they intended to send each other the bell code '5-5-5' to re-open their boxes in readiness for the early morning 'Edinburghs' (6.25 a.m. off Dundee and 7.04 a.m. off Burntisland) and other local services which, of course, were never going to run that day.

The emergency train arrived at Leuchars Junction in the wee small hours at about 4 a.m. where Stationmaster Thomas Robertson noted Sir Thomas Bouch in a 'pitiful state of mind'. His evidence, seeing as he actually met Sir Thomas, seems to rule out the story that Bouch travelled to Dundee that night via the Caledonian Railway, as some chroniclers have averred. Poor Stationmaster Robertson had had a very rough evening because just after the 'Edinburgh' had left for St Fort at 6.59 p.m. his wife had complained about the shaking of the west wing because of the gale hitting the station house. This was where his children were trying to sleep, so he moved them all to the east wing, which was more sheltered. Then, a while after that as we've seen, John Watt from Tay Bridge South Signal Box appeared with his tale of woe. The NBR officials had disembarked from their special train and held a brief conference in the station office. They heard by telegraph from Stationmaster Morris at St Fort, who seemed to have returned from his outing, his estimate of 300 passengers aboard the train. It shows something of the agitation and distress of the NBR officials that they should take this number count as anything like accurate. There is no way that 300 people could have possibly been squeezed into the six little carriages of the 5.27 from Burntisland. However, Manager Walker used this data when he framed a press release, sent by telegraph from Leuchars Junction at 4.30 a.m. which read:

> From reports made to us here of the terrible calamity at the Tay Bridge, it appears that several of the large girders of the bridge, along with the last train from Edinburgh, were precipitated into the river about half past seven last night. There were, I deeply deplore to say, nearly three hundred passengers, besides company servants in the train, all of whom are believed to have perished. The cause of the accident is not yet ascertained.

Back in Dundee, further proof of the train's demise came in with news from Broughty Ferry, 5 miles downstream from the bridge, that mailbags had been washed up along the shoreline there along with a carriage destination board that read 'DUNDEE & BURNTISLAND'. The mailbags had been taken to the Custom House and then delivered to Miss Barclay, the postmistress. She immediately sent them by cab to Dundee.

The next morning, the Post Office sent men to search the north bank of the river. They found several more mailbags washed up on the beach at Carnoustie, 11 miles downstream from Dundee. These were taken to Dundee Head Office and after being dried, the letters were delivered by second post on the Monday afternoon with apologies from the GPO for the lateness of delivery.

A few days later the valet to the Bishop of Glasgow presented his master with a damp letter and apologised for its condition. 'It's been in the Tay,' he said.

On the Monday morning, 29 December, the dawn was sluggish in coming up, almost as if it was unwilling to reveal the destruction in the cold light of day. Everything appeared paralysed. The scene was unreal, the silence complete. The storm had vanished, leaving a deathly calm. Smooth leaden waters covered everything as if it had all been a bad dream – except for the brutal reality of the stumps of the lost spans sticking up from the tideway. Dundee Tay Bridge station was a wilderness of broken glass.

The NBR's arch rival for many years was surprisingly magnanimous in its attitude concerning the disaster. The Caledonian Railway did its very best to help the re-timetabling of NBR services over their lines and was sympathetic in very many ways, for instance organising ticketing, and making arrangements for goods traffic and the use of its railway lines. The Caledonian may have been implacable in battle but was ever merciful to an enemy in distress.

Notes

1 This of course is not what was done. Fireman Marshall would never have started to draw his fire and throw it overboard because that duty was all down to the fire-dropping crew at Dundee Engine Shed. Apart from anything else in footplate practice the whole idea constituted a fire risk, one reason why the entire bridge had been ballasted the whole way across just a few months earlier in order to absorb any live coals falling from engine grates.
2 Night glasses are binoculars with large-diameter objective lenses which can gather and concentrate more light, enabling the user to see better in low-light conditions.
3 However, the artist shows the bridge decking as plain planking, without the ballast that had been added some months previously.
4 They were: Mr Walker (NBR Manager/Company Secretary), Inspector McClaren (NBR Passenger Superintendent) and Mr James Bell (NBR Civil Engineer).

14

INQUIRY

〜

'A scientist will never show any kindness for a theory
which he did not start himself.'
'First get the facts. Then distort them at your leisure.'

Mark Twain

Truth and history rarely rhyme.

Unknown source

Two of a trade cannot agree.

Old Proverb

Der Teufel steckt im detail
(The Devil resides in the detail)

Goethe

You'll note that this chapter heading is 'Inquiry' not '*the* Inquiry'. I don't wish to iterate the verbatim proceedings of the official inquiry, which have been well quoted and at length by other authors on this subject. But I have cited references from it when appropriate. Some material evidence that did not make it to the official grilling of the Board is of great interest and throws up some fascinating data, indeed some of it deliberately suppressed by the machinations of the North British Railway and their legal team. It has been alleged that the lawyers 'nobbled' some of the witnesses they thought possibly hostile to the interests of the NBR by regaling them in a pub or a bar and getting them drunk the night before their testimonies were due to be heard, the aim being to make them so intoxicated that their subsequent hangovers caused them to fail to appear as witnesses.

In the very early hours of the Monday morning after the debacle, newspaperman John Malloch from the *Dundee Advertiser* was able to use the Caledonian Railway's cable line to send out the first reports to the world. The headlines included a figure of 200 casualties, which was obviously wrong – the number of seats available in the five passenger-carrying vehicles was less than half that figure; but the apparent death toll deeply disturbed Queen Victoria when she was told. Sir Henry Ponsonby, on behalf of Her Majesty, sent Provost Brownlee in Dundee a telegram expressing her shock. It wasn't until Station Agent Morris from St Fort station, came over the river by ferry later that morning with a cardboard box of fifty-seven collected tickets, that the casualty list was revised downwards. Morris reported that ten or eleven through passengers kept their tickets, as did two season-ticket holders. There were quite a few children under 5 years of age who didn't require tickets, plus seven railway employees, making an apparent total of seventy-five persons. As dawn broke and the sun came up at 7.48 a.m., the river was running smoothly, lapping gently around the stumps of the broken piers with all the ferocity of the previous night gone. It was almost as if it were saying, 'Who, ME?' like a child caught next to a broken window with a ball in its hand. The government immediately ordered the Board of Trade to begin an inquiry. It didn't take long to pick the investigators and they were very soon on their way to Dundee. Meanwhile, a relief fund was hastily set up to help those families who had lost their main breadwinner in the disaster.[1]

Across Britain, all the newspapers swept their planned lead stories aside to report the Tay Bridge Disaster. The Kabul massacres in Afghanistan lost their front-page status in the stead of the Tay Bridge collapse. The news impacted upon the nation as a whole. Not only the bridge but also Great Britain's pride in her engineering industry and prowess had fallen into the Tay and the populous were very angry indeed at this seeming betrayal of the nation's reputation. How could this gigantic 3,465yd-long bridge (all but 55yd short of 2 miles), the pride of Scotland which strode high over the Tay estuary and a worldwide-acknowledged icon of British achievement, have come to grief so early in its life? The outraged public at large needed someone to blame and vilify, wanted explanations as to how this could possibly have happened, and it needed such information fast.

On the river and around the broken piers, the first tentative explorations as to what had happened the night before were being made. Various divers made descents into the muddy sand-fugged depths of the Tay near the bridge site to see what they could find. Everyone waiting ashore wanted bodies but in this wish they were to be sadly disappointed, at least at first. At Dundee Tay Bridge station a room was laid out with tarpaulins (actually goods-wagon sheets) ready to accept the bodies as they were recovered so that relatives could make positive identifications and examine the personal effects of the victims. On Tuesday 30 December, three divers were at work. John Cox went down north of the fourth collapsed pier when he found a carriage but no bodies. Diver Simpson found engine No 224 near the fifth pier but again, no bodies. Diver John Barclay also found no trace of the passengers. This underwater exploration continued for some days and the results gave some evidence to the newly convened Board of Inquiry a day or so later. But what everyone wanted was bodies. Ann Cruickshanks was the first to be pulled out of the river, the alleged jewel thief whom we first met in chapter nine. It took some weeks for all the corpses to be washed up or retrieved from the Tay but in the end, only forty-six bodies were recovered.

Before seeing the evidence presented by the witnesses at the Board of Inquiry and noting the findings of that board, it's worth examining the qualifications and experiences of the Board members. The court was set up by Lord Sandon, President of the Board of Trade and included three gentlemen of note in the engineering world: Mr Rothery, Colonel Yolland and Mr W.H. Barlow.

Taking them in alphabetical order, let us examine their fitness to judge the reasons for the failure of Bouch's structure. What were their CVs?

William Henry Barlow was born in 1812 and lived just into the next century, expiring finally in 1902. His credentials as a qualified engineer included the wonderful train shed at St Pancras station, the London terminus of the Midland Railway. He built this single-span of 240ft out of wrought iron between 1864 and 1868. He was born in Charlton in south-east London, the son of engineer and mathematician Professor Peter Barlow, and grew up close to Woolwich Dockyard, spending his formative years studying engineering with his father and working in Woolwich Dockyard's machinery department. Then there were six years working in Constantinople, building an ordnance factory, before returning to England as an assistant engineer on the Manchester & Birmingham Railway in 1838. He joined the Midland Railway in 1842 but by 1857 had his own consulting practice. He was always an active member of the Institution of Civil Engineers and was involved in the design for the Great Exhibition building (later known as the Crystal Palace) in 1851. He finished off the work on the Clifton Suspension Bridge in Bristol in 1864 after the untimely demise of its designer, Isambard Kingdom Brunel. After the Tay Bridge Inquiry, he and his son Crawford went on to design the replacement viaduct across the Tay.

Henry Cadogan Rothery, the Chairman of the Inquiry, was a maths graduate and a trained barrister. Born in 1817 in London, his father, William Rothery, was the Chief of Office of the King's Proctor in Doctors' Commons. Educated at St John's College Cambridge he graduated in 1840 with a BA and then later as an MA. After leaving university, he entered Doctors' Commons and from 1842 practised in Ecclesiastical and Admiralty courts. He married Miss Madelina Garden in 1851 but the union was childless. On 26 November 1853 he was appointed Registrar of the Admiralty Court and soon became the Registrar of the Privy Council in Ecclesiastical and Admiralty cases. By 1860 he was the legal advisor to Her Majesty's Treasury, especially with regard to proceedings arising from the slave trade. Because of his large experience gleaned from the Court of Admiralty, he was appointed, in 1876, Commissioner of

Wrecks, the post extant today, the new title being Receiver of Wrecks. His duties were to investigate shipwrecks and casualties at sea. His inquiries indicated many preventable causes of maritime loss. His judgements on fire at sea, methods of stowing grain, ship stability and overloading were especially valuable inputs to maritime safety.

The last of the triumvirate, Colonel William Yolland, was born in 1810 in the village of Plympton St Mary[2] in South Devon, the son of a land agent to Lord Morley.

He was a military surveyor, astronomer and engineer. He became the Chief Inspector of Railways from 1877 until his death in 1885. He was ever a redoubtable campaigner for railway safety, often after strong opposition at a time when railway investment was being directed towards the expansion of the networks rather than the prevention of accidents.

So one may conclude that these were a highly qualified team to form the Board and get to the bottom of the tragedy. Not only were the members very experienced in the world of engineering but also all had an inclination to dispense justice and a sharp eye for scotching future faux pas. The *onus probandi* for what had happened to the bridge during design, construction and service sat squarely upon their shoulders, and they acquitted themselves admirably until perhaps the final report, where some members begged to differ, particularly about the apportionment of blame.

The proceedings were conducted by Mr Trayner, the Sheriff of Forfarshire, who later went on to become one of the top judges in Scotland. In addition, lawyer Mr J.B. Balfour was there to represent the interests of the North British Railway and lawyer Mr Bidder appeared for Sir Thomas Bouch throughout the hearings. All six men were able to ask questions of witnesses and to cross-examine if they so wished. The whole thing was definitely not a trial as there were no accused defendants and no guilty/not guilty/not proven verdicts (don't forget we are dealing with Scottish law!) to be pronounced. No one was in the dock. However, later in the inquiry, when Sir Thomas Bouch was called to give his evidence, the atmosphere certainly seemed more like a trial and Bouch began to look like he was in the dock.

The first sitting began at Dundee Courthouse on Saturday 3 January 1880 and heard evidence from eyewitnesses on the night of 28 December. It adjourned on 6 January and reconvened on 26 February, hearing more testimonials from a wider viewpoint of subjects, including the preposterous activities at the Wormit Foundry, of which we've already heard about in the 'Iron and Cupar' chapter. Adjourning again on 3 March, the inquiry venue moved to Westminster Hall on 19 April, this time to hear evidence from, among others, Sir Thomas Bouch himself.

During the court sessions, alarming evidence arose from witnesses, who were convinced that the trains were going too fast. Some of them began to time their crossings and calculated speeds of up to 40mph instead of the set limit of 25mph. This seemed to occur especially in the mornings with the commuter trains from Newport to Dundee. Since the Tay Bridge had opened, the little towns of Wormit, Newport and Tayport had swollen into dormitory towns for Dundee and the morning trains to Dundee quite often were made of up to eleven packed carriages. It appeared that the drivers were racing the passenger ferries still in use from Newport on Tay to Dundee. Some of these passengers were upset enough about the bridge movements that they could feel through the carriage floors that they stopped using the northbound trains and went back to the ferries. Provost Robertson was one regular passenger who became, like many others, perturbed at the excess speed of the trains and the damage being done to the bridge. Once Robertson timed a morning local at 43mph and on arrival at Dundee complained to Stationmaster Smith. He said (paraphrasing the court transcript) that 'I noticed a frightful vibration of the bridge both lateral and vertical. Undoubtedly the bridge was moving laterally, both vertical and lateral motions were quite perceptible. It was a very bad ride.'

Robertson shared his misgivings with John Leng, the editor of the *Dundee Advertiser* newspaper who was also a regular morning commuter. He estimated that one in ten of the local trains exceeded the speed limit. Altogether Robertson complained to Stationmaster Smith three times and although Smith claimed he'd cautioned the train drivers, nothing seemed to change. By November 1879 Robertson was so disturbed at the excess speeds and the bridge's behaviour that he went back to using the ferries.

The court quizzed all the drivers of the morning locals about the speed of trains on the northbound crossings. To a man, they stuck to their guns and flatly denied going too fast. Of course they were in fear of their jobs if they said anything that might put any responsibility on the North British Railway and consequently perjured themselves.

When Henry Noble, the inspector of brickwork (but not iron!) gave evidence, he told of hearing chattering noises in the piers which were caused by the tie-bars becoming loose. Without telling Bouch, on 21 October 1878 he bought a five-pound length of iron bar from Nicholls, the ironmonger in Ward Road, Dundee. He sawed this up into discs and used these pieces to pack out the looseness between the gibs and cotters where the tie bars were fixed to the cast-iron lugs. In his ignorance, all he was doing was setting the columns in their already distorted configuration, but the traffic was making the cross bracing more and more slack so that more tie bars were chattering. Noble had twice more to buy iron bars to cope with the increasing demand.

In August 1878 the Dundee Water Commissioners began the construction of a six-inch water pipe to cross the bridge beside the track. The water main was to serve the inhabitants of Newport and district and also gave the NBR a free water supply for putting out any fires on the bridge. Mr Bailey Thompson laid the pipe and during this work he observed that when trains passed, the bridge oscillation had a range of several inches. Then Alexander Stewart, who was a Dundee joiner, got the job of making wooden boxing for the pipe at a quote of £512 8s 4d. He and his men worked on this task from May to about the end of October 1879. He described the side-to-side movement of the bridge which was especially noticeable where the high girders and the low girders joined. When a train passed, an up-and-down movement was also readily felt. Stewart estimated the lateral movement to be about 3in, which was visible when he looked along the line of the girders.

Engineer Charles C. Lindsay travelled over the bridge in late December 1879, very close to the time of its demise. He remarked that he was surprised at the bad treatment the bridge received from passing trains but he was never called to give this kind of evidence at the inquiry. Whenever possible, the NBR picked its witnesses carefully. Anyone who seemed liable to give evidence of any shortcomings in the bridge was not invited to be a witness.

When Henry Noble found evidence of some of the columns actually splitting, due to their having been filled with Portland cement which had since expanded inside, he did tell Sir Thomas Bouch, who then recommended the fitting of iron straps around the cracks. We've already heard in the Rainbow Bridge chapter how Noble had his own way of testing cracks in the columns with a wet notebook page and a ginger-beer bottle stopper wire. This kind of ignorant inspection would be hilarious were it not for the fact that a great loss of life would shortly occur because of its shortcomings and, as we know, the NBR board reduced Noble's maintenance staff and cut their wages so that in the end, the entire bridge was in the sole charge of Mr McKinney, the lamplighter. The inquiry board never got to hear of this state of affairs and thus the NBR escaped censure for their cheapskate methods.

Now to the vexed question of the wind and what part it might have played in the demise of the bridge. At the Board of Inquiry Sir Thomas Bouch was asked if he'd made any allowance for wind pressure when designing his bridge and he'd answered 'not specially'. Some historians have since taken this reply out of context when in fact the truth is somewhat different. Bouch had really been to great lengths to get expert advice about wind pressure on bridge structures and wanted very much to include any data available to help him in his designs. He collected all the available information on the subject and wrote firstly to the Astronomer Royal, Sir George Airey, to expand his information.

Regarding Sir George Airey, many British scientists of the period ventured to pronounce on engineering matters and frequently made complete fools of themselves, such as Dr Dionysius Lardner.[3] Even the great Sir Humphrey Davy (inventor of the miner's safety lamp) was arrogant in his refusal to believe that an unlettered colliery engine-wright such as George Stephenson could possibly have invented a miner's lamp as good as his own. Which of course is what George Stephenson had done and according to history he gets no credit for it.

Only the pontificating of Sir George Biddel Airey, the Astronomer Royal, equalled Lardner's pseudo-scientific drivel. He announced in a pamphlet that the Crystal Palace, the building housing the Great Exhibition of 1851, would most certainly blow down. He then damned the idea of the transatlantic telegraph project saying: 'it was a mathematical impossibility to submerge a cable at so great a depth. Even if it were possible, no signals could be transmitted through so great a length.'

A characteristic of such men was an impossible-to-penetrate self-esteem, which led them to persist in their follies no matter how many times the engineers and cold hard facts proved them wrong. Sadly, Aireys's final fatuity may have had disastrous consequences. Thomas Bouch consulted Sir George Airey as to what wind pressure he might expect to blow against his projected Forth Bridge. On 5 October 1869 Airey replied: 'I think we may say that the greatest wind pressure to which a plane surface like that of the bridge will be subjected in its whole extent will be ten pounds per square foot.' Bouch then assumed he could use this figure for his Tay Bridge. In view of Airey's earlier dogmatic pronouncements on other matters, Bouch should have known better than to trust such a statement.

However, Bouch was indeed very concerned about the wind forces that might play against his bridge but there was a dearth of material to consult. Bouch tried to collect all the available data on the subject, including John Smeaton's paper for the Royal Society in 1759 wherein he stated that a high wind would produce a pressure on a structure of 6lb/sq. ft or, with a very high wind, 8 to 9lb/sq. ft. Clearly this was not only wrong but also hopelessly out of date.

There was a particular irony concerning Bouch and wind pressure. Not content with Airey's opinion, he then consulted Colonel Yolland at the Board of Trade with the same queries. Bouch wrote to him on 5 October 1869:

> In calculating the strain of malleable iron girders will you kindly tell me what you take the live load as per running foot for spans over a hundred feet and is it necessary to take the pressure of the wind into account for spans not exceeding two-hundred feet, the girders being open lattice-work? My own opinion is that one and a quarter tons per foot run for live load is sufficient for spans over one-hundred feet and that it is not necessary to take the force of the wind into account where open-work girders are used with spans less than two hundred feet. <u>I merely ask this information that I may act in accordance with the views of the Board of Trade.</u>

It's clear from that last sentence that Bouch was trying his humble best to do what was right and was not ignoring the problem.

However, Colonel Yolland's prompt reply on 8 October 1869 was emphatic:

> A ton and a quarter per foot run will be sufficient for spans over one hundred feet and we *do not take the force of the wind into account when open lattice girders are used for spans not exceeding two-hundred feet.* [Author's italics]

The supreme irony here of course is that Yolland was now sitting in judgement on Bouch for implementing the very information that he himself had supplied! Yolland was most aware of this, which may very well have led to the two separate inquiry reports, Mr Rothery's and the Barlow/Yolland version which begged to differ from Mr Rothery's far more scathing pronouncements. Barlow himself, like Yolland, had approved of Bouch's bridge design and had said so in writing. Which put two-thirds of the Board's members in a very difficult position indeed. They could hardly vilify Bouch after they'd agreed with his pre-construction plans and intentions without calling into question their own professional reputations.

On 30 April the witness everyone had been waiting for was called to give his evidence: Sir Thomas Bouch. One wonders if he thought about some of the illustrious predecessors who had sat to be judged in this very same Westminster Hall – men like Sir Thomas More or King Charles I. They ended up going to their doom and very soon Bouch was to follow. He stuck tenaciously to his theory that his bridge was not at fault but that it was the violence of the wind that had derailed the second-class carriage, causing that vehicle to collide with the girder work and bringing on a shockwave that was sent along and down the bridge, causing it to collapse. The North British Railway was very much on Bouch's side here. It was anxious that the inquiry should show that the collapse was due to the unprecedented force of the storm. The NBR Board did not want any hint of structural weakness, which could lay it open to claims for damages from the families of those killed. Mr Trayner asked the crucial question as to why the bridge fell. Sir Thomas maintained that the fracturing of two of the tie-bars as a result of the carriage hitting the girder work would be enough to bring the bridge down. He basically admitted that if just two struts were to go, then the whole of the high girders section would go as well. This was tantamount to saying that his design couldn't even take the light shock of a 5-ton vehicle's bump without causing a fatal structural failure. This was a shocking self-indictment and he was a ruined man from that moment on.

Benjamin Baker, a member of the Institution of Civil Engineers, was called as an expert witness to the inquiry on 6 May 1880 and initially examined by Mr Bidder. Baker's credentials and achievements in the world of civil engineering may be found in the chapter Coda. He thought that the failure of the bridge was something much more than just wind pressure. Referring to pictures taken not only of the bridge remains but also of Dundee and its environs just after the accident by Valentines (the Dundee photographers hired by the court for evidence) it will be noted that most structures do not appear to have been much damaged by the wind. Mill chimneys are still standing and the signal boxes have no broken windows. Baker described how he'd experimented with window glass panes and wooden doors and figured the wind pressure was nothing like as bad as had been assumed.

Nevertheless, a glass windowpane can take a wind force of 80lb/sq. ft if evenly distributed, but of course Baker was unaware of the 'gust within a gust' phenomenon as explained by climatologist Dr Dennis Wheeler of Sunderland University. Dr Wheeler could be described as an 'archaeological meteorologist' as he is convinced that the weather holds the key to many crucial historical events. He has analysed the weather factors in great battles such as Waterloo and the Spanish Armada, finally making sense of some of the enigmas surrounding these events when the weather at the time was carefully considered. When consulted on the Tay Bridge storm, Dennis provided information that helped to reconstruct the weather that night. Analysis of observations from many sources such as ships' logs and other watchers often miles apart, enabled a detailed weather picture hour by hour to be produced. Most importantly Dr Wheeler stated that it is the buffeting caused by the sudden stress of strong gusts of wind that causes the most amount of damage. It is peak wind speeds that matter. Gustiness arises from the turbulent eddies formed by, and carried along with, the wind. It is now widely acknowledged that embedded within severe storms there are pockets of notably more violent winds. In a storm area there is general damage, some zones of little damage, but patches of real devastation which may be no more than a few hundred yards in extent. One of these sudden buffets was felt by many Tay Bridge Disaster witnesses at the time, at around 7.16 p.m. So although the general maximum wind speed on the night was calculated by Benjamin Baker to be not that high and many structures were left undamaged, this does not preclude a highly destructive and turbulent eddy being carried along within the main storm itself.

The total side area of the train presented to the wind that night was 1,758 sq. ft, including the engine, tender and the six carriages. The whole entourage weighed in at approximately 125–130 tons, this figure being vague to the extent of the weight of the passengers and their luggage not being known exactly. As Benjamin Baker had figured, the wind pressure that night was no more than 15 lb/sq. ft; it would require a pressure of more than 30 lb/sq. ft to capsize the train, a total pressure of 26,370 lb all up, but this was without considering the hidden 'super gusts' inside the main storm. Also, there are, strangely enough, the 'Principles of Flight' to be considered, which may help bolster theories pertaining to the second-class carriage derailment.

Daniel Bernoulli was a Dutch/Swiss mathematician who published his ideas in a book called *Hydronamica* in 1738. His idea, known as 'Bernoulli's Principle', is the reason that aeroplanes can fly. In a nutshell, the principle is that as a wing passes through the air, its curved upper surface and flat underside makes the air travel faster over the top of the wing than beneath it because it has further to go. This causes a reduction of pressure on the top surface making a higher pressure on the bottom surface. The pressure difference causes the wing to be pushed upwards, creating lift. You can prove this at home, using nothing more than a big tablespoon with its 'wing' cross-section and a running cold-water tap. Turn the tap on full blast and dangle the spoon loosely from two fingers and then gently introduce the spoon into the downward water flow. Imagine that the water flow is the moving air and the spoon the wing of an aircraft. You'll find that far from the water repelling the spoon, it is sucked into the water flow, pulling the spoon sideways with quite a noticeable tug. Of course, the force is going sideways but just imagine the whole thing turned through 90 degrees – you've got lift! I can just picture you all running for the kitchen cupboard and finding a tablespoon to stick under the tap. You won't be disappointed, the effect will occur and this is why aeroplanes fly and why also a light carriage such as the second-class vehicle in the train just before the luggage van could have been affected. All the carriages had curved roofs and flat undersides, much like a wing cross-section and with a strong wind blowing at right-angles to the vehicles, under Bernoulli's principle maybe the vehicle could have lifted a tiny amount above the rails, perhaps enough for its wheel flanges to derail, especially as the vehicle was just negotiating the kinked rail in the first high girder.[4] This fact was never brought out at the inquiry.

Physicist Bill Dow has always asserted that this kink in the rails was an important factor in the demise of the bridge. He states that the very light second-class carriage could possibly have derailed because of the extreme wind pressure on its left side, helped out by Bernouilli's principle, then run along the bridge deck until it collided with an iron trunnion bracing the girder work. Severe abrasion marks and damage to the right-hand side of the fourth high girder span certainly suggests that the second-class carriage may have scraped the girder work, but the marks seem too high, above carriage-roof level, for this to have happened while the span was still upright and the carriage would not have run along the decking that easily because the whole track bed had recently been ballasted with granite chippings which would have caused a severe drag on the wheels.

However, something happened to the last two vehicles that was different from what happened to the rest of the train and whatever it was remains an enigma. The other four carriages were damaged to a degree, mostly by the action of water and air pressure sweeping through them. But the guard's van and the second-class carriage were completely wrecked. Nothing was left of the second-class carriage above the solebars. Its whole bodywork had been reduced to matchwood. The entire scenario looks as if the guard's van had rear-ended the little second-class vehicle as if it had suddenly stopped and been telescoped.

Maybe if the light little carriage was off the rails, the ballast might have acted like a sand-drag on the wheels, giving the effect of a sudden brake application. The instant deceleration would have let the guard's van crash into it and smash it up, which looks like being the case. But this begs a further mystery in that one would expect severe physical injury to the passengers. Instead, the recovered bodies who were travelling in that carriage were hardly harmed and showed no traumatic or horrific injuries consistent with the damage to the vehicles.

However, Bill Dow's theories do offer the reason for all the carriage axles being bent except for those of the second-class carriage and the guard's van. This damage has never otherwise been satisfactorily explained. When the two last vehicles stopped almost dead, that shock would have broken the couplings between them and the rest of the train. A whiplash action of the five joined high girders sections then occurred as their support piers gave way, throwing the front four passenger vehicles into the air. The effect would have been like 'a clothes-line being plucked', as Bill Dow puts it. As the carriages crashed back down onto the decking (they would have missed the rails due to the gale still blowing them eastwards) the impact distorted the 4in steel axles. The engine and tender axles were not bent, indicating they were never off the rails until they were in the river. Being so very much heavier, No 224 and her tender would have been immune to the whiplash action.

Prior to the Tay Bridge Disaster, there was no known fact about a railway train being blown off a viaduct or bridge. It wasn't until the Owencarrow Viaduct Disaster of 30 January 1925 that a train was indeed actually blown off a viaduct.[5]

In 1875, Staithes Viaduct was built on the North Eastern Railway's Loftus to Whitby branch in the North Riding of Yorkshire. It was actually designed and built by Benjamin Baker himself and resembled Bouch's Belah Viaduct in that it was a pipe bridge with tubular cast-iron columns and was single track, similar in concept to the Tay Bridge but without using cast iron under tension. Only four years after the Tay Bridge fall, and obviously as a result of a lesson learned from that event, it had a special feature regarding wind. The bridge was fitted with an anemometer to warn the signalman at Staithes should the wind pressure be too great to allow the safe crossing of a train. This precaution was felt necessary as the viaduct, being near the coast and exposed to the full force of north sea gales, could be at risk when a train was crossing it. The anemometer was installed in 1884 and if the wind pressure reached 28lb/sq. ft, it rang a bell in the signal box. Staithes Viaduct was 770ft in length and stood 152ft above the bed of the beck[6] it crossed.

In recent years, several engineers and mathematicians have explored computer analyses concerning the factors involved in the fall of the bridge, some of which have never previously been considered. Tom Martin and Ian Macleod, both highly qualified mathematicians and engineers, carried out a series of computerised simulations of what might have caused the collapse. They found that the bridge was not strong enough to withstand the wind pressures on the fateful night. Their conclusions were that the wind alone precipitated the downfall. Fundamentally Martin and Macleod concluded that the bridge was blown over due to being under-designed for wind loading. With the weight of the train passing over at the moment of collapse, this merely raised the already high centre of gravity, which certainly didn't help the bridge's chance of survival.

However, Martin and Macleod's analysis was static. Dr Peter Lewis undertook a dynamic computer analysis where, in his words, 'things get much more complicated'. Dr Lewis's investigations also took into account the subject of metal fatigue. This was especially looked at in respect of the cast-iron lugs holding the cross bracing in the piers. It now seems clear that the constant tensioning and relaxing on the cast lug bolt-holes would eventually cause the brittle cast-iron lugs to facture, allowing the bracing bars to become detached and thus leaving the upright columns with ever-lessening support. This is borne out by the examination of the excellent wreckage pictures taken by the Dundee photographic firm of Valentine's for use at the inquiry. Dr Peter Lewis made a careful study of these pictures and referred the whole thing to forensic metallurgists Ken Reynolds and Professor Roderick Smith, who, after poring diligently over these photographs with the cast lugs at high magnification, confirmed that fatigue stresses had indeed been present and had caused many of the lugs to snap. Professor Smith mentioned that a low-cycle fatigue, such as was found in the Comet jetliner aircraft failures in the 1950s, was probably present in the Tay Bridge collapse. Referring once again to Lewis's dynamic analysis, the towers became more and more un-braced over time as lugs failed, unnoticed by the cursory and wholly unsatisfactory so-called 'inspection' methods. Side winds and the passage of trains on the bridge decking above conspired to cause oscillation to occur. The bracing bar connections in the towers failed at first one by one, in small numbers, and went unnoticed by the tiny maintenance crew. These failures probably happened slowly over most of the nineteen months the bridge was in use but, as more and more went, the structure became more and more vulnerable to resonance, a vicious downward circle. By the night of 28 December 1879 the bridge was in a very critical condition indeed and only needed a strong enough wind plus the weight of a train to cause an oscillation which the structure was unable to stand any longer.

Far from needing a full-on gale to do this, even a relatively light wind would have been sufficient. On the fateful night, the wind was the agent of the resonance and oscillation taking place. The actual passage of trains across the bridge exacerbated the resonance problem further.

Two famous cases of wind causing oscillation and resonance in bridge structures are the Tacoma Narrows Bridge in Washington State USA, near Puget Sound, in 1940 and the Millennium Bridge over the Thames in London in 2000.[7]

Both of these are examples of what happened to the Tay Bridge when resonance occurs and is allowed to run on unchecked.

Very strong suggestive evidence that the Tay Bridge was indeed subject to severe oscillation came from the testimonies of the bridge painters at the inquiry. David Pirie had the chance to tender for the bridge-painting job during 1879. He carried out an inspection and although he didn't get the contract from the NBR, he was able to supply the Board with some fascinating evidence. He was checking out the bridge so as to calculate a quote for the job, which entailed him having to walk over the structure to ascertain the size of the task before putting in his figure. He saw bolts and screws lying in the booms but didn't know whether or not they were leftovers or had fallen from the structure. He noticed that vibrations occurred as soon as a train entered upon the bridge, which he described as a 'wavy motion'. When questioned further, he admitted that the motion increased as the train got nearer to him. The latticework in the high girders he said 'vibrated very much and noisily so'. He described it as a very violent vibration dependent upon the speed of the trains. There was a wavy motion in the bridge as an approaching train neared him and this motion was very great as the train passed him.

Peter Robertson was a painter on the bridge and employed by Mr Bamlett of Sunderland, who was finally contracted to paint the bridge. Mr Robertson worked from four to five weeks during June and July of 1879 in and around the area of the high girders and he also came across large quantities of loose screws, nuts and bolts lying in the booms of the girders. Other members of the painting crew such as John Milne, Peter Donegany, David Dale, John Gray and John Nelson all testified to finding considerable numbers of bolts and screws all along the length of the bridge. They also all agreed to being concerned and somewhat frightened by the way the bridge shook from side-to-side and also appeared to have an up-and-down movement whenever a train crossed. They reported that if they hadn't actually tied their paint pots to the girders with string, the pots would have been shaken off into the river, such was the extent of the shuddering.

Thomas Bouch was convinced that the wind had blown his bridge down. In his inquiry evidence he proposed that the second-class coach had derailed and then collided with the girder ironwork. In his view the shock of such an impact was enough to cause the failure. If he thought that a 5-ton vehicle could collide with his bridge girders and thus precipitate a collapse, it was tantamount to saying that his huge iron construction could be compromised by a tiny jolt, as delivered by the light second-class vehicle, which doesn't say much for the integrity of the bridge design. He condemned his work out of his own mouth.

Having scoured all the evidence not only from the inquiry but from all the well-qualified luminaries such as Bill Dow, Tom Martin, Iain Macleod and Peter Lewis, I must confess that as an unqualified amateur I dare not come to a complete conclusion as to why the bridge collapsed that night the way it did. To think about Mark Twain's epithet at the front of this chapter, these highly qualified experts all fail to agree with one another. I can only conclude after immersing myself in all the evidence that maybe they were all correct in one way or another.

When the hearings finally were over on Saturday 8 May 1880, the Board retired to consider its findings. The Board had convened for a total of twenty-five days in three separate sittings and had asked 121 witnesses 19,119 questions. It made its report to parliament in June 1880.

In fact, two reports were submitted: Mr Rothery's and the one of Messrs Barlow and Yolland. They agreed on most aspects of the evidence. There had been no movement or settlement of the piers since construction and the wrought-iron girder work was of fair quality. The cast iron used in the columns was of fairly good quality although it had been very sluggish in melting and during the casting process, with probable 'cold shuts' occurring, causing unequal dimensions in the column thicknesses. These columns, although sufficiently strong enough to support the vertical weight of the girders and trains, were unfit to resist lateral wind pressure because of the weakness of the cross bracing and its fastenings. The imperfections in the work turned out by the Wormit Foundry were mostly due to bad or non-existent supervision. Maintenance and supervision of the bridge after construction and while in service was unsatisfactory. If, by the loosening of the tie-bars, the columns had gone out of shape, then merely introducing packing, as Henry Noble had done between the gibs and cotters, would only keep them tight in their distorted positions. The Board was critical of the allowance of trains to run through the high girders at much greater speeds than the 25mph limit imposed by Hutchinson after his original inspection prior to the opening. The fall was probably due to the ultimate failure of the cross-bracings, and imperfections in the columns would have contributed to the same result. However, Mr Rothery went on to criticise certain design problems such as the narrow base, the too-slight 'batter' or inclinations of the outer columns of each pier and the omission of spigots at their bases. He laid the blame for everything on Sir Thomas Bouch and ended his report thus (leaving the punctuation and grammar as originally written):

> The conclusion then, to which we have come, is that the bridge was badly designed, badly constructed and maintained, and that its downfall was due to inherent defects in the structure, which must sooner or later have brought it down. For these defects both in the design, the construction and the maintenance, Sir Thomas Bouch is, in our opinion, mainly to blame. For the faults of design he is entirely responsible. For those of construction he is principally to blame in not having exercised that supervision over the work, which would have enabled him to detect and apply a remedy to them. And for the faults of maintenance he is also principally, if not entirely, to blame in having neglected to maintain such an inspection over the structure, as its character imperatively demanded.

Not a word about the NBR and its cost-cutting maintenance manoeuvres.

Yolland and Barlow were not at all happy with Mr Rothery's use of the pronouns 'we' and 'our' in his report as these statements were Mr Rothery's opinions alone and did not reflect what Yolland and Barlow thought at all. From 9 July 1880, A.J. and J. Dickson, Bouch's solicitors, had an exchange of correspondence with Yolland and Barlow on the matter. They wrote:

> On perusing Mr Rothery's report we find it contains several most injurious (and, as we think, unjust) statements and charges reflecting on Sir Thomas Bouch, which appear to us to be inconsistent with the opinions and findings

contained in the joint report of yourself and Mr Barlow and which certainly are not countenanced by anything therein contained.

Barlow and Yolland acknowledged the letter and added that Mr Rothery was not warranted in representing their opinions as concurring with his own in matters not referred to in their report. The Dicksons sent a copy of these letters to the editor of *The Times* but it was all too late. Mr Rothery's report was the one that everybody had read and now believed word for word. Initially, the North British Railway had thought to let Sir Thomas carry on with the rebuild but was forced, after the public outcry against him, to dispense with his services. With Sir Thomas's name attached to the rebuilding proposal, it would never have got through parliament, so low had his fortunes and reputation now sunk.

On the upside, as a result of the inquiry, several measures were implemented immediately, and these are outlined below.

All Bouch-built bridges were to be examined, reinforced or rebuilt as necessary.

The Board of Trade approved the use of steel in bridge construction and outlawed any designs that involved cast-iron columns.

Regular and frequent inspections of bridges were to be made both during and following construction by Board of Trade personnel.

A Royal Commission was set up in 1881 with the subject to be examined being 'Wind Pressure on Railway Structures'. The Commission members included Barlow, Yolland, W.G. Armstrong, John Hawkshaw and G.G. Stokes. They carried out an extensive survey of wind speeds and pressures using anemometers at numerous locations. They set a maximum wind pressure of 56lb/sq. ft for the design of future bridges and recommended rules for applying this specification to bridges of differing construction in their report to the Board of Trade on 20 May 1881.

Far from merely 'shutting the stable door after the horse has bolted' these measures and the many more to follow made railway bridge building a far safer and more reliable undertaking for the future.

Notes

1   The Tay Bridge Disaster fund, with cash inputs from a myriad of sources including Sir Thomas Bouch and the NBR, was transferred in 1988 to the Piper Alpha Oil Rig disaster fund when all possible Tay Bridge claimants had long died. The balance of monies remaining, £4,068, was transferred to Aberdeen lawyers administering the oil rig fund, which catastrophe occurred in July 1988 and claimed 167 lives.
2   Oddly and irrelevantly that's where I just happened to attend primary school in the late 1950s and first heard of Yolland as one of Plympton's famous sons.
3   Dr Dionysius Lardner, an Irish scientific writer in the 1830s and 1840s was responsible for some of the most fatuous drivel of the time on matters such as Brunel's Box Tunnel, when he predicted the asphyxiation of passengers. In 1838 he said, 'Men might as well project a voyage to the moon

as attempt to employ steam navigation against the stormy North Atlantic ocean.' He was having a go at another of Brunel's creations, the *Great Eastern* steamship. The good doctor was ever the bane of Brunel while building the Great Western Railway. Strangely (or not, given his reputed sense of humour), Brunel allowed the doctor to make an idiot of himself by giving Lardner his personal train in which he roamed the partly completed GWR system to collect evidence that the enterprise was doomed to fail.

4   Refer to 14 (i) 'Bernoulli's Principle' in the chapter note section.
5   Refer to 14 (ii) 'The Owencarrow Viaduct Disaster' in the chapter note section.
6   Northern English word for a pebbly mountain stream.
7   Refer to 14 (iii) 'Wind-caused Oscillation and Resonance in Bridge Structures' in the chapter note section.

15

The Rebuild

Upon the wreckage of thy yesterday
Design thy structure of tomorrow

From a headstone in Rye Parish Churchyard, Sussex

One should not expect to solve a problem with the same level of intelligence that caused it.

Albert Einstein

Great as the worldwide shock had been, not to mention the damage to the bubble-burst boom economics of Dundee's industries because of the fall of Bouch's bridge, it was obviously essential that the bridge should be replaced as soon as possible, either by rebuilding the existing partly ruined structure or by erecting a brand-new construction in its stead. Many proposals were put before various parliamentary committees. They all suggested a double-track bridge which would give far greater stability than the first single-line effort, being that much wider at the base. One idea was to build a new bridge on the site of the old, sinking new caissons next to each original one and uniting the pair with a brick arch, so spreading the weight of the new superstructural girders over a wider base. On these duplicated caissons, the projectors of this new bridge intended to erect masonry piers supporting a wrought iron superstructure. No more cast iron in any shape or form to be used, let it be noted! There were various disabilities, however. To begin with, this was a reversion to Bouch's original plan and there was no clear evidence that the original caissons had not moved out of position in places. It was also doubtful whether the old caissons would be capable of bearing the much greater weight of the new masonry piers.

Furthermore, it was known that some of the old caissons had not been sunk anywhere near far enough into the riverbed and that considerable scouring had since occurred. During the short life of the old bridge, vast quantities of rubble had been frequently dumped around the caisson bases to prevent them from becoming undermined and dangerously unstable.

The North British Railway Board actually wanted Sir Thomas Bouch to build the replacement bridge but it was plain very quickly that this could not be countenanced because of the anti-Bouch feeling amongst engineers, the press and the public at large. So the Board regretfully dropped him from its plans.

The Parliamentary Committee urged the building of an entirely new bridge on different foundations and so the NBR duly commissioned W.H. Barlow to provide a feasibility study on restoring the bridge connection between Wormit and Dundee.

Barlow and his son Crawford, who were destined to become the designers of the new bridge, first undertook an elaborate and thorough programme of riverbed soundings and experimented to determine the amount of scour sustained by the piers of the old structure.

They carried out their borings at 500ft intervals along a line parallel to the centre line of the old structure. One can be sure that after sitting on the Board of Inquiry into the collapse of the first bridge and hearing all the horror stories, Barlow was determined not to make any of the mistakes perpetrated by Sir Thomas Bouch.

They sank a trial cylinder into the worst riverbed material, loaded it heavily and watched for the results. Their experiments showed that the building of the old bridge had caused the riverbed to sink near the piers, especially where the current of the ebb tide was most powerful. The trial cylinder was sunk in silt to a depth of 20ft. Then a concrete bottom was put in and the cylinder loaded until it exerted a gross weight of 7 tons to the sq. ft – twice the maximum anticipated for the new bridge. The settlement amounted to 5¼in. The weight was kept on for ten weeks but no further settlement occurred. In addition to this, the Barlows loaded two of the old piers with 1,500 tons of old railway metals, thereby exerting a gross pressure of 3 tons 12½cwt per sq. ft. One of the piers stood in clean sand and settled a mere ¼in. The other was in micaceous sand (that is chemically and physically related to aluminium silicate minerals) and this pier settled just 2in.

While carrying out their very thorough programme of riverbed soundings, such a far cry from Jesse Wylie's benighted efforts a few years previously, the Barlows plotted that on and near both riverbanks, the substratum consisted of rock. For about 900ft from the Fife shore at Wormit there extended a bed of sandstone, leading away from the shore material, which was whinstone. On either side of the rock bed was a layer of hard clay for a further 900ft and between the two clay beds lay an area of sand mixed in some places with 70ft-thick veins of clay.

Barlow and Son began to prepare their plans which they duly submitted at the end of 1880.

But a new difficulty arose regarding the attitude of the Board of Trade, which was insisting that all traces of the old bridge must be removed before work could commence on the new one. The Barlows had reckoned on using what was left of Bouch's structure as staging to assist the construction work on their bridge and this edict from the Board of Trade would make the rebuilding much more difficult. A great deal of wrangling and horse-trading went on about this matter until finally an agreement was struck that the old piers could be allowed to stay in position so long as they were cut down to high-water level and provided with visible warning lights for passing shipping. It is these stumps that can be seen today (a 28ft water-gap downstream of the present bridge or about 60ft bridge centre to centre), appearing seemingly as a long line of tombstones stretching out across the river and a grim reminder as to what happened on Sunday 28 December 1879. The parliamentary act green-lighting the new construction, the North British Railway (New Tay Bridge Viaduct) Bill received the Royal Assent in July 1881.

The engineering contractor appointed in October 1881 to actually build the new bridge was William Arrol & Company.

Arrol had evolved a method with cross-water bridges of building the bridge actually on land and then rolling and floating it out to its position later, making the construction that much safer for the workmen as well as it being easier to monitor the work quality. He invented and built a mechanical driller and a hydraulic riveter which also saved time and money as well as doing the jobs far better than by hand. No difficulty ever arose on his works which, by his ingenuity, he was not able to overcome by some new resource.

It is both ironic and sad that the North British Railway didn't engage Arrol as contractor for the first Tay Bridge when the chance was there, but the NBR Board went for the cheapest quote. If it had chosen a man such as Arrol to undertake the construction work, the bridge would never have fallen.

One cannot imagine William Arrol[1] being satisfied with Mr Jesse Wylie's cursory river-borings, or running the Wormit Foundry in the ramshackle way it operated, or countenancing the practices prevalent there due to lax supervision. He would certainly have questioned the use of inferior iron and would definitely have vetoed the use of cast-iron lugs as physical parts of the pipe uprights for the pier cross-bracings. Disagreement over this point could have instigated some heated debates and forceful arguments if Mr Arrol had worked with Thomas Bouch!

Not yet aware of the design faults and dubious constructional practices inherent in Bouch's Tay Bridge, Arrol did accept the contract for Bouch's outrageously bold suspension bridge across the Firth of Forth and had spent some thousands of pounds in preparatory work. Then the Tay Bridge fell down along with Bouch's reputation, ending the whole enterprise. Fresh plans were laid for both structures and Arrol got the job for both of them.

The general configuration of the new bridge would resemble the old because the same topographical factors that influenced Bouch applied to the Barlows' design. The approach from Fife is at a considerable height, the shore being bounded by high cliffs. On the Dundee side, the final spans had to come down to the level of the existing railway, which was only a few feet above the level of the Tay and also ran at right angles to the centre line of the bridge.

For these reasons both bridges resembled the letter 'J' with the tail cut short coming into Dundee on a sharp curve and a down gradient.

The total length of the replacement bridge which stands today is 10,711ft or 2 miles 50yd and 1ft. The straight section is 1 mile 1,038yd and 2ft. The structure begins at the south side with a brick-built approach viaduct consisting of four 50ft spans, known locally as 'The Wormit Arches'. These arches, at a height of 83ft at the southern abutments, also carried the double-track junction with the Tayport line and the main line from Leuchars Junction. Today that junction is redundant after the closure of the Tayport branch in 1969, which was no longer a necessary part of the Dundee commuting system after the Tay Road Bridge, opened in August 1966 by HM the Queen Mother,[2] connected Newport on Tay directly into the centre of Dundee. This structure was 7,312ft long and built at a low level across the Tay, approximately 31ft above the water and was the second Tay Bridge in less than a hundred years to be built by Sir William Arrol & Company. The great man had died in 1913 but his company lived on for many years as an international contractor for bridges and other works before being taken over by Clarke Chapman in 1969.

The new Tay Bridge maintained a height of 83ft over a level section as far as the fourth pier. Thence to Pier 28, the bridge deck follows a downgrade of 1 in 762, bringing it down to a height of 79ft. The section from Pier 28 to Pier 32 is level. After that the bridge follows a continuous downgrade on an incline of just over 1 in 113, the height at the northern abutment being only 26ft 6in above high water level. The north end curve of the 'J' is 21 chains radius and bears eastwards until the line of the bridge is parallel with the river.

The spans which lie over the water vary considerably in length and in this respect the bridge is identical with its predecessor. Certain of Bouch's girders were used again by the Barlows as there was nothing wrong at all with the wrought-iron work that Bouch had built. However, these originals were considerably reinforced by new girder work. To cross the bridge today means that one is actually travelling over large sections of Bouch's old Tay Bridge. More of the original wrought-iron girders surplus to use in the reconstruction were apparently employed in the structure of another Tay crossing, this being the Victoria Bridge which carried the B9099 road across the river at Caputh about 30 miles upstream from Dundee. By 1993, the bridge was replaced by a new parallel structure and subsequently demolished. The sets of cast-iron columns which had formerly supported the girders to the north of Pier 14 were removed during the construction of the new bridge and it is not known to what purpose, if any, these were put. Over the years, the remains of the high girders themselves were lifted from the riverbed and sold for scrap to an English engineering company, which used the wrought iron to build numbers of small railway engines for export. Each engine bore a cast plate recording the origin of its metal and John Prebble notes that up to 1955 or thereabouts, one of these engines was still at work in southern Spain.

After the Wormit Arches comes a single span of 118ft, then ten of 129ft each, followed by thirteen of 145ft and then the new 'high girders' in the same mid-stream position as Bouch's old high girder section. Like the original bridge, the railway lines pass through the girders rather than sitting on top of them. However, these new navigation spans are at a height of only 77ft above high water, rather than 88ft and there are only eleven of them at 245ft in length as opposed to thirteen in Bouch's original work. After this part comes two spans of 227ft, one of 162ft, eleven of 129ft, twenty-four of 71ft and one of 56ft. Finally, the esplanade spans connect the main part of the bridge with the original brick arching leading downhill towards the yards and Dundee Tay Bridge station. They comprise two wrought-iron skew arches, four 66ft girder spans, a curved-top or bowstring span of 108ft and a short brick arch connecting with the old arching.

The foundation stone for the new bridge was laid on 6 July 1883 and soon afterwards, the Arrol company got on with the job. Any difficulties were solved as they occurred by the intrepid and inventive Mr William Arrol.[3] After four years of steady construction progress, the Tay had a railway crossing once more. On 12 June 1887, goods trains began to cross the new bridge. On 18 June Colonel Rich and Major General Hutchinson inspected the bridge for the Board of Trade.

For the test, the North British Railway supplied sixteen engines having a total weight of 955 tons. These were placed in groups of eight, one on either track, and run backwards and forwards over the bridge. The slight movements of the structure under the weight were observed first by levels and then by stretched steel wires. The only permanent set observed was a deflection of one-hundredth of a foot on the 245ft span between Piers 30 and 31 and this took place on the west side only. So the new Tay Bridge was passed with honours and the triumph of the Barlows and William Arrol with all their assistant engineers was complete. The whole thing had cost in the money of the day, £670,000 or about £62 10s a foot. It also cost the lives of fourteen workmen, mainly by drowning after falling off the bridge. It was declared fit for passenger traffic on 20 June 1887 and began carrying a full passenger train service on 13 July 1887. The bridge has given irreproachable service ever since.

In 2003, a £20.85 million budget was allocated for the strengthening and refurbishment of the bridge, which figure expanded to £24.6 million by 2010. Over 1,000 metric tons of bird droppings were scraped off the ironwork and millions of rivets were replaced. For this effort the bridge won the British Construction Industry Award in consideration of the staggering scale and logistics involved, as well as appreciating that all the work done was in a very exposed position high over the firth, with its fast-running tides.

The dream of Thomas Bouch was to bridge both the Forth and the Tay to make a complete rail route from Edinburgh to the north of Scotland. This was to be a ferry-free route and one that would establish forever the superiority of the North British Railway over the Caledonian Railway. Bouch's plans for the Forth Bridge lay stillborn as a lump of concrete on Inchgarvie Island and nothing further was done about that scheme since his Tay Bridge fell, plunging Sir Thomas into the realms of engineering oblivion. However, the NBR, knowing that its existence was at stake, really needed to build a Forth Bridge. William Arrol, doing so well with the replacement Tay Bridge, was employed to come up with a way of bridging the Forth too. He wasn't required to design the structure, just to be the contractor to physically build it. The chosen designers were Benjamin Baker and John Fowler. Benjamin Baker had already been an expert witness at the Board of Inquiry into the Tay Bridge collapse and was painfully aware of the follies of using cast iron under tension. Consequently he opted for an entirely steel construction.

The full and fascinating story of the Forth Bridge construction is outside the remit of this book but a hint of what went on is included here as both the firth crossings, not just the Tay, were part of Thomas Bouch's Big Plan and consequently find a place in this essay. His Forth crossing was to have been a suspension bridge with 1,600ft spans and towers 600ft high, but work on them had hardly begun when his Tay Bridge failed.

In 1881, W.H. Barlow and Thomas Eliot Harrison were appointed to a commission to review Thomas Bouch's plans for the crossing of the Forth. This was just as Barlow was carrying out preliminary work on the replacement Tay Bridge. Harrison was the grand old man of British civil engineering, still working aged 73 years old and clearly not a man who was ready to hang up his gun belt. He was a highly experienced railway surveyor who had worked with the famed Stephenson throughout the 1840s and 1850s on a myriad of projects, plus doing his own work as a docks designer, and he had been President of the Institution of Civil Engineers in 1873. The Commission threw out Bouch's suspension bridge plans entirely and recommended a cantilever bridge built entirely of steel. The bridge, 1½ miles long, was opened in 1890 as the triumph of the age and to this day does what it was supposed to do – carry railway trains from the south to the north of Scotland, with weights far and above those envisaged at the time of construction. Sadly, Thomas Harrison died aged 80 in 1888 so he never saw the finished Forth Bridge, to which he had provided so much valuable input. The designing engineers were Benjamin Baker, whom we've already met at the Tay Bridge Inquiry, and Mr John Fowler. Fowler was a specialist in the construction of railways and railway infrastructure. In the 1850s and 1860s he was the engineer for the world's first underground railway, London's Metropolitan Railway.

Later in his career, with partner Benjamin Baker, he consulted for the first two of London's Tube railways, the City & South London and the Central Line.

THE REBUILD

What with William Arrol as contractor and Benjamin Baker plus Fowler as design engineers, the Forth Bridge construction could hardly have been in better hands. All three participants were knighted for their efforts on the Forth Bridge. The bridge was the last element in what Cuthbert Hamilton Ellis christened 'The Great Bridges Route', referring to the whole East Coast route from London to Scotland and the north, comprising as it did and does, Welwyn Viaduct, Durham Viaduct, the Tyne bridges, the Royal Border bridge at Berwick, the Forth Bridge and the Tay Bridge. This route stood the East Coast main line in very good stead when it came to what were known as the Railway Races to the North, against the West Coast system, which included the NBR's old rival the Caledonian Railway in 1895 and later – but that is another story.

Notes

1. Arrol was a Scottish civil engineer and bridge-builder who'd been born in 1839, the son of a cotton-spinner in Houston, Renfrewshire. He started work at only 9 years old at a cotton mill in Johnston, but started training as a blacksmith with Reid's of Paisley when he was 13. He attended night school to learn Mechanics and Hydraulics and in 1863 was appointed foreman with Laidlaw & Sons which was a boiler-making firm in Glasgow. By 1872 he had established his own business called Dalmarnock Ironworks in the city's east end at Dunn Street. By the late 1870s this company was known as William Arrol & Co. and was both busy and successful under its enterprising and highly inventive namesake. Arrol had already built bridges for the suburban railway lines above the streets of Glasgow and also the bridge over the Clyde that brought the Caledonian Railway into the centre of Glasgow.
2. Ironically the British government code name for funeral plans for the Queen Mother when she should pass away was 'Tay Bridge'.
3. Refer to the Appendix which gives the full technical details of the new construction.

16

CODA

The follies of Mankind are innumerable and time adds hourly to the heap.

Jonathan Swift

A reasonable man adapts to conditions, an unreasonable man tries to change them; therefore all progress depends on the unreasonable man.

George Bernard Shaw

The Tay Bridge Disaster, that is, the bridge actually falling down, occurred on the night of Sunday 28 December 1879, but really and truly the disaster began to happen in small increments as early as 1854. The day of 28 December 1879 was merely the climax to a catalogue of disastrous decisions and events that stretched back over twenty-five years. The benefit of hindsight of course enables us to see this in perspective.

Marion K. Pinsdorf's 1997 treatise on the Tay Bridge debacle, 'Engineering Dreams Into Disaster', is subtitled 'a museum of management mistakes', and how absolutely true that is.

The boom period of railway building, the era of railway companies at war with one another to increase their shareholders' dividends at the expense of other companies (in this case the Caledonian versus the North British), plus the rivalry between the cities of Perth and Dundee, were factors that compromised the design of the first Tay Bridge.

Further compromises were the cost-cutting exercises after the many changes of design made necessary because of the poor surveying. Added to that, the ultra-sloppy maintenance and quality controls during the construction as well as after the bridge was in service almost guaranteed the whole structure would fall down eventually, gale or no gale on 28 December 1879.

CODA

Over the years, lessons in every conceivable sphere of human endeavour never seem to be learned. It's worth looking at a few examples of past engineering management disasters to trace the parallels that caused the Tay Bridge to fail as it did. Indeed, the same sorts of blunders were being made well after the Tay Bridge fell and all for the same reasons. It is because humans were involved and decisions were not made on the basis of logic and cold science alone.

A sad litany of repeated mistakes in engineering projects stretches down the centuries, most of which could have been avoided with careful heeding of history; but greed and hubris often conspired to overrule sensible thought.

Perhaps the earliest structural faux pas known in history occurred during the construction of Stonehenge, the Neolithic monument on Salisbury Plain in England.

A highly sophisticated stone-age society, provenly capable of extraordinary engineering achievements, built this huge, complex and mathematically spot-on temple to the sun, stars and the seasons with incredible accuracy some 4,500 years ago, yet there were management and design problems, if not quality control lapses even back then. Archaeological evidence from 2004 indicates that some of the cross-lintel stones with the laboriously chiselled holes that were to receive the lugs in the upright sarsen stones, were positioned backwards, in other words against the diameter of the circle to be, so that nothing fitted properly. These mistakes, although probably not causing fatalities, must have cost months of wasted work and effort, plus the fact that the wrong positioning of the holes meant that everything had to be done again, overrunning any projected construction time.

The continued use of cast iron in bridges throughout the nineteenth century, even when better materials such as wrought iron and eventually steel were available, is another example of lessons not being learned. When Robert Stephenson built the Dee Bridge at Chester as part of the London to Holyhead railway route, he used cast-iron girders. Now cast iron, as we have learned, is fine under compression but brittle and unreliable when under tension. When the Dee Bridge was built in 1846, large cast-iron girders were laid upon the piers in the River Dee and carried traffic for less than a year before disaster occurred. On 24 May 1847, one of the cast-iron girders cracked and broke near the centre of the third and last span under a passenger train. Five passengers died and sixteen were injured. The Railway Inspectorate examined all the details of the accident and concluded that:

> the girder did not break from any lateral blow from the engine, carriage or van [as Stephenson maintained and just like Thomas Bouch in defence of his theory as to why his bridge failed] or from any fault or defect in the masonry of the piers or abutments but from its being made of a strength insufficient to bear the pressure of quick trains passing over it.

The Inspectorate further concluded that:

> no girder bridge of so brittle and treacherous a metal as cast iron alone, even though trussed with wrought-iron rods, is safe for quick or passenger trains. And we have in evidence before us that there are upwards of one hundred bridges similar in principle and form to the late one over the river Dee. All are unsafe [sic].

This was in 1847! It was recommended that 'Her Majesty's Government, as the Guardians of public safety, to institute an inquiry into these bridges as shall either condemn the principle or establish their safety to such a degree that passengers may rest fully satisfied there is no danger'. Brunel took note of this and never used cast iron again for structural usage in bridges.

It was well known at the time that cast iron was a very brittle material and indeed, the first iron bridge at Coalbrookdale built in 1779 was designed especially so that all of the structural members were in compression and not in tension. It stands today as evidence of using cast iron in the right way. The curved arches on such bridges as that famous Iron Bridge were useless for a railway as they did not give the necessary flat roadbed needed. Therefore engineers attempted to use straight cast-iron girders in bridges with predictable failure of the material under tension sooner or later. Meanwhile, Thomas Bouch continued to use cast iron in the piers of some of his bridges, notably the Belah Viaduct and the Tay Bridge. Now this usage was fine, given that the metal was under compression in this role. His blunder with cast iron was to cast integrally with the upright pipes the lugs for the cross bracing, a task of 'under tension' which was doomed to fail. Nevertheless, and against all current knowledge of engineering practice of the use of cast iron, the London Brighton and South Coast Railway (LB&SCR) built a cast-iron girder bridge over a road at Norwood Junction in 1860 in the south London suburbs. It amazingly lasted for thirty-one years but, in June 1891, the Portland Road Bridge (as it was known) suddenly fractured as a train from Brighton to London was passing over it.[1] Luckily, no one was killed, the only injury being a passenger's dislocated ankle. The cast-iron beams had broken but the track itself did not, remaining festooned over the gap. There were large casting defects in the main girder which had remained undetected since manufacture. In his report, Board of Trade investigating officer Major General Hutchinson (who had approved the Tay Bridge and had escaped censure at the time because of his wish to observe the bridge in a high wind, although never carried out) failed to mention the possibilities of metal fatigue. Nevertheless, as a direct result of this and after an edict issued by the Board of Trade, all cast-iron bridges were to be checked out. The Board issued a circular requesting details of all cast-iron bridges in the UK railway network, of which there were literally thousands. Sir John Fowler undertook this survey and recommended replacement of all of them with wrought-iron girders. A very similar cast-iron girder had failed on the self-same bridge at Norwood Junction in 1877, when an engine overran the track on a disused siding. The driver was injured as the engine fell into the roadway below. This warning about poor design and girder strength went unheeded until the second failure in 1891. Yet another cast-iron bridge failed at Inverythan, Scotland in 1882 and five passengers died with many more injured. This was on the Great North of Scotland Railway between Auchterless and Fyvie, where cast iron was yet again being used in tension. Much replacement went on with girders being rebuilt with steel or wrought iron. The LB&SCR reconstructed twenty such bridges immediately and another sixty within three years. Why such cast-iron bridges had not been replaced years before and certainly after the Dee Bridge collapse, was not explained. At least one lesson was painfully learned and that was that no new cast-iron beam bridges were built after August 1883.

A much more recent example of the fatal consequences of poor management, design and failure to communicate in an engineering project is the NASA space shuttle *Challenger* disaster on 28 January 1986. This event has so very many likenesses (albeit not literally) to the Tay Bridge Disaster it is uncanny. Yet again, no one seems to have learned anything from the past. To tell the tale quickly, the morning of 28 January 1986 was particularly cold at 31°F (-1°C). The shuttle *Challenger* was launched at 11.38 a.m. but, after only seventy-three seconds into the flight, the craft suffered a catastrophic failure and disintegrated. An 'O' ring, one of a number of large synthetic rubber rings sealing off the Solid Rocket Boosters or SRBs on the right-hand side booster, failed at takeoff. As a result, hot pressurised gas escaped and impinged on adjacent hardware and the external fuel tank, leading to a separation of the SRB attachment and structural failure of the fuel tank. Aerodynamic forces then promptly destroyed the craft. These 'O' rings were well known to be suspect to failure at low temperatures yet still the launch had gone ahead.[2]

The Rogers Commission, set up to investigate the catastrophe, said in effect that failures in communication resulted in the decision to launch the shuttle based on incomplete and misleading information, conflict between engineering data and management judgements, plus a NASA management structure that permitted internal flight safety problems to bypass key shuttle flight managers.

One Commission member, physicist Richard Feynman, argued that the estimates of reliability offered by NASA management were wildly unrealistic. He said: 'for a successful technology, reality must take preference over public relations, for nature cannot be fooled.'

Just after Shuttle Pilot Michael J. Smith radioed a laconic 'Uh Oh!', the whole craft blew apart at 48,000ft but the crew cabin stayed intact. It described a ballistic arc reaching 65,000ft before falling into the sea. This took two minutes forty-five seconds and there is every chance the crew was conscious and aware throughout, an unimaginably terrifying experience. The crew cabin hit the Atlantic at around

200mph and colliding with water at that velocity has the same effect on human bodies and metalwork as crashing into concrete.

The tragic death of the seven dedicated individuals putting their trust in the system that had attempted to put them into orbit is perhaps the worse case scenario of such misplaced faith since the Tay Bridge in 1879.

Although NASA made some significant changes in its management organisation after the accident, some commentators have mooted that these changes were neither deep nor long lasting. When the shuttle *Columbia* disaster occurred in 2003, the investigation board concluded that NASA had failed to learn the lessons of the *Challenger* accident. The self-same flawed decision-making processes that killed *Challenger* were responsible again for *Columbia*'s doom seventeen years later.

Up to date (2012) in Australia, there is the pathetic availability state of the Royal Australian Navy's Collins Class submarines. The situation regarding these six boats[3] is a catalogue of design failures and mechanical failures because of mismanagement or underperformance of contractors, allowed to occur through poor project supervision, ending up with built-in points of failure. No lives have been lost but they nearly were in a succession of at-sea accidents. The boats are constantly in the yards undergoing modifications and equipment repairs so that usually only two of the class are seaworthy and operational at any one time. Translating the principles of these shortcomings into the mid-nineteenth century, the situation is highly reminiscent of the design and construction of Bouch's Tay Bridge.

What of Sir Thomas Bouch? The story has always popularly been that after his professional mauling in Mr Rothery's report, he became a broken man with his world in ruins, fell ill, went to Moffat and died. That he did retreat to Moffat is true, after his doctor had advised him to have a complete rest to recuperate from his recent stresses and nervous strains. But far from giving up his professional activities, at least before the inquiry verdict was delivered, he doesn't seem to have stopped at all. He had a full professional agenda ahead of him and applied himself diligently to it.

He beavered away in his chambers at 111 George Street, Edinburgh, on several schemes. Firstly (or so he thought then) there was the restoration of his Tay Bridge, for which he had to submit new designs. He was completely confident that his bridge would be rebuilt and quickly too. In this, the North British Railway and all the business interests in Dundee completely concurred. However, when the inquiry report came out, the NBR, with regret, got rid of him, since his name associated with the parliamentary bill for the rebuild would have seriously jeopardised its passing. Since the first bridge was opened there had been a continuing escalation of coal traffic to Dundee from the Fifeshire coalfields. This coal fuelled the jute and flax mills whose output went up and up, week by week. The transportation costs were very much lower now that the coal could come directly across the Tay from Fife and not have to arrive in Dundee by the much longer and circuitous inland routes via Perth and the Caledonian Railway. What with all the other goods traffic coming across the bridge,

Dundee effectively became a boom town and its businessmen, loom- and mill-owners were delighted. And in reverse, the bridge had become a vital link to the south and its markets, carrying tons and tons of Dundee-made goods for Scotland and the rest of England. All that had suddenly been stopped in one awful night and all the old high transportation costs were back, glaring malevolently from the pages of the balance sheets.

Also there were miles of approach railway and stations lying idle until a replacement crossing could be effected. The capital invested by the North British Railway tied up in such assets was enormous and was, for now at least, useless and unproductive.

Bouch had longer-term plans for his projected Forth Railway Bridge and also the remaining work to be done on the Arbroath & Montrose Railway in which his son William was involved as an indentured engineering apprentice. On top of all that, there was the Edinburgh South Side & Suburban Junction Railway plans to be completed and submitted for parliamentary presentation.

Moffat is a nineteenth-century spa town, its name derived from the Scottish Gaelic 'Am Magh Fada'. It is a town and burgh in Dumfries & Galloway on the banks of the River Annan and is also the ancestral seat of Clan Johnstone. Bouch's wife Margaret brought Thomas here in mid-1880 to help his recovery from a chest infection, given that the sulphurous waters of Moffat Spa were believed to have healing properties.[4] During the Victorian era the high demand from visitors seeking curatives led to the waters being piped down to a specially built bath-house in the town centre, which building is now the present town hall. To cope with all the visitors, the Hydropathic Hotel was opened in 1878. However, the Bouch family owned a country retreat in Moffat called Spa House which is where they stayed until Thomas caught a chill and died on 30 October 1880, just ten months after the fall of his dream bridge. He had a splendid funeral at Dean Cemetery in Edinburgh, the ceremonies attended by many luminaries in the railway and engineering world including Edgar Gilkes and Sir William Arrol, who had just begun to wrestle with the problems of building the Forth Bridge and was the contractor for the new Tay Bridge.

Bouch was only just in his grave when a final metaphorical nail was driven into his coffin. Colonel Yolland, who had sat on the Tay Bridge Board of Inquiry, was one of the Board of Trade's inspecting officers. He was sent up to Scotland by the Board to examine the South Esk Viaduct on the Arbroath & Montrose section of the NBR. This bridge, designed by Sir Thomas, was another pipe bridge with cast-iron columns, much resembling the Tay Bridge in concept and design, albeit not in length.

The work on it had been overseen by Bouch's son William. During April 1880 Bouch actually visited the South Esk Viaduct. It looked like a smaller version of his Tay Bridge but only crossing a sea inlet some 500yd wide with thirty spans and not a 2-mile wide estuary. The lattice girder superstructure was, like the Tay Bridge, supported by cast-iron columns and amazingly with the flanges for the cross-bracing once again cast into them as one piece. One would have thought that after the fall of his Tay crossing that Bouch might just have decided not to perpetrate the exact same design and casting techniques in another bridge. But no, he seemed to have learned nothing although the lesson had cost so many lives. Hopkins Gilkes were once more the contractors and the bridge parts were built at Middlesbrough, a replay of the Tay Bridge build, especially as Bouch was using the same old team and construction systems again. He can't have been thinking straight or maybe he didn't care – pride and vanity reared their heads as they do with people who are too sure of themselves. There was a comeuppance – when the girder lengths were added together, they were 5ft short of the designed bridge length. Gilkes in conversation with Bouch suggested cutting a girder in half and inserting a distance piece in the middle. This Heath Robinson affair (a byword for bizarre and obviously impractical inventions), almost as if they were children experimenting with Meccano on the sitting-room floor, was carried out with all the signs of another 'Bouch botch'. From the plans submitted to parliament the bridge was supposed to be straight. Yolland observed that because several of the piers were not at 90 degrees to the axis of the bridge, the structure was anything but straight.

Yolland carried out some tests with rolling loads (that is, sending engines and vehicles backwards and forwards across the bridge) during a period of thirty-six hours and noted that some piers sank over 2½in and generated distortions felt across the whole of the bridge. The only safety factor to prevent a train falling off the structure should a derailment happen was a mere handrail which doubled, as on the Tay Bridge, as a gas pipe. No way could a thin tubular iron handrail hold up against the weight of a train if a derailment happened. Engines and carriages would be precipitated easily into the river below.

Colonel Yolland thought that such a derailment was 'not a very remote contingency'. He condemned the whole structure as unsafe and it was demolished, never having carried a revenue-earning public train. The archetypal Greek tragedy for Sir Thomas had been played out to the very end.

Thomas Bouch's memorial to his life and dreams is simply a long row of stumps stretching out across the Tay for 2 miles from Wormit to Dundee upon which seagulls perch and caw, indifferent to the meaning of these truncated piers which are a pathetic reminder to us today about shattered dreams. These are not the only bridge relics, as deep beneath the surface of the Tay and invisible under the water lie some of the brick columns, only discovered recently by side-scan sonar investigations. On the Wormit shore still lie the broken and weed-encrusted remains of the first two demolished brick piers.[5]

There were survivors of the Tay Bridge Disaster, albeit by default. Alice Upton, who was 16 years old, lived with her mother in Union Street, Dundee, and had been on a weekend visit to some friends in Edinburgh. She was supposed to return home to Dundee on the Sunday 5.27 train. When she didn't appear that night her mother, of course thinking her daughter had been lost in the disaster, was utterly distraught and consumed with weeping. She even waited at Dundee Tay Bridge station all the night of 28 December but had no news whatsoever. But in the early hours of Tuesday 30 December, she received a telegram from Alice begging her mother's forgiveness for having stayed over in Edinburgh that Sunday night. Mrs Upton roused all her neighbours to tell them the news and fell to her knees in thankful prayer for her daughter's safety.

There were two William Browns who escaped death in the train that night. Mr William Brown, a salt merchant from Green Market, Dundee, was in Edinburgh and about to return home from his honeymoon on the Sunday Edinburgh service but he and his wife changed their minds at the very last moment.

The other William Brown was Lizzie Brown's brother who was supposed to have gone with Lizzie and her grandmother to Leuchars on a family visit but was made to stay at home because of naughtiness – naughtiness which saved his life! The ladies boarded the 'Edinburgh' at Leuchars Junction and their bodies were never recovered from the Tay.

Mr William Linskill was saved as we have seen earlier by the last-moment arrival of the Dean's carriage at Leuchars. And there was of course Jamie Lee, my great-grandfather. There were probably more people who missed the train by luck or providence, leaving the only true survivor of the disaster as North British Railway's engine No 224 which had plunged into the River Tay along with the six carriages and their human cargo.

She was surprisingly little damaged by her dive into the Tay but also seemed reluctant to leave it when it came to the salvage operation. Dugald Drummond, the dour and explosive Scot in charge of the NBR Mechanical Engineering Department, was keen to recover the engine which, according to the divers, still lay on its right side inside the fifth high girder span.

Drummond, in his imperious way, rode roughshod over Sir Thomas Bouch's anxiousness to retrieve high girder span four, as Bouch believed that this might provide him with the evidence he needed to show a derailment of the second-class carriage and thus justify his theories as to the bridge collapse. However, Drummond's high-handed bluster prevailed and he commandeered the lifting pontoons and chains to recover engine No 224 from the river.

Drummond was present on 7 April 1880 when the engine appeared from beneath the Tay and he noted that very little damage had been done. The cab was fine as were all the steampipe connections but the lifting chains broke, dropping the engine back into the river. The engine got itself stuck in a sandbank and it took two days for divers to set up another lift. This happened as planned until the anchor cable of the recovery ship *Henry* got entangled with the cab, pulling it off and ripping away the injector steam cock. Only a very short way to the planned beaching point at Tayport the chains parted again and into the Tay went No 224 for the third time. Finally the pontoons beneath which she was hanging were towed to Tayport where the engine was beached. Drummond examined her there and reported to the North British Board that:

> the engine is very slightly damaged and it will not cost more than fifty pounds to put it in working condition. With the exception of the left hand trailing axle-bar, which has a small portion of the outer end broken, the tender is not in any way injured and this damage will not prevent it from being serviceable.[6]

It is interesting to note that Driver Mitchell could have had absolutely no warning that the disaster was about to happen, as the regulator was found to be wide open, the reversing gear at the third notch and the brakes fully off.

The engine and tender were quite able to run on their own wheels and were towed back to Cowlairs Works, Glasgow – No 224 was soon repaired and in service once again. With a new boiler fitted in 1897 she lived out a useful life, was renumbered 1192 in May 1913 and was finally sold to a Glasgow scrap yard in 1919 after a service career of forty-eight years, forty of which were after the Tay Bridge Disaster. Mostly she seems to have worked south of Edinburgh on the Waverley route through the Borders counties to Carlisle and also down the NBR main line as far as Newcastle. Engine crews nicknamed her 'The Diver' and she didn't work across the Tay again for many years. Superstitious engine roster clerks may have been responsible for this but nevertheless, ironically and exactly on the twenty-ninth anniversary of the disaster, 28 December 1908, No 224 once again hauled the self-same Sunday evening mail train from Edinburgh to Dundee, this time of course over the fully completed ferryless route now using both the Forth and Tay Bridges.

The final ghost had at last been laid to rest.

In some other accounts of the Tay Bridge Disaster, the death roll of passengers and crew on the 5.27 from Burntisland has been quoted as seventy-five persons. It may be noted that in this version of the story, the number has been raised to a possible eighty-five victims. This is because research over the years has revealed another possible ten casualties, most of whom were children under 5 years old and consequently not requiring a ticket when travelling with the rest of their families, so they didn't show up as passengers from the ticket count. Also railway employees like George Ness, for example, travelled free on their workmen's passes and weren't counted. The Tay Rail Bridge Disaster Memorial Trust disagrees with my estimate and, after its own research, cites fifty-nine victims.

Ian Nimmo White, a prolific poet living in Leslie, Fife, is the Vice-Chairman of the Memorial Trust and recently carried out some historical detective work concerning driver David Mitchell who was born in Leslie. Ian found Mitchell's great-grandson and great-great-grandson after many blind alleys and much 'sherlocking'. He was responsible for raising a stone for Driver Mitchell in Leslie Cemetery on 20 April 2011 and has kindly allowed me to include some facts concerning the Mitchell family after the disaster. Driver Mitchell's wife was Janet (*née* Moyes) and after the demise of her husband took his body to Leslie on 4 March 1880 for interment. She then moved her family to Leslie where they lived in the High Street, according to the 31 March 1881 census. Their 2-year-old daughter Margaret sadly died a few days later.

The poetic doggerel of Mr William MacGonagal has been studiously avoided as previous story tellers have used him to the full. Instead, these verses below seem to encapsulate the thoughts of those left behind. Sadly, these lines are anonymous but pay tribute, respect and sorrow for those who died that night, 134 years ago.

>Christmas Time while mirth abounded,
>Thro' the country far and wide,
>Happy homes are turned to sadness,
>Dear friends in death lay side by side.
>Young and old upon the railway,
>In that fatal train that day.
>Little thought to death were going,
>From this life they've passed away.
>(Refrain)
>Tay Bridge gave way the train went hurling,
>Down into the deadly deep,
>Just a crash and all was over,
>Many there in death now sleep.
>Mothers with there [sic] little infants,
>Fathers sons and sweethearts true
>Laugh'd and jok'd so free together,
>As along the rails they did pursue.
>No thought of danger was among them,
>Thinking of old Christmas cheer,
>All was merry and light-hearted,
>Returning home they had no fear.
>That Sabbath night while the storm was raging,
>The Edinburgh train went on its way,
>Watch'd by a few who felt the danger
>As on Tay Bridge she steamed away.
>Sparks of fire they saw ascending,
>While down went crashing, bridge and train,
>Into the river smash'd to pieces,
>Buried in the watery main.
>At the railway station friends were waiting,
>For the arrival of the train,
>But when the news to them was broken

It filled their hearts with grief and pain,
Mothers cried 'Give me my children'
Fathers shed a silent tear,
Brothers, sisters, friends and sweethearts
Wept for those they lov'd so dear.
Many now are sad and lonely,
Thinking of a poor dear friend,
Little orphans now are weeping,
For their parents' fearful end,
None of us can tell the moment,
When from this earth we'll have to go,
Those poor souls little thought of dying
In that fateful train below.

Notes

1. Refer to 16 (i) 'Norwood Junction Accident – Additional Information' in the chapter note section.
2. Refer to 16 (ii) 'Challenger Disaster' in the chapter note section.
3. Submarines are always called 'boats' and not ships.
4. The sleepy little town of Moffat was not yet done as a host to an important historical event. It saw the death of a national figure with Sir Thomas and then, only two years later, it was host to a birth of greater import for Britain, because Hugh Caswell Tremenhere Dowding was born there on 24 April 1882. As Air Chief Marshal Dowding, he led Royal Air Force Fighter Command to victory in the Battle of Britain in 1940.
5. Refer to 16 (iii) 'The Remnants' in the chapter note section.
6. Refer to 16 (iv) 'Locomotive 224 Arises' in the chapter note section.

Appendix

DETAILS OF THE SECOND TAY BRIDGE VIADUCT CONSTRUCTION

After the foundation stone ceremony on 6 July 1883, work began in earnest. Firstly all the foundations for the piers the whole way across had to be sunk into the riverbed. Four pontoons were used to sink a pier-base cylinder, each pontoon consisting of five watertight tanks. Two of the tanks were long and sandwiched the three shorter ones. The complete pontoon resembled a letter 'H' with the top and bottom openings filled in. Through the spaces in the middle the cylinder was sunk, and the pontoon was made secure meanwhile by legs passing down through its corners to the bed of the firth. The cylinders themselves were riveted together in sections on shore and then carried out by boats to the waiting pontoons. As each length was lowered through its respective well in the pontoon, it was bolted to its predecessor through an internal flange. The upper parts were lined with brickwork and then slowly lowered by hydraulic jacks until they rested safely on the riverbed.

For excavating the silty sand in the cylinders, the engineers arranged two 6in hosepipes in the bottom of each cylinder. Twenty feet from their open ends, these hoses were united to form a single 12in pipe, the upper end of which connected with a powerful centrifugal pump on the pontoon. Divers manipulated the pipes so that one sucked up sand while the other took in only clean water, thus preventing the choking of the pump by diluting the flow through it. As much as 40cu. yd of sand and silt per hour could be removed from the riverbed with this system, realising a subsidence of the cylinder of 2ft per hour.

When each cylinder had reached the required depth, it was cleaned out down to the cutting edge at the bottom and then concreting took place. Having been completed as far as low water level the cylinders were then tested by subjecting each one to a weight one-third more than it would ever have to bear, assuming this maximum weight to be that of each line of rails occupied completely by the heaviest locomotives. Thus the test allowed a wide margin of safety for the considerable increase in weight of railway rolling stock as the years went on. In fact the test weight on each pier was 2,348 tons.

After these tests, the builders attached temporary wrought-iron caissons to the cylinders before completing the masonry work and building the foundations for the superstructure.

Each pair of cylinders was joined above high water level by a horizontal connecting member. Above this, the pier rose in the form of two octagonal pillars of iron, hollow but united at the top by a semi-circular arch of the same material. The design varied slightly in different places and the relatively short piers at the northern end were of a simpler construction altogether. The octagonal pillars and the arches were dispensed with and a simple rectangular structure was imposed on the iron cylinders. Except where the piers rested on hard rock, the foundations were carried down to a depth of at least 20ft further than the lowest part of the bottom of the firth in the vicinity. This acted as a precaution against the scouring action of the river that had so plagued the piers of Bouch's bridge.

Special provision was made in the Barlow plans for the expansion and contraction of the structure in climatic extremes. Scotland is a country of vastly changeable weather and its eastern counties have known the coldest times ever experienced in Great Britain. At intervals of approximately 500ft, the girder ends were supported on rocker bearings at one end of each length, the other being firmly fixed to its pier. An observation made over a year showed that the variation in a 512ft length during a temperature range of 55°F amounted to 1ft 7½in. The whole bridge therefore could be 3ft 9in longer on the hottest of days!

Several distinct operations attended the erection of the girders upon the piers. The first was concerned with the removal of sound and undamaged girders from the old bridge to the new. For this process, large pontoons were prepared upon which were mounted telescopic lattice girder supports which could be adjusted to any required height. These pontoons were floated under the old girders at low tide and allowed to rise with the tide beneath the girders, the telescopic members being pushed up and made secure underneath the section to be moved. This gradually rose clear of its bedplates and thus floated with the pontoon which was then manoeuvred upstream until it was between two piers of the new bridge and secured again, the girder being carefully lowered into position on the new piers. The tops of those piers were slightly lower than those on the old bridge. This process was not feasible with the final spans at the north end because of the sharp curve. Here, the builders transferred each girder in turn by steam cranes.

Meanwhile, erection of the new girders for the northern and southern sections (that is, exclusive of the navigation spans of the central section, the 'high girders') was taking place in the contractor's yards adjacent to the bridge. Preliminary work had already been done in Glasgow. Arrol was using his tried and tested method of building spans on land and then floating them out to their sites on the bridge. The new sections were needed because the bridge deck was now for double track and Bouch's girders were, of course, too narrow on their own. Consequently the new pieces had to act as spacers between pairs of the Bouch girders. Rails had been laid on the tops of the old girders which were now all in their new positions and the new girders were run out in series on traversers running on the rails and dropped into position between the old girders like the filling in a sandwich.

The flooring was built up from corrugated steel and eventually supported an ordinary ballasted roadbed with standard cross-sleepered track.

With the high spans of the central section, the builders had to adopt a totally different series of operations. In the old bridge it was this section, the 'high girders' that had fallen into the river and there was no question of using these over again even if their wreckage could be prised from the riverbed in any state of usability. Furthermore, as the tracks run inside the girders on the navigation spans, there would only have to be two great girders to each span with a clear space between them. The various members of the girders were made and drilled ready in the Glasgow works and the girders were then erected complete from these parts on the south side of the firth. The only parts left unfinished were a small section of the connecting members at each end. On completion, each girder span, weighing 514 tons, was lowered onto a pontoon and towed out to its site by four tugs. Here the engineers lowered the span onto beech blocks on the piers, the pontoon being meanwhile anchored to the old and new piers. The pontoon was floated away while the tide was ebbing and was generally free of the span some two and a half hours after high tide.

The next step consisted of erecting the superstructures of the piers on which the spans were to rest. Only when these had reached their full height did the process of raising the spans themselves begin. To give effect to this, the engineers mounted a steam boiler and a set of powerful pumps on the middle of the span, the pumps being connected to a set of four hydraulic rams, two at either end. A system of stopcocks enabled these pumps to operate alternately on either pair of rams. Thus stage by stage, the great central spans rose to a level above their final position, when the engineers inserted the connecting cross-girders, rockers and bearings beneath them. Finally each span was lowered gently into place and secured to the fixed bearings or adjusted to the rocker bearings as required.

For those who like figures, the building of the new Tay Bridge accounted for 13,425 tons of wrought ironwork in the parapets and girders, 7,626 tons of wrought ironwork in the cylinders and superstructures of the piers, 2,705 tons of cast iron in the cylinders, 3,588 tons in the flooring, 37,024cu. yd of concrete and 26,419cu. yd of brickwork. Nearly five years were occupied in the construction. Operations on the ironwork began in the Glasgow yards on 22 June 1882. In July 1883 the engineers on site began operations on the sinking of the cylinder foundations in the bed of the firth. Three hundred men were employed in the Glasgow yards, and the number at work on the bridge site was at times as many as 900.

Chapter Notes

PREFACE

The *Princess Alice* Disaster

The *Princess Alice* was one of a pair of paddle steamers built by Caird & Company at Greenock, Scotland, in 1865. They were originally named SS *Bute* and SS *Kyle*, both of 251 tons displacement and both set to work as Isle of Arran ferries for the Wemyss Railway Company. In 1866, the Waterman's Steam Packet Company (later called The London Steamboat Company) bought the SS *Bute* and transferred her to the River Thames in London, renaming her *Princess Alice* after Queen Victoria's third daughter, the Grand Duchess of Hesse-Darmstadt. *Princess Alice* plied as a pleasure steamer up and down the Thames for the next twelve years.

Sunday 3 September 1878 was warm and pleasant. *Princess Alice*, with Captain William Robert Hattridge Grinsted in command, left her dock at Swan Pier near London Bridge at 10 a.m., setting off on a cruise to Gravesend and Sheerness. By 6 p.m. she had re-boarded all her passengers, most of whom were Londoners going back home after an afternoon stroll in Rosherville Gardens, Gravesend. By 7.40 p.m. *Princess Alice* was nearly home, passing Tripcock Point and entering Gallions Reach just before Woolwich Town. At the same time, a steam collier, SS *Bywell Castle*, under the command of Captain Harrison, entered Gallions Reach from upstream. The 890-ton collier was sailing from Millwall dry dock where she'd just been repainted and on to Newcastle. There she was to pick up a cargo of coal and head for Alexandria, Egypt.

As the *Bywell Castle* entered Gallions Reach she was travelling at slow speed in the middle of the river. Captain Harrison observed *Princess Alice* approaching and turning towards the north shore, appearing to cross his bows. To avoid a collision Harrison told his river pilot, Christopher Dix, to angle towards the south shore. He was aiming to pass safely astern of *Princess Alice*. However, at this dangerous moment Captain Grinsted, aboard *Princess Alice*, confused the *Bywell Castle*'s intentions by turning *Princess Alice* to the south as well and straight into the path of the big collier. Harrison ordered 'full astern' but it was too late. *Bywell Castle* knifed into *Princess Alice* just abaft her starboard paddlewheel. The pleasure steamer stood no chance against a ship four times her size and was cut completely in two. *Princess Alice* took a mere four minutes to sink to the bottom of the Thames. She was licensed to carry 936 passengers and although no exact figures are available, she was thought to have had about 750 people aboard.

Bywell Castle's holds were empty and she was riding high in the water. As a consequence very few of the hundreds of people thrown into the Thames could scramble aboard her to safety; most had to cling to the wreckage from the collision. Unfortunately for those struggling in the water, just to the north was Becton North Outfall Sewer, which daily pumped thousands of gallons of raw sewage into the river. Industrial plants in North Greenwich and Silvertown also let their waste flow into the river untreated, making this section of river one of the most polluted in Britain.

As news of the accident spread, hundreds of relatives gathered at the London Steamboat Company's office. Mr W.T. Vincent was one of the first newspaper reporters on the scene, which he described thus in his own words and punctuation:

> Soon policemen and watermen were seen by the feeble light bearing ghastly objects into the Steampacket company's offices for a boat had just arrived with the first consignment of the dead – mostly little children whose light bodies and ample drapery had kept them afloat even as they were smothered in the festering Thames. I followed into the Steamboat office, marvelling at the fate which had brought the earliest harvest of victims to the headquarters of the doomed ship, and entering the boardroom, the first of the martyrs was pointed out to me as one of the companies own servants, a man employed on the *Princess Alice* and brought here thus soon to attest by his silent presence the ship's identity. The lifeless frames of men and women lay about, and out on the balcony, from which the Directors had so often looked upon their fleet through the fragrant smoke of the evening cigar, there was a sight to wring out tears of blood from the eyes of any beholder. A row of little innocents, plump and pretty, well-dressed children, all dead and cold, some with life's ruddy tinge still in their cheeks and lips, the lips from which the merry prattle had gone for ever. Callous as one may grow from frequent contact with terrors and afflictions, one could never be inured to this. Then to think what was beyond out there in the river ... it was madness!

It soon became clear, after about 100 people had been saved, that this was going to be an operation of recovery of the dead, not rescuing the living. Local workmen were paid 5s for each body recovered and they were pulling bodies out of the river for weeks after the event. Probably not all the bodies were recovered but a large number were found inside the ship when the two halves were raised later.

The work must have been ghastly for the watermen as the pollution would have been horribly disfiguring to the corpses, and this would have confounded attempts at identification. In the end, over 115 people were buried as 'Unknown' and the exact death toll is itself unknown to this day. There were 544 inquests in Woolwich alone and at least 46 elsewhere. The final toll is estimated at around 600 persons.

1 WORKING ON THE RAILWAY

Westinghouse Brakes

In the mid-1870s all railway companies were becoming aware of the importance of brakes. It seems unbelievable now but engines themselves often didn't have any brakes at all. Trains were belting along at over 80mph and stopping was dependent upon handbrakes on the engine tenders and the co-operation of guards in their vans. In 1871, after a series of nasty accidents because of this hopeless situation, the American inventor George Westinghouse came to England. Regardless of his ability to show how American trains were using his air brake, British railway companies were sadly quick to dismiss his ideas. Westinghouse's first design proved the ability to stop but did not include a system whereby if a train parted, the whole ensemble would stop. So by 1874 he'd thought up the triple valve system that would cause this to happen. At the time, useless brake systems were in use in Britain, like the LNWR's chain brake.

However, companies like the NBR were much more far-seeing and tested the Westinghouse system in 1876. They loved it and started fitting out both engines and coaching stock with it. By the time of our story, most engines and passenger rolling stock were Westinghouse fitted.

Injectors

The injector for forcing water into the boiler seems a scientific paradox. The system uses steam from the boiler to inject water into that boiler at the same pressure! To explain, let us imagine for a moment that steam is cold and not boiling hot, so that someone could stand in a jet of it without being scalded. Now imagine two hose nozzles, from one of which steam at, say, 30lb pressure is issuing and from the other, a jet of water at the same pressure. If anyone walked past these nozzles he'd pass the steam jet with no discomfort but on meeting the water jet, he'd probably be knocked over. The steam, being gaseous, can be resisted but not so the solid jet of water. So by firing the steam jet through a series of cones, the water is carried over against the boiler pressure into the boiler itself, thus topping it up.

2   TAY TO FORTH: ACROSS FIOBHA, THE KINGDOM OF FIFE

One Train at a Time

There was one incident on the bridge where things appeared to have gone wrong with this supposedly foolproof safety device. Robert Dempster of Newry was riding the 4 p.m. Dundee–Burntisland train on 7 December 1878 and he sent a letter to the railway department of the Board of Trade. To paraphrase, he stated that as his southbound train was on the first sharp curve of the bridge having passed the North Signal Box, a lady passenger screamed that there was a train coming from the opposite side. When everyone looked out of the carriage windows there indeed seemed to be steam blowing out of the southernmost high girder section. In moments, their train came heavily to a stand. The approaching train in the 'high girders' also seemed to stop very suddenly. The guard of the 4 p.m. train was then seen running back across the bridge accompanied by the fireman who exclaimed that, 'we've gotten the wrong ticket!' Then the Down train shunted itself back to Wormit, out of the way. The Board of Trade demanded an immediate explanation from the North British Railway. It seemed that two trains were supposed to cross the bridge southwards, one at 4 p.m. and the other at 4.05 p.m.. The driver of the first train was given the ticket so that the second train could take the baton. The North Box signalman had given a ticket to the 4 p.m. but in error it was the Down ticket collected from the previous train to arrive at Dundee. The fireman noticed the mistake when his train was about 300yd out on the bridge. Even after running back, the signalman refused him the right ticket on the grounds it must be handed to the driver. The NBR flatly denied that there were two trains on the bridge at the same time. The NBR's propensity for fudging the truth was thus demonstrated and would occur again during the disaster inquiry.

Royal Railway Journeys

Royal railway journeys were definitely subject to economic strictures. As it was, the Queen spent £10,000 annually on train travel. Just one return trip to Scotland would set the royal coffers back by £5,000. But Queen Victoria insisted on lookout men being posted at 200yd intervals for the entire mileage! At approximately eight men per mile, that was 4,500 lookouts from Windsor to Balmoral, each needing to be paid. Plus there was the cost of the new white gloves for all the signalmen en route, from whom the Queen expected a salute as she passed.

The Queen didn't like going too fast on her train journeys. The maximum speed set was 50mph. In 1850, her private secretary, The Honourable Alexander Gordon, wrote from Osborne House to a British railway company:

> I am desired to intimate Her Majesty's wish that the speed of the Royal Train should on no account be increased at any one part of the line in order to make up for the time lost by an unforeseen delay at another, so that if any unexpected delay does take place, no attempt is to be made to regain the time by travelling faster than what has been agreed upon in the Time Bill you have sent me. I have to request you will communicate Her Majesty's wishes to the secretaries of the other railways concerned.

From 1845, the Royal Saloon carried a miniature semaphore signal on its roof, and this was visible to the engine driver. It indicated Her Majesty's wishes as to whether the train should 'go quick, go slow or stop'. The signal box bell code for a Royal Train was four rings repeated three times and the telephone call sign was RX.

3 CROSSING THE FORTH

Edmondson's Visiting Cards

'Edmondson's Visiting Cards' was the nickname for the humble pieces of pasteboard that served as railway tickets as part of a ticket system devised by Thomas Edmondson. He was the Stationmaster at Milton on the Newcastle & Carlisle Railway in the middle 1830s and noticed the inefficiencies and disadvantages of existing ticket-issuing. His duties at Milton were not onerous and he had time to apply his craftsman's training to improve the dispensing of tickets. Firstly, he devised the idea of pieces of pasteboard printed with printer's type set into a small wooden block. These ticket blanks he numbered by hand and placed in vertical tubes for each destination with a counterweight device to push up the next ticket. He then invented a foot-operated date-stamping press. The invention which made Edmondson's fortune was a machine which could print tickets in large batches complete with individual serial numbers. He patented this machine and charged royalties to railway companies on the basis of 10s per mile of route. For example a line 100 miles long would earn him £50 per annum. However, his employers (the Newcastle & Carlisle) showed little interest in these inventions so Edmondson then approached the Manchester & Leeds Railway when it opened in 1839. That company loved all of his ideas and appointed him Chief Booking Clerk in Manchester. M&L tickets had various tricks in their printing to prevent fraud, all devised by Edmondson. Eastbound tickets had a picture of a woollen fleece on the back, while Westbound tickets carried the image of a cotton-bale. Edmondson's machines and their improved successors became the standard for all British railway companies.

as well as in many other parts of the world. He died in 1851, a very wealthy man. His idea was used almost to the end of the twentieth century before being superseded by electronic devices.

The Treaty of Perpetual Peace

The Treaty of Perpetual Peace was signed between England and Scotland in 1502. It gave Berwick the special status as being 'of' the Kingdom of England but not 'in' it. As a result the town thereafter needed a special mention in all royal proclamations. When Queen Victoria signed the declaration of war with Russia in 1853 she did so in the name of 'Victoria Queen of Great Britain, Ireland, Berwick-Upon-Tweed and the British Dominions beyond the sea'. However, Berwick was not mentioned in the Treaty of Paris that ended the Crimean War in 1856, leaving the town still technically at war with Russia! The matter remained unresolved until 1966 when a peace treaty was signed by a Russian diplomat and the Lord Mayor of Berwick, who said to the diplomat, 'You can tell the Russian people that they can now sleep peacefully in their beds!'

Edinburgh Waverley Station

Edinburgh Waverley station has had a complex gestation to the site we see today. In the early 1840s three railway termini were established in quick succession. The first was the North British Railway's route from England and south-eastern Scotland and the second was the Edinburgh & Northern's line to the docks for ferry connections across the Forth to Fife and the north. This second station, Canal Street, was built at right angles to the NBR platforms and its trains left northwards through the 1,000yd-long Scotland Street tunnel beneath Princes Street. The tunnel was designed by Thomas Grainger and engineered by William Paterson, whose son was later to lay the foundation stone of Bouch's Tay Bridge at Wormit. The bore was on a stiff gradient of 1 in 27 and trains were rope-hauled up the incline by a stationary steam engine. Scotland Street tunnel was abandoned in 1868 when trains for the docks used the NBR route to Granton via Abbeyhill Junction. The tunnel became a mushroom farm from 1887 until 1929 and later was both an air-raid shelter in the Second World War and one of ten emergency control centres for the LNER (London & North Eastern Railway). The third station was the eastern terminus of the Edinburgh & Glasgow Railway which made an end-on connection with the NBR and ran through Princes Street Gardens to Haymarket, thence on to Glasgow. This conglomerate of stations was first called North Bridge. The link through the gardens was only established after extended arguments and parliamentary debates as the residents of Princes Street, led by Lord Cockburn, defended their environment. The title 'Waverley' was applied to the three stations from 1854, named after the series of Sir Walter Scott novels.

The Edinburgh Time Signal

The Edinburgh Time Signal was devised for sailors at Leith Docks and in the Firth of Forth to check their chronometers. Originally, time balls were used and had been invented by Captain Wauchope of Midlothian, Scotland. They were installed at Greenwich, St Helena and the Cape of Good Hope. Not until 1852 did Edinburgh get its own time signal on the Nelson Monument. This one was devised by Charles Piazza Smith, Astronomer Royal for Scotland after his experiences working with the time ball at the Cape of Good Hope. The actual design work was carried out by Edinburgh clockmaker Frederick James Ritchie. The ball was raised a minute or so before 1 p.m. and dropped exactly at 1 p.m., providing a visible signal for miles around. Then it was decided to fire a gun from the Half Moon Battery on Edinburgh Castle battlements. A 4,200ft electric cable was strung across the valley in 1861 from the Nelson Monument to the castle, enabling a cannon to be fired automatically at 1 p.m. Being an audio signal rather than visual, it took several seconds for the sound of the gun to carry to Leith, about 3 miles north-north-east of the castle. 'Gun Maps' were published in Post Office directories from 1861 which showed the delay times taken for the report to travel across Edinburgh. Hislop's Time Gun Map, published in 1862, performed the same function.

4   DURESS NON FRANGO

Pre-Bouch Train Ferries

The building of the great breakwater in Plymouth Sound, Devon, to defend the harbour from the vagaries of weather and tide coming in from the English Channel, began in March 1812. The work was overseen by Scottish engineer John Rennie, who had used a 25-acre quarry site at Oreston on the edge of Plymouth Sound bought from the Duke of Bedford for £10,000. A 3ft 6in gauge tramway with metal rails and horse-drawn wagons was built to carry the quarried stone down to a jetty. From there, ships conveyed the building material out to the breakwater work site. These ships had rails laid in their holds to carry the stone wagons which were unloaded at the breakwater onto another 3ft 6in railway complex. Thus the stones travelled by wagon from the quarry out to the breakwater construction site with no transhipment. Cranes hoisted the wagons in and out of the ships at both ends of the trip.

In 1842, another train-ferry enterprise in the north-east resulted in the first case of 'taking coals to Newcastle'. In that year, the management of the Bedlington pit in Blyth, Northumberland, took delivery of a twin-screwed steamer named *Bedlington* which was specially constructed for the carriage of chaldron wagons. This enterprising step was taken as the result of the continued and no doubt intentional delays to which the Bedlington wagons were subjected at the coaling staithes of their rival, the neighbouring Netherton Colliery. Furthermore, to gain access to the staithes in question (at that time the only convenient waterside facility available in the area) the Bedlington wagons were forced to use the Netherton firm's 3-mile wagon-way.

It was to remedy this state of affairs and to expand the business that the steamer *Bedlington* was conceived. Immediately after her arrival at Blyth she was put into service between that port and Newcastle, 10 miles to the south. There, the contents of the conveyed wagons were transhipped into colliers lying alongside by means of powerful steam derricks with which she was fitted. *Bedlington* could carry forty loaded chaldron wagons which had curved sides and carried one chaldron each, a chaldron being an official weight measure of 2 tons 13cwt. The vessel operated for ten years, substantially assisting the Bedlington company in securing fresh markets for its rapidly increasing coal output. She was eventually sold in April 1851, improved rail and quayside accommodation having since been provided at Blyth. Under her new Scottish owner's house flag she plied across the Firth of Forth, although not as a wagon ferry, until she was transferred to government service at the outbreak of the Crimean War in 1854. *Bedlington* was lost in the Baltic Sea while acting as a military transport. *Bedlington* represents a most successful attempt at mechanical co-operation between rail and sea transport. Whoever was her designer, it is improbable that he realised that from this beginning as a local stopgap, would be evolved a system of transport used extensively worldwide.

Part of a letter from Wilkie (Company Secretary Leven Railway) to Thomas Bouch

The unsuitability of the engine raised double in the minds of the directors that all was not right, but to them you made no disclosure of the defective condition of the works. Again and again they required you to make a private report on those points in regard to which there seemed cause for dissatisfaction, but this request you did not accede to until 21st May last after the line had been open upwards of nine months when you made a communication to me to the effect that the contractor might be paid under deduction of 25 pounds. But in this letter for the first time you made known the secret that the curves had not been executed according to the contract and that the special instruction given for their improvement had not received your attention. The details of the curves you then furnished were totally different from those you had previously returned to the Board of Trade and equally different from those in the contract plans.

The Directors have had a minute inspection made by an engineer of eminence and have ascertained that in the execution of the works the variation from the plans have been of the most disgraceful character, that the statutory powers of the company have been violated, the Board of Trade misled and that the Leven company are exposed to the danger of having the line shut up until the railway is rendered conformable to the authorised plans and consistent with public security.

The Directors, I can assure you, have taken up this matter with great pain and reluctance, but as has been seen, while implicitly trusting you, they have been grievously disappointed in the works of the railway and they feel that they have the very strongest claims on you for relief for the consequences [sic].

5 STRANGERS ON A TRAIN

Paraffin Oil

Paraffin oil gave a much brighter light than rape oil and was cheaper. It was made from the output of the West Lothian and Midlothian shale fields and supplied in 25,000-gallon batches at a halfpenny per gallon. Shales are laminated deposits of clay which vary considerably in appearance and composition and are found in all geological epochs from the Cambrian to the Tertiary. Bituminous shales or oil shales are valuable sources of petroleum products and exist in considerable quantities in parts of Scotland. As early as the seventeenth century attempts were made to distil mineral oil from shales but not until the middle of the nineteenth century were any real advances made. A large supply was discovered a few miles east of Bathgate, its abundance and cheapness providing a considerable expansion to the industry. By 1865 there were more than a hundred works in operation using the oil shales of the Lothians and the cannel shales of the coal measures.

6   THE TAY AND TWO CITIES

Assassination of James I

The actual murderer was a man called Robert Graham but the whole plot was set up by the Duke of Atholl. Here fact merges with Scottish mythology because there is an old story of the King's death being foreseen on his way to Perth by a woman calling out to him when he boarded the ferry across the Forth at Queensferry. She said if he crossed these waters he'd never return alive. However, the King, having reached Perth, was made welcome by the Duke of Atholl. While playing chess with this falsest of hosts, the old woman mysteriously reappeared (and this is 50 miles further on than her previous manifestation!) and called upon the King once more. Because of the late hour, King James commanded her to return the next morning, when he promised to speak with her.

She left muttering, 'hit shall repent you all that bye will not let me speke nowt with the kyng [sic].' During the night, King James was murdered in his bed. According to the historian Buchanan, certain witches, 'for whom the county of Athole [sic] was always infamous', had told Atholl that he would be 'crowned a king in sight of all the people'. Prior to his execution his tormentors placed a diadem of red-hot iron upon his head for all to see, thus fulfilling the prophecy, though not in the way that Atholl had expected.

The Stone of Scone

The Stone of Scone, pronounced 'scoon', is the greatest Scottish icon of all time and was used in Iona and Scone in Scottish Coronation ceremonies. It is an oblong block of red sandstone 26in by 16¾in by 10½in and at each end is an iron ring, presumably to help lift it when required. In 1292 John Balliol was the last Scottish King to be crowned upon it because in 1296 the stone was looted by King Edward I of England and taken to Westminster Abbey in London where it remained for 700 years. The last monarch to be crowned upon it was Elizabeth II in 1953. On St Andrew's Day, 30 November 1996, the stone was restored to the Scottish people and now resides in Edinburgh Castle. The stone had a Celtic name, 'Lia fail', which means 'the speaking stone' and an old prophecy states that 'except old seers do feign and wizard wits be blind, the Scots in place must reign where they this stone shall find'.

Falkland Palace

The name derives from the Old English 'Fealca', meaning a falcon, plus 'land' giving Falkland 'land for hawking'. In the village below East Lomond Hill (which has two prehistoric forts) stands Falkland Palace which is on the site of an earlier castle destroyed by English invaders in 1337. In 1371 another castle was owned by Robert Stewart, Duke of Albany and in 1402 he imprisoned his nephew the Duke of Rothesay here and starved him to death. In 1424 the castle reverted to the Crown and later became a favourite hunting seat of the Stuart kings.

Falkland Palace itself was built between 1502 and 1541 and is a fine example of Renaissance architecture. The royal tennis courts in the grounds were built in 1539 for King James V, who died here in 1542. His widow, Mary of Guise, lived here as Regent with their daughter Mary Queen of Scots. Charles II was the last monarch to hold court here and during the first Jacobite Rebellion in 1715, Rob Roy MacGregor and his men occupied it.

7 THE RAINBOW BRIDGE

The Art of Bridge Construction

These artists/engineers put new life into bridge construction, and Italy, where the Renaissance movement originated, still has many fine examples of their work extant. Later in France, the Corps des Ponts et Chaussées (literally, the Body for Bridges and Roadways) was formed in 1716, which truly advanced civil engineering in that country. The need for qualified engineers to further the work of the corps led to the founding in 1747 of the Ecole des Ponts et Chaussées (School of Bridges and Roads). The first director of the school was Jean-Rodolphe Perronet who himself became one of the foremost bridge builders in the world and who has since had a great influence throughout the world of bridge building. His greatest surviving opus is undoubtedly the Pont de la Concorde in Paris, built in 1791 just after the French Revolution. That event caused a shift in the centre of civil engineering development to Britain, where the environment was much more stable than France which was in a state of upheaval and where heads were quite literally more liable to roll!

There were some wonderful stone bridges built in Britain at this time, such as William Edwards's work at Pontypridd, the first Westminster Bridge and Blackfriars Bridge across the Thames in London. The famous Thomas Telford, with his eye on earlier French works, built a bridge at Over, across the River Severn. But stone bridges merely continued with the art of bridge building as it was already known.

The Bends

Nothing about the 'bends' could ever be funny but this anecdote is at least amusing. When the Thames Tunnel was nearing completion in 1843 after nearly eighteen years' work by Sir Marc Brunel, assisted by his son Isambard, the directors of the venture held a banquet in the middle of the tunnel. The tunnel at that time was still pressurised like a compressed air caisson, as last-minute work was still in progress. The feasters were puzzled when champagne bottles failed to fizz when uncorked in the compressed air environment. However, when the revellers emerged from the tunnel later into the non-pressurised outside air, the champagne bubbles began to fizz inside them, leading, to put it politely, to much gaseous effusions from the rear end of their digestive systems, which must have been acutely embarrassing for the straight-laced Victorian ladies and gentlemen!

William Innes Hopkins

William Innes Hopkins was a flamboyant figure who certainly enjoyed the good life. He was a member of the Tees Conservancy Commission and a Middlesbrough town councillor. He'd even been elected mayor for two years running. He'd also married well, his bride being Miss Everald Hustler of Acklam Hall. The Hustler family had occupied Acklam Hall for nearly three centuries. Hopkins wished to set up similar standards for his bride; he spared no expense in building Grey Towers Hall at Nunthorpe with extensive gardens and an ornamental lake. Hopkins had arrived on Teesside in 1850 to manage a fuel plant. Three years later he met a Mr Snowdon and together they formed Teesside Ironworks, which eventually merged to become Hopkins, Gilkes & Company with the addition of Edgar Gilkes, and it became a construction firm for bridges and also locomotives. Unfortunately the company suffered a grave blow to its reputation when a boiler supplying steam to a rolling mill exploded, the blast hurling many men into the River Tees. Sixteen men were badly injured by scalding steam and debris. Even back then, Middlesbrough had a population of 15,000 and yet the nearest hospital was at Newcastle, some 30 miles to the north. Consequently many of the injured died on the journey there.

The Collapse of the Ashtabula Bridge

On Friday 29 December 1876 at about 7.30 p.m., the small town of Ashtabula in north-east Ohio was being hammered by a blizzard. Twenty inches of snow and a wind that whipped along at more than 50mph were not the best recipes for train time-keeping but despite the weather the town train depot was bustling. Most of the passengers were leaving for their New Year's holidays and were waiting the arrival of the No 5 Pacific Express which was running more than two hours late because of the snowstorm. Weather delays had kept their train in Erie station, Pennsylvania until after 6 p.m. that night. Just short of Ashtabula Depot, the Howes truss-iron bridge (built for cheapness eleven years previously) spanning Ashtabula Creek gave way under the double-headed Pacific Express leaving a 60ft gap into which were precipitated all the passenger and baggage cars which caught fire when the heating stoves were tipped over. At least eighty people died and sixty-three were injured. The Court of Inquiry found the accident was the result of defects and errors in design, construction and maintenance, an eerie precursor to the findings of the Tay Bridge Inquiry. The American court stated that 'the bridge was liable to have gone down at any time in the last eleven years and it is remarkable that it did not'. The parallels here are the court's conclusions, the close time and date of the accident (7.30 p.m. on 29 December), the corner-cutting in the bridge construction, the storm itself, the death toll and the early deaths after the disaster by the designer and builder, Amasa Stone and the maintenance chief Charles Collins, who both shot themselves.

NBR Tay Bridge Excursions

Many excursions and tours to promote the Tay Bridge appeared in the 1879 NBR timetables. The cheapest trip and one that involved crossing the Tay Bridge twice in one day was the afternoon excursion from Dundee to St Fort and St Andrews. This ran every Wednesday and Saturday at 2.45 p.m., stopping at St Fort and St Andrews only and returned at 8 p.m. (and 8.20 p.m. from St Fort). Fares were St Fort and return: first class 1s, third class 8d, and for St Andrews and return: first class 2s, and third class 1s.

Listed under 'Tourist Ticket Arrangements' in the 1879 NBR timetable were also the following Circular Tours:

Tour No 16 was 'Aberdeen, Inverness, Caledonian Canal, Oban and West Highlands, via Fife, Tay Bridge and Aberdeen'. Tickets were valid for one month and cost, for example, from Edinburgh £3 5s 6d for first class.

Tour No 17 was similar except that it was via Stirling and the Tay Bridge while Tour No 18 covered the same ground as No 16 but cost slightly less at £3, commencing from Edinburgh and terminating in Glasgow.

Tour No 28 was much shorter, being from Dundee and Perth to Helensburgh. Outward bound it was via the Tay Bridge, Fife and Edinburgh but returned via Stirling. First class was £1, and third class was 10s 3d.

Tour No 31 offered St Andrews and Dundee as a circular tour from Grangemouth costing 19s for first class.

8 HEAVY WEATHER

Michael Fish, BBC Weather Presenter

Michael Fish was a BBC Television presenter for the weather slot following the evening national news bulletin in the UK. On the night of 15 October 1987 he said in his weather report:

> Earlier on today apparently, a woman rang the BBC and said she'd heard there was a hurricane on the way. Well, if you're watching, don't worry, there isn't. Having said that, the weather will become very windy but most of the strong winds will be down over Spain and across France.

His reassurances were unfulfilled and within a short time, the most destructive storm to hit Britain since 1703 ravaged the south-east of England, blasting forests down, ripping house-roofing clean off, blocking roads and railways with debris and taking the lives of eighteen people. So much for modern weather forecasting and the populist faith in it. Poor Michael Fish's career never recovered, somewhat unfairly since he was only iterating the information given him from the Met Office and it was not his own opinion.

Demonstrate Air Pressure

You can demonstrate the pressure of the air for yourself with a plastic milk or drinks bottle (not glass!). Boil a kettle and hold the mouth of the bottle over the kettle spout until the bottle is filled with steam, then replace the bottle-cap and run cold water over the bottle from a tap. The steam in the bottle will condense and leave a partial vacuum inside the bottle which will instantly crumple and collapse due to the 15lb/sq. in air pressure on it.

9 IRON AND CUPAR

Life as a Housemaid

Ann Cruickshank's possible motives for the robbery she may have committed might have been connected with her terms of employment as a housemaid. Of course aside from money, her reasoning must remain a matter of conjecture. But, it is possible that after many years of probably thankless service to Lady Baxter, she was fed up with being a doormat and having a life of spinsterhood. She would have had years of low wages (about £20 per annum) and would have had to conform to a strict code of behaviour. To quote from *The Servant's Behaviour Book* published in the 1850s:

'Never let your voice be heard by the ladies and gentlemen of the house except when necessary and then as little as possible.

'Never begin to talk to your mistress unless it be to deliver a message or ask a necessary question.'

'Never talk to another servant or person of your own rank in the presence of your mistress unless from necessity and then do it as shortly as possible and in a low voice.'

'Never call out from one room to another.'

'Never speak to a lady or gentleman without saying, "Sir", "Ma'am" or "Miss" as the case may be.'

'Never take a small thing into a room in your hand. Any small thing should be handed on a tray kept for the purpose.'

'Never choose gay patterns or colours. Not only are such dresses unfit for morning work after they are a little worn but also they can never look becoming for servants.'

'Always stand still and keep your hands before you or at your sides when you are speaking or being spoken to.'

'Always answer when you receive an order or reproof.'

It is plain that the object here was to widen the gulf between employers and their domestic staff, creating a deep class difference. Girls coming from poor families often had to enter domestic service and as soon as they had done that, they were turned into virtual robots. However, a household like the Baxters' was already aristocratic and had an accepted social status. Lady Baxter therefore might not have required such strict adherence to *The Servant's Behaviour Book* code but enough perhaps to rankle Ann after thirty-five years of service.

12   THE LONG DROP

The 'High Girders'

The 'high girders', unlike all the others, were not all firmly bolted to the piers beneath them. To allow for heat expansion effects, a mixture of rollers and expansion joints were used, meaning that most of the girders sat upon their piers simply by their own weight. Counting the high girder spans from the south, the first was joined to the low girder section preceding it with rollers alone. The next span had rollers at each end and span 3 was bolted to its pier at the north end. Spans 4, 5, 6 and 7 all had rollers except at the extreme ends of the group. The next four spans had a similar arrangement of rollers. Spans 12 and 13 were again more rollers except for the south end of span 12. Therefore spans 4 and 5, where the train was at the moment of collapse, had a fixed joint at one end, a roller in the middle and an expansion joint resting on Pier 5. This meant that the entire high girders section was held together as a unit, over a distance of 1,050yd, with rollers and expansion joints and only actually anchored to piers in three places. It is not surprising therefore that if any one went down, the others would be dragged down with it.

14   INQUIRY

Bernoulli's Principle

I tried an experiment at home which I stress was in no way scientific. I took a 1930s Hornby, 7mm/ft scale O gauge model luggage van weighing 180 grams, placed it on a piece of tinplate Hornby track and put the lot on a fairly sensitive (within 2 grams) electronic scales. I then turned a domestic hairdryer at a range of about a foot broadside to the van and watched the digital readout of the scales. The 180-gram vehicle lost about 8 grams in weight due to Bernoulli's Principle because of its curved roof and flat underside causing lift. If the light second-class vehicle in the train was brought to the very limits of its wheel-flange connection with the rails due to the wind, then the wheel rims may possibly have climbed over the rail surface and derailed the carriage. If it indeed happened, such a derailment could have been abetted by the kink in the rails at the start of the first high girder, the point at which workers on the bridge, drivers and guards reckoned that the engines 'nodded' their way into the girder.

The Owencarrow Viaduct Disaster

On the Londonderry & Lough Swilly Railway in Ireland, the 7 p.m. train from Letterkenny to Burtonport on 30 January 1925 was approaching Owencarrow Viaduct, 3 miles from Creeslough. Driver Robert McGuiness, with his fireman John Hannigan, slowed down to 10mph because of the hefty winds blowing. The gale was so strong that a great gust lifted the first carriage off the rails when the train was about 60yd onto the viaduct. Guard Neily Boyle was helpless to intervene as everything happened so fast. McGuiness stopped the train with the vacuum brake but already the last carriage had carried the tail wagons halfway over the bridge parapet – this all happened at about 8 p.m. The roof of a carriage was ripped off in the windy blasts and precipitated four people to their deaths in the valley below the bridge. Other carriages such as the six-wheeler were upside down with their rooves smashed. The masonry parapet then gave way and fell down on top of the surviving passengers, mangling five more. The whole train consisted of two carriages, a wagon and a van. It was a 40ft drop from the bridge into the valley. Philip Boyle, his wife Sarah, Una Millgan and Neil Duggan were among the fatalities that night.

Wind-caused Oscillation and Resonance in Bridge Structures

One of the most famous and visually amazing cases of wind causing fatal oscillation and resonance in a bridge structure is the Tacoma Narrows Bridge in Washington State, USA, near Puget Sound.

Opened on 1 July 1940, the road suspension bridge had a main span of 2,800ft. The engineers didn't fully understand the forces that may have acted upon their bridge or how a suspension bridge might react to these forces. Furthermore, because of carrying road vehicle traffic only, it was thought that the deep truss girders as used in railway bridges were unnecessary because of the lighter loads, so they used shallow plate girders for the span. Wind simply passes through open girder work but obviously not through continuous plate work. From the outset, the bridge experienced rolling undulation brought on by the wind and earned itself the nickname Galloping Gertie. Just four months after opening, disaster struck. On 7 November 1940, a 35mph wind was blowing at the bridge: a strong wind but not anything like a gale. It was enough to set off a transverse vibration in the bridge. The resonance fed on itself, with the amplitude worsening from 1½ft to an amazing 28ft in three hours. The torsional mode happened in two halves, each out of phase with the other so that half the bridge was trying to twist clockwise while the other was going anticlockwise. Thus the deck twisted itself until the materials finally succumbed and a 600ft section fell into the river below.

An up-to-date case of an oscillating bridge is the Millennium Bridge, a pedestrian-only suspension bridge 325m long crossing the River Thames in London from Bankside to the City. It was the first pedestrian crossing of the river to be built for more than a century and cost £18 million. It opened on 10 June 2000. Like the Tacoma Narrows, it soon received a nickname, the 'wobbly bridge', because an unexpected uncomfortable swaying motion started happening during the first two days the bridge was open. On the first day, 1,000 people assembled at the south end with a band in front. As the entourage began to cross, there was an immediate pronounced lateral movement of the deck. Only a lightish wind was blowing that day and it was obviously not wind buffeting that was setting off the resonance. However, 80,000 people crossed on the first day while the bridge swayed to and fro. The agency causing this was the uncoordinated foot treads of the pedestrians themselves. By the simple act of hundreds of people walking across at the same time, they were transferring their body weights from one leg to the other as they strolled. This caused lateral excitation in the structure and had not been foreseen by the most complex of modern computer modelling programmes.

The structure was then closed for nearly two years while modifications were made to eliminate the wobble. The bridge uses lateral suspension, an engineering innovation that allows a suspension bridge to be built without tall supporting columns.

The engineers decided on dampers to absorb the resonance, ones much like car shock absorbers and also tuned mass-dampers. After a £5 million bill for this work, the bridge was re-opened in 2002.

16 CODA

Norwood Junction Accident – Additional Information

On May 1891, as the 8.45 a.m. Up express from Brighton to London Bridge was passing over Portland Road Bridge, Norwood Junction, one of the 20ft span cast-iron girders gave way. The whole train, consisting of locomotive No 175 Hayling of Mr Stroudley's 0-4-2 Gladstone class and fifteen vehicles, was derailed. The last van, a four-wheeler, fell through into the roadway below after the train had come to rest, which it did within its own length, the driver having applied his Westinghouse brake immediately he had left the rails. The train concerned was that known in later years as The City Limited and, in those days, slipped three coaches at East Croydon for Victoria.

On the day in question the train was made up as follows, counting from the rear: a four-wheeled brake van, four six-wheeled firsts, two bogie firsts, a Pullman car, three bogie firsts, two four-wheeled brakes, a first-class bogie carriage and a six-wheeled first.

The accident caused much concern not only to the LBSCR but to all other railways in the country owing to the large number of bridges built with cast iron that were still in use.

On the LBSCR, replacement work cost £100,000 and was finished by 1895.

Challenger *Disaster*

The disaster resulted in a thirty-two month hiatus in the shuttle programme. President Reagan appointed the Rogers Commission (named after its Chairman William P. Rogers with Neil Armstrong as Vice-Chairman) to investigate the accident. The Commission found that NASA's organisational structure and decision-making processes had been a key factor. NASA managers knew that since 1977 contractor Morton Thiokol's design of the Solid Rocket Boosters contained a potentially catastrophic flaw in the 'O' rings but had failed to address the problem. They also disregarded warnings from engineers about the dangers of launching posed by the low temperatures that morning and failed to report these misgivings adequately to their superiors. The cold weather forecast for the morning of 28 January 1986 prompted concern from the Morton Thiokol engineers as 'O' rings were low-temperature sensitive. The rings became brittle when cold, lost their springiness and would no longer re-sit themselves into their grooves. In other words, they would no longer seal.

A teleconference was held between the engineers, Morton Thiokol's managers and NASA managers at both Kennedy Space Centre and Marshall Space Flight Centre.

Several engineers, most notably Roger Boisjoly, were worried about the effect of low temperature on the resilience of the 'O' rings. They argued that if the rings became colder than 53°F (12°C) then there was no guarantee the joints would seal properly. This was a very important consideration indeed since the SRB (Solid Rocket Booster) 'O' rings were designated as 'Criticality One' components, meaning there was no back-up should both primary and secondary rings fail for any reason. Such a failure would be sure to destroy the Orbiter and her crew. NASA managers argued against the concerns of the contractor's engineers saying that if a primary 'O' ring failed then the secondary would still effect a seal. This is unproven and in any case was an illegitimate argument for a Criticality One component. It was forbidden to rely on a back-up for a Criticality One component. Back-up is there to provide redundancy in the case of a completely unforeseen failure, not to replace a primary device leaving no further back-up. In any event Thiokol's management overruled its own engineers and recommended to NASA that the launch proceed as scheduled the following morning. Apparently it was alleged, albeit unproven, that NASA managers frequently evaded safety regulations to maintain launch schedules. The Rogers Commission further concluded that a main cause of the disaster had been the failure of both NASA and Thiokol to respond adequately to the dangers posed by the faulty joint design. Rather than redesign the joint, they simply redefined the problem as an acceptable flight risk. Marshall Space Flight Centre's managers had known about the design problem since 1977 but never discussed it outside Thiokol.

This was a breach of NASA regulations. Even when it became more apparent how serious were these flaws, no one at Marshall saw fit to ground the shuttles until the problems were fixed. On the contrary Marshall managers issued waivers for six launch constraints related to the 'O' rings.

The Remnants

In 1994 a paper was published in *Geoarcheology Volume 9* co-authored by Professor Rob Duck at St Andrews University and physicist William M. Dow of Carnoustie. It was found that side-scan sonar surveys, augmented with echo-soundings, have revealed a series of columnar bodies, broken into segments, lying on the bed of the Tay estuary at the southern end of the first bridge. These are, identified with the aid of archive material, the remains of eleven twin brick uprights (Piers 4–14) that survived the disaster collapse. These eleven of the fourteen brick piers of the first bridge were lost, apparently, forever. According to Brotchie and Herd (1982) they were 'soon blasted away to high water level' after the opening of the new bridge on 20 June 1887. However, this is slightly inaccurate. The method employed for demolition was to remove a line of bricks near to the base, about 5ft above mean high water level and replace these with hard wooden bricks impregnated with paraffin or a similar flammable substance. These bricks were later set on fire and as they burned away the structure, denied its support, fell into the water. The insertion of the bricks was such that the piers fell to the north. Photographs clearly show smoke rising from the burning bricks at the base of the piers and that the process of demolition began with Pier 14 and progressed southwards. In this way each set of two brick columns fell into the gap immediately north of the former upright pier position. The angle of the fall of the columns during their demolition would have been critical in view of the fact that the new structure was being built with only 28ft of clearance (i.e. 60ft, centre-to-centre spacing) from the old.

The demolition process must have been very precise indeed so as not to endanger the new works. These underwater remains appeared on the side-scan sonar investigations almost by accident, as the survey was undertaken in 1992 as part of a sedimentological examination of the Tay riverbed and not ostensibly to discover relics from the first bridge. Nevertheless the results have identified items of great historical interest.

Locomotive 224 Arises

Examining the damage to No 224, Drummond noted that the lever on the motion shaft connecting to the reversing lever was broken and the spring beams of the front bogie were also broken. The Westinghouse brake gear was all there but the left-hand buffer and sandbox had gone. A photograph of the right-hand side of the engine taken at Cowlairs Works shows some bending of the running plate ahead of the coupled wheels, the chimney and safety valve bonnet are missing, as is the cab roof metalwork and some of the external pipe work is mangled. Most of this damage was caused by the salvage operations and not when the accident occurred. In the plunge to the water and on down to the riverbed, the engine and tender had been largely protected by the iron cage of high girder span number 5. When Matthew Holmes arrived in 1882 to take up the post of NBR Locomotive Superintendent (Drummond having moved on to the Caledonian Railway) there was a lot of talk in railway engineering circles about the value of compounding, which was the use of steam twice in an engine. The first was through the normal high-pressure cylinders but when the steam was exhausted from these, it was further sent through low-pressure cylinders to maximise the energy it contained. So as an experiment, in 1885 Holmes's cousin, engineer W.H. Nesbit, proposed a tandem compound arrangement and converted No 224 to this system. She ran in this form for two years but was not as successful as hoped, so, in 1887 she reverted to her original 'simple' configuration.

Bibliography

A.J. Cronin, *Hatters Castle* (1931).
A.R. Bennett, *The Chronicles Of Boulton's Siding*, David & Charles, New Impression Edition (1971).
Adrian Vaughan, *Signalman's Morning*, Amberley Publishing (1981).
Andrew Murray Scott, *The Wee Book Of Dundee*, Black and White Publishing (2003).
Anthony Burton, *On The Rails*, Aurum Press Ltd (2004).
Brian Hollingsworth, *How To Drive A Steam Locomotive*, Penguin Books Ltd (1979).
British Railways Pre-Grouping Atlas, Ian Allen (1976).
British Transport Commission, *Handbook for railway steam locomotive enginemen*, British Transport Commission (1957).
Christian Wolmar, *Blood Iron And Gold*, Atlantic Books (2009).
Christian Wolmar, *The Subterranean Railway*, Atlantic Books (2004).
Christopher Harvie, *Scotland: A Short History*, Oxford University Press (2002).
Christopher McGowan, *Rail, Steam And Speed*, Columbia University Press (2004).
Clarence Winchester, *Engineering Wonders Of The World*, vols 1 & 2 (1936).
Clarence Winchester, *Railway Wonders Of The World*, vols 1 & 2, Amalgamated Press (1935).
David Swinfen, *The Fall Of The Tay Bridge*, Mercat Press (1994).
Denis P. Smith, *David Kirkaldy (1820–90) and Engineering Materials Testing* (1980).
Description of articles found after the Tay Bridge Disaster and brought to Tay Bridge Station 1879/1880, Dundee Central Library.
Ellis C. Hamilton, *The North British Railway*, Ian Allan, 2nd edition (1955).
Great Storms, Laughton & Heddon (1930).
G.W.N. Sewell, 'North British Railway Locomotives/Coaches/Wagons' (1992).
H. Gasson, *Firing Days*, Littlehampton Book Services Ltd (1973).
H. Gasson, *Footplate Days*, Littlehampton Book Services Ltd (1976).
H. Gasson, *Signalling Days*, OPC Railprint (1989).
H. Lamb, *Historic Storms Of The North Sea, British Isles and Northwest Europe*, Cambridge University Press (1991).
H. Raynar Wilson, *Railway Accidents. Legislation and Statistics, 1825 to 1924*, The Raynar Wilson Company (1925).
J.B. Priestley, *Victoria's Heyday*, Penguin Books Ltd (1974).
J.P.M. Pannell, *Man The Builder, An Illustrated History of Engineering*, Book Club Associates, London (1977).

BIBLIOGRAPHY

John Prebble, *The High Girders: Tay Bridge Disaster, 1879*, Penguin Books Ltd (1959).
John Thomas, *Forgotten Railways: Scotland*, David & Charles, Revised edition (1976).
John Thomas, *Tay Bridge Disaster: New Light on the 1879 Tragedy*, David & Charles (1972).
John Thomas, *The North British Railway*, vols 1 & 2, David & Charles (1969).
L.T.C. Rolt, *Isambard Kingdom Brunel*, Penguin Books Ltd (1957).
L.T.C. Rolt, *Red For Danger*, The History Press (2009).
L.T.C. Rolt, *Victorian Engineering*, The History Press (2007).
M. Howell and P. Ford, *The True History Of The Elephant Man*, Allison & Busby (1980).
Major General Hutchinson, *Report On The Tay Bridge: Fitness For Public Usage*, Board of Trade Inspectorate (1878).
Marion K. Pinsdorf, *All Crises Are Global*, Fordham University Press (2004).
Marion K. Pinsdorf, *Engineering Dreams Into Disaster* (1997).
Noel Botham, *The Ultimate Book Of Useless Information*, Blake Publishing (2004).
O.S. Nock, *British Steam Railways*, Bounty Books (2009).
O.S. Nock, *Historic Railway Disasters*, Book Club Associates (1966).
Ordnance Survey Maps: Landranger Series, nos 59 (Fife) & 66 (Edinburgh).
P.R. Lewis, *Beautiful Bridge Of The Silvery Tay*, The History Press (2004).
P.W. Smith, *Footplate Over The Mendips*, Littlehampton Book Services Ltd (1978).
P.W. Smith, *Mendips Engineman*, Littlehampton Book Services Ltd (1972).
Prof. Rob Duck and William M. Dow, '1992 Sedimentological Survey of Tay Riverbed: Paper on side-scan sonar', in *Geoarcheology*, vol. 9 (1994).
R.H.N. Hardy, *Steam In The Blood*, Littlehampton Book Services Ltd (1971).
Ray Gwillam, *A Loco Fireman Looks Back*, D.B. Barton (1972).
Ronald Inglis, *An Introduction to Railway Engineering*, Chapman & Hall (1953).
Ronald Smith, *Dundee Street Plans*, Ronald P.A. Smith (2001).
Sidney Weighell, *A Hundred Years Of Railway Weighells*, Robson (1984).
Simon Garfield, *Last Journey Of William Huskisson*, Faber and Faber (2002).
The North British Railway Timetables 1879, National Archive of Scotland.
Transcript of the Tay Bridge Disaster Court of Inquiry 1880, HMSO.
W.A. Tuplin, *Great Western Steam*, Allen and Unwin (1957).
W.G. Chapman, *Track Topics*, Great Western Railway (1935).

Magazines and Newspapers

Dundee Advertiser, 1872–80.
History Today magazine, 1950–70.
Illustrated London News, 1880.
Railway Magazine, 1920–2000.
Railway World, 1960–2000.

Libraries and Archives

AMRA Reference Library, Western Australia.
Dundee Central Library Local History Section.
Melbourne Library Reference Section.
National Archives of Scotland.

Index

Airey, Sir George, Astronomer Royal 172–173
Arrol, William 185–189, 195, 202

Baker, Benjamin 174–175, 177, 188–189
Barclay, Thomas 37, 125–128, 131, 139, 146–148, 154, 161, 163, 166, 169
Barlow, William Henry 169, 174, 179–181, 184, 188, 202
Beeching, Dr Richard 95
Bernoulli, Daniel 175
Beynon, William Henry 49, 80, 105–106, 136, 138–139, 142–143
Black, John 125, 131
Board of Trade 66–67, 70, 100–101, 109, 136, 168–169, 173, 181, 184–185, 187, 192, 195, 206, 210
Bouch, Sir Thomas 36, 41, 51, 54, 56–68, 83, 86–87, 93–99, 102–103, 109, 114–116, 144, 156, 164–165, 169–174, 177, 179–181, 183–188, 191–192, 194–197, 202, 208–210
Brassey, Thomas 57, 96
Brunel, Isambard Kingdom 36, 57, 94, 169, 192, 212
Buick, John 125, 129, 131
Burntisland 20, 23, 30–31, 38–43, 48, 50, 52–54, 57–59, 61, 63, 69, 71, 73, 75, 77, 79, 101, 120, 125, 131, 134–135, 137, 143, 151, 165, 198, 206

Cupar 28–29, 38, 59, 113, 117–122

de Bergue, Charles 97
Dougall, Admiral William Herriot Maitland 43–44, 110, 112, 124
Dow, Bill 176–177, 179
Dundee 13–14, 19–21, 23, 27–31, 37–44, 46–47, 49–50, 54, 57, 59–60, 71, 73, 77–79, 81–90, 92, 94, 96, 98, 100–102, 105–106, 109, 112–113, 115–116, 118–122, 124–125, 130–131, 133–145, 147–148, 153, 155–157, 159–162, 164–166, 168, 170–171, 174, 178, 184, 186–187, 190, 194–198, 206, 213
Dundee Advertiser 36, 95–96, 168, 171
Dundee Courier and Argus 119

Edinburgh, Dundee and Perth Railway 14, 61, 63–64
'Edinburgh' 14, 20, 28, 37–38, 43, 72–73, 79–80, 89, 105–106, 112, 117, 120, 125–126, 128, 132–133, 136–137, 139–140, 147, 149, 159, 161–163, 165, 197

Firth of Forth 20, 39–40, 51–52, 56, 59, 185, 208–209
Forth railway bridge 195
Fowler, John 188–189,192
Friend, Willam 142–143, 163

Grant, Ulysses S. 100

Harrison, Thomas Eliot 188

INDEX

Ingles, Alexander 142–143, 163

Kennedy, Alexander 125–132, 134, 160, 217

Lewis, Peter 177–179
Linskill, William 79, 106, 136, 138–139, 143, 164, 197

Macleod, Ian 177, 179
Marshall, John 22, 24, 26–27, 29–32, 34–36, 38–42, 77–79, 89–90, 106, 118, 121, 138, 140–141, 145–147, 149–150
Martin, Tom 177, 179
Matthew, Patrick 92–93, 95–100, 103
McBeath, David 30–31, 38, 41, 50, 54, 78, 90, 106, 121, 125, 138, 148
McKinney, Mr 43, 102, 156, 172
McMahon, Hugh 44, 110, 158–159, 163
Mitchell, David 13, 19–23, 26–27, 30–31, 34–38, 40–42, 77–78, 89–90, 106, 118, 121–122, 135, 138–141, 145–147, 149–150, 198–199
Morris, Robert 141–143, 163, 165, 168
Murray, Donald 30–31, 38, 41, 50, 54, 148

Ness, George 134–135, 138, 143, 145, 147, 150, 198
Noble, Henry 97, 102–103, 171–172, 180
North British Railway 13, 19, 22–23, 25, 30–31, 42, 46–52, 54, 71, 75, 96, 100–102, 118, 121, 125, 127, 131, 134–135, 138–139, 164, 167, 170–171, 174, 181, 184–185, 187–188, 194–195, 206
North Eastern Railway 46–47, 54, 208

Perth 21, 23, 34, 38, 51, 59, 61, 63–64, 81–89, 92, 94, 105–106, 139, 141, 143, 157, 190, 194, 211, 213

Queen Victoria 41, 47, 120, 126, 168, 186, 207–208, 217

River Tay 34, 38, 51, 56, 81, 84, 97, 150, 197
Robertson, Provost 155–157, 171
Robertson, Thomas 138–139, 163–165
Robertson, William (Carriage and Wagon Inspector) 137
Robertson, William (Harbourmaster) 159–160, 162–163
Rothery, Henry Cadogan 169, 180–181

Shand, Robert 125, 129–132, 160
Somerville, Henry 34, 126, 128, 130, 132, 146–147, 154, 157, 161
Stephenson, Robert 188, 191
St Andrews 29, 37, 64–65, 79, 85, 106, 134–136, 138–139, 143, 164, 213, 218

Tay Bridge 16–18, 20, 23, 27–30, 34–37, 39, 41, 44, 46, 51–52, 56–58, 63–66, 68, 72–73, 78, 80–83, 85–87, 89, 91–103, 107–109, 114–116, 121–122, 125–126, 131, 133–136, 139, 141, 145–146, 151, 154–155, 157, 160, 164–166, 168–170, 173, 175, 177–178, 185–199, 203, 208, 213

Watt, John 139, 147–148, 154, 163–165
Westinghouse 25–27, 30, 36–37, 43, 71, 77, 90, 118, 122, 129, 138, 141, 143, 205–206, 217, 219
Wheeler, Dennis 175
Wylie, Jesse 86, 98, 147

Yolland, Colonel William 169–170, 173–174, 179–181, 195–196
Young, Inspector James 42, 135, 137

If you enjoyed this book, you may also be interested in…

The Beautiful Railway Bridge of the Silvery Tay
PETER R. LEWIS

Over 125 years ago, barely a year and a half after the Tay Railway Bridge was built, William McGonnagal composed his poem about the Tay Bridge Disaster, the poem about Britain's worst-ever civil engineering disaster. Over eighty people lost their lives in the fall of the Tay Bridge, but how did it happen? The accident reports say that high wind and poor construction were to blame, but Peter Lewis, an Open University engineering professor, tells the real story of how the bridge so spectacularly collapsed in December 1879.

978 0 7524 8763 2 EBOOK

Death, Dynamite and Disaster
ROSA MATHESON

Life in Britain was revolutionised as the railways flourished in the nineteenth century. Cities were linked and the masses could travel; railway mania was born. Yet these early days were dramatically different o the present in terms of health and safety! In this fresh approach to railway history, Rosa Matheson explores the grim and grisly railway past. These horrible happenings include the lack of burial grounds for Londoner's dead, leading to the 'Necropolis Railway', disasters and accidents, digging up the dead, and how the discovery of dynamite gave rise to the 'Dynamite Wars' on the London Underground in the 1880s and 1890s … long before the terrorist attacks of the twentieth century.

978 0 7524 9266 7

Wheels to Disaster
PETER R. LEWIS & ALISTAIR NISBET

On Christmas Eve in 1874 the worst accident in the history of the GWR occurred at Shipton-on-Cherwell, several miles from Oxford, when the 10 a.m. from London Paddington to Birkenhead derailed, killing thirty-four passengers. The fracture of a single tyre was enough to cause this catastrophe due to the lack of continuous braking and inadequate communication between the driver and passengers. Using the accounts of eyewitnesses, archive newspaper articles and reports, *Wheels to Disaster!* tells the story of the worst incident in the history of the GWR.

978 0 7524 4512 0

Visit our website and discover thousands of other History Press books.

www.thehistorypress.co.uk

The History Press